Designing Applications with MSMQ

Message Queuing for Developers

Alan Dickman

Addison-Wesley

An imprint of Addison Wesley Longman, Inc.

Reading, Massachusetts • Harlow, England

Menlo Park, California • Berkeley, California

Don Mills, Ontario • Sydney • Bonn

Amsterdam • Tokyo • Mexico City

Many of the designations used by manufacturers and sellers to distinguish their products are claimed as trademarks. Where those designations appear in this book and Addison Wesley Longman, Inc., was aware of a trademark claim, the designations have been printed in initial caps or all caps.

The author and publisher have taken care in the preparation of this book, but make no expressed or implied warranty of any kind and assume no responsibility for errors or omissions. No liability is assumed for incidental or consequential damages in connection with or arising out of the use of the information or programs contained herein.

The publisher offers discounts on this book when ordered in quantity for special sales. For more information, please contact:

AWL Direct Sales
Addison Wesley Longman, Inc.
One Jacob Way
Reading, Massachusetts 01867
(781) 944-3700

Visit AW on the Web: www.awl.com/cseng/

Library of Congress Cataloging-in-Publication Data

Dickman, Alan.
    Designing applications with MSMQ : message queuing for developers
    Alan Dickman.
        p.   cm.
    Includes bibliographical references and index.
    ISBN 0-201-32581-0
    1. Microsoft Message Queue Server.   2. Queuing theory.
    3. Middleware.   I. Title.
    T57.9.D53   1998
    519.8'2—dc21   98–25737
                                                CIP

ISBN 0-201-32581-0
1 2 3 4 5 6 7 8 9 10—MA—0201009998
First printing, August 1998

To Hilary and Alex

Contents

Foreword

This book is about an important new technology from Microsoft Corporation called Microsoft Message Queue Server (MSMQ). MSMQ falls into the category of message queuing middleware (MQM) because it enables applications to communicate with other applications over a network via a series of messages that are stored in queues while they are awaiting delivery. Because message delivery is asynchronous and connectionless, and queues enable extremely high levels of delivery guarantees, MQM solves many challenging communication problems.

Despite MQM's power, most developers have never built an application that uses message queuing. In certain industries—most notably telecommunications, airlines, and financial services—systems based on message queuing have existed for years. As recently as five years ago, however, most solutions were largely developed in-house—regardless of cost and complexity—because reliable, asynchronous communication products from mainstream software vendors were not available or were prohibitively expensive. Given that relatively few companies are in a position to build and to maintain their own complex communication technology, the number of developers who have built MQM applications is accordingly small. This situation is poised to change as software industry giants—most notably Microsoft and IBM—moved to create powerful, affordable, and widely available MQM products, based on their recognition of two important industry trends

First, the trend toward deploying Internet networking has created a ubiquitous—yet marginally unreliable and completely nonsecure—ability for any two computers in the world to communicate with each other. While fine for Web browsing and file downloads, the Internet alone is not suitable for business-quality communication. MQM products enable applications to use Internet networking to communicate with mission-critical reliability, security, and in a way that senders and receivers do not need to be reachable and running at the same time. This enables a whole new class of mobile, collaboration, business-to-business, and electronic commerce applications that simply were not possible (or cost-effective) in the past.

Second, competitive trends have forced companies to achieve a higher level of application integration.

- Customer-care systems need to provide unified access to data from many different applications.

- The once-per-night frequency of batch/file transfer approaches (once the standard for application integration) is no longer timely enough to meet business requirements. In many line-of-business applications, such as supply chain management, competitive advantages are increasingly coming from near–real time data collection and propagation.

- Business managers want activities in one system—such as a debit to an inventory system—to cause other systems (from replenishment applications to modeling spreadsheets) to perform related actions.

Conventional approaches often failed because of the variety of data formats and protocols involved in most integration efforts and because synchronous connections between applications are not always practical. Here MQM is ideal because of its reliable store-and-forward features and the ease with which messages can be transmitted across various protocols and translated from one format to another.

IBM was first to address the broad market need by delivering a product called MQSeries. Given the significant investment that it has made in marketing MQSeries, IBM deserves much of the credit for driving broad awareness of MQM, particularly MQM's potential as a catalyst for application integration. More recently Microsoft released Microsoft Message Queue Server and includes MSMQ with every copy of Windows NT Server, making powerful MQM technology available to millions of users. Such features as integrated public key–based security and dynamic message-routing capabilities will help developers build the next generation of Internet-ready applications. And the availability of interoperability products ensures that MSMQ will play an important role in application integration as well.

Ironically MSMQ is already in the hands of many more people than know how to use it. For most developers the challenge is not just learning a new programming interface. Rather, building and deploying well-behaved applications with MSMQ (like other MQM products) requires a number of design, programming, and management paradigm shifts. For example, developers need to learn the best ways to design applications, deal with common error conditions, exploit such capabilities as security features, and maximize application performance. Administrators need to understand how to design MSMQ networks efficiently and to manage the day-to-day issues of running an MSMQ-based infrastructure.

There is perhaps no better resource for learning about MSMQ concepts, features, application design, and management than this book. Author Alan Dickman has a unique gift for explaining sophisticated technology in a way that makes it accessible to all developers. Alan's style is effective: He explains MSMQ concepts and features in detail, provides well-written sections of reusable sample code, and—most important—provides invaluable tips and hints drawn from his personal experience acquired over years of building successful, mission-critical systems based on message queuing middleware. The tips and hints alone are worth much more than the price of the book.

PETER HOUSTON
MSMQ Product Manager
Microsoft Corporation

Preface

There may be no more fascinating arena to work in these days than the computing industry. We seem to be continually challenged by technological and design revolutions and counterrevolutions, especially in the area of distributed processing. Today software architectures are evolving, and new languages compete for mind share and market acceptance. Processor speeds and network technologies accelerate to accommodate increased distribution.

The world is witnessing several shifts in the way it develops distributed applications.

- Windows NT is already becoming the middle-tier platform of choice. It will not displace mainframes or UNIX, but we will see its acceptance as a high-performance platform in the next several years.

- Object-oriented concepts are being adopted within application architectures as they grow to support previously unimaginable degrees of distribution and granularity.

- Technologies that make distribution possible are setting new standards for ease of use.

Into this space Microsoft has introduced two key technologies: Transaction Server and Message Queue Server. Microsoft Transaction Server (MTS) adds transactions to the object model defined by Microsoft's Component Object Model (COM). Message Queue Server (MSMQ) supports asynchronous transaction processing, whereby applications exchange messages through a message queue. Although less understood by the developers of smaller, two-tier applications, queued messaging has provided the bulk of transaction processing in non-Windows environments for decades.

But MSMQ stands apart from queued messaging technologies of the past. It combines the high-performance communications and reliability of mainframe transaction processing technologies with the flexibility of objects and the large-scale distribution of intranets and the Internet.

Great! MSMQ is an exciting new technology. But why would you be interested in this book? Simply stated, this book offers a lot to various groups of readers.

- Queued messaging and MSMQ are new to Windows developers. This book will help them to design and to develop messaging applications by using Message Queue Server (MSMQ).

- Distributed transactional, component systems are emerging as the preferred way to implement Internet and intranet systems on Windows and other platforms. MSMQ is presented in that context.

- Developers are not the only individuals who must venture into the world of distributed transactional components. Executives and midlevel managers also need to understand the benefits and issues associated with distributed processing and transaction processing (TP).

Although this book has an MSMQ and COM orientation, I have attempted to convey information that is useful outside those contexts. Selected chapters, sections, and paragraphs will be of value to readers who use other messaging environments or other component frameworks.

About This Book

If you are a programmer who will be developing MSMQ applications, I assume that you are proficient in Visual Basic or C/C++. In addition, you should be familiar with Windows as a user. This text does not assume Windows programming knowledge, but that knowledge certainly helps. Also, information systems executives and managers need not be developers to derive value from this book.

This book does not go step by step through MSMQ Enterprise, Site, Server, and Client setup. I discuss design trade-offs in Chapter 2 and demonstrate creation of queues in Chapter 4. However, MSMQ makes setting up an Enterprise, Sites, Servers, and Clients straightforward. It does not warrant duplication here.

This book also ignores the creation of e-mail and connector applications. I would be interested in hearing from readers as to whether they want these or other topics covered in a future release of this book.

Organization of This Book

Chapter 1 tells how queued messaging is similar and different from other forms of communications. Then it describes how MSMQ can be used in two-tier, three-tier, Web, and component architectures. This chapter will be useful to IS executives, development managers, and programmers with limited backgrounds in distributed applications or object-oriented concepts.

MSMQ delivers terrific deployment flexibility and administrative ease of use. These features are highlighted in Chapter 2 as part of a detailed overview of the MSMQ architecture. Level 8 Systems technologies are also described, since most companies will need to integrate non-Windows resources with MSMQ (and vice versa).

Any MSMQ application needs to understand how queues can be configured and messages can be exchanged. In an MSMQ architecture, queues and messages are modeled as objects and have properties associated with them. Chapter 3 introduces queue and message properties. It also describes the kinds of queue names that MSMQ applications must use.

Chapter 4 uses Visual Basic to teach basic queued messaging. In this chapter we implement a version of the well-known Hello World application, using COM components. In Chapter 5 the exercise is repeated, using Visual C++ and the MSMQ (C language) API. COM components can be used in C++ programs and Java applets. (The COM examples contained in Chapter 4 and other chapters could easily be converted to those languages.)

Chapter 6 begins with a critique of the Hello World applications developed in Chapters 4 and 5. Using those applications, we illustrate queue and messaging architectures that satisfy various project goals, requirements, and assumptions.

Several processing scenarios are common in messaging environments. For example, client applications usually need to correlate a request and a response. Also, servers may want to conserve processing resources by triggering processing only when a message is available. These and other processing requirements are implemented in Chapter 7.

One of the differences between queued messaging and on-line kinds of communication, such as remote procedure calls (RPCs), is that they provide much richer failure handling. Messages can be made recoverable and can be copied to journal queues on the source and destination machines. You also have the ability to trace the route that the message takes through a network and can receive acknowledgments that a message reached a receiver or its target queue. Chapter 8 demonstrates how to use these facilities in your program and suggests how they may be used in administrative programs.

MSMQ security is particularly attractive. Chapter 9 discusses MSMQ administrative and programmatic security features. Administrative operations, including configuring access control and auditing, are demonstrated. Program-to-program authentication and message encryption are implemented.

Chapter 10 introduces transaction processing concepts. It begins by describing the value of transaction processing. Atomicity, consistency, isolation, and durability are explained. Then the chapter elaborates on several issues relating to distributed transaction processing. It examines the strengths and weaknesses of on-line distributed transaction processing systems and queued messaging. Compensating transactions and the two-phase commit protocol are also reviewed.

A transactional queued messaging application is developed in Chapter 11. It illustrates how to transactionally send and receive messages, as well as how to combine these operations with other transactional operations, such as database updates.

Appendix A provides a brief reference to COM components and the MSMQ API. Appendix B describes how to set up MSMQ projects in Visual C++ and Visual Basic. MSMQ performance test results are described in Appendix C, and hints are offered.

Gaining Additional Help

The industry is still in the early stages of delivering infrastructures for the development of distributed transactional object systems. Likewise the art of developing distributed transactional object applications is in its infancy. This book attempts to address many basic questions a reader might ask. Complete coverage is a noble goal but is one that no author can hope to achieve.

Luckily resources are available to help you solve your problems. Microsoft does a great job of making its products accessible to users through the Web. You can expect to see Microsoft place white papers on its Web site. Information related to MSMQ can be found at:

`http://www.microsoft.com/NTServer/Basics/AppServices/MSMQ/`

PSW Technologies also has several resource pages devoted to MSMQ, transaction processing on Windows NT, and porting applications from UNIX to Windows. Please visit our Web site at:

`http://www.psw.com/`

I will also place information about message queuing, MSMQ, transaction processing, and COM at:

`http://www.tpmq-experts.com/`

For information about connecting MSMQ to non-Windows platforms, visit the Web site of Level 8 Systems for information about their message queuing solutions:

`http://www.level8.com/`

When all else fails, you can communicate via e-mail. Please address questions to:

`alan@psw.com`

Thanks

Writing a book is challenging and tiring. Above all, it is a humbling experience. I have benefited in so many ways from numerous people.

My book reviewers were terrific. Thanks to Oran Bodner, Ilan Caron, and Alexander Dadiomov at Microsoft, who helped me sort through a lot of technical details. Melodi Gates, Jay Lang, Ken Walker, and Gene Belitski offered great suggestions and practical insights.

Others at Microsoft were very helpful, too! Peter Houston made human and intellectual resources available to me. Amnon Horowitz, Doran Juster, Nir Katz, and Syed Yousef contributed a lot of time. I owe a tremendous debt to Dr. Frank King, as well as to Brian Baisley, Bill Cason, Dennis Thompson, Christine Kungl, Mike McCown and others of PSW Technologies for giving me the time to explore MSMQ and the resources to write. Thanks to Reid Spencer of PSW Technologies for reviewing parts of this book. Also, thanks to several readers of Microsoft's MSMQ newsgroups for sharing their questions and experience.

Special thanks to Carter Shanklin, Elizabeth Spainhour, Genevieve Rajewski, John Fuller, Krysia Bebick, and others who have made working with Addison-Wesley such a pleasant experience.

Finally, my family and friends stayed out of my way when I was working and distracted me when I needed a break.

ALAN DICKMAN
PSW Technologies, Inc.
April 1998

1 Chapter

Distributed Architectures and Microsoft Message Queue Server (MSMQ)

This chapter discusses how MSMQ can be used in various distributed application architectures. The chapter is intended for IS managers and developers who need to know more about designing two- and three-tier systems, Web applications, and object-oriented or component-based systems.

Microsoft Message Queue Server (MSMQ) provides services for designing and developing distributed applications. Although it is a newly released Microsoft product, MSMQ is a powerful enabling technology for developing distributed applications, and future enhancements will make it even more useful.

But why use a message queue server? Isn't queued messaging an out-of-date way for application communication? Distributed objects are in vogue today. Why would we want to go back to communication technologies of yore?

The answer is simple: Good ideas never die; they just get facelifts. And Microsoft has given queued messaging quite a facelift!

At the heart of MSMQ are the basic strengths that have made queued messaging so important to high-performance transaction processing. A message is a flexible way for two applications to exchange information. The sender and the receiver must agree on the content of a message. A message exchange represents something akin to a contract: Both the sender and the receiver understand the information the message contains and how it will be processed.

Using queues with messaging adds processing flexibility. A sender places messages in queues managed by a queue manager. The receiver reads messages from queues. Since messages flow through an intermediate process, the queue manager, messages can be sent even when an intended receiver is off line. Although a queue represents a first-in, first-out store, a receiving application can also remove messages out of order, and priorities can be used to implement various qualities of service.

But the strengths of MSMQ extend far beyond queued messaging. An important element of MSMQ is its architecture, which provides a unifying way to organize computing across a far-flung enterprise. Therefore the management of communications and networks is highly scalable. A second architectural feature enables connectors to be built. Connectors make it possible for developers to exchange messages with non-MSMQ environments by using standard MSMQ APIs and services.

But MSMQ consists of much more. Exceptional security features are built into the technology. MSMQ enforces access controls on all operations and audits operational activities. Message senders can be authenticated to receivers. And messages can be encrypted for transmission across the network.

Further, MSMQ sports two interfaces. Microsoft's Component Object Model (COM) components will appeal to programmers who are fluent in object-oriented programming languages and have used component development solutions. This interface is especially important for the future of MSMQ because today we are witnessing a revolution in architectural thinking. This revolution relates to the design of distributed applications and the technologies that facilitate distributed application development. Many, or perhaps most, theorists embrace design principles that promote the definition of smaller, reusable computational entities called components.

MSMQ defines a set of simple, easy-to-use COM components that developers can use to quickly leverage the power of queued messaging. Ideally these MSMQ components will find their way into customized component software that is developed for private use and off-the-shelf components that are available at retail stores and through mail-order outlets.

But what about companies that face challenges in the design of distributed component systems? Many development groups lack design skills for distributed component systems, and the design skills are also difficult to acquire on the market.

UNIX and mainframe transaction processing experts should feel quite comfortable working with MSMQ's C language API. This interface enables companies and developers to leverage their existing transaction processing skills as they turn to Windows NT for the majority of their new-systems development work.

Don't worry about your company's ability to design distributed component systems. MSMQ can be used in a variety of system architectures, including two-tier, three-tier, and Web-based systems. Let's begin this book by discussing architectures that fit the use of MSMQ.

1.1   Introduction to MSMQ Application Architectures

In this section we'll focus initially on differences between queued messaging and on-line forms of communications. Then we'll describe typical queued messaging application architectures.

1.1.1   Communications within Distributed Applications

There are many ways to categorize the communication mechanisms and features that enable a distributed application to function. Perhaps the most basic attribute of a communication mechanism is whether the communicating applications exchange information in a *synchronous* or an *asynchronous* manner. In synchronous communications an application establishes a connection to a peer application, sends a request to the application, and waits for information to be returned by the peer. Frequently the application is blocked from performing other work until a response is returned. Here synchronous means that the applications are engaged in the communication process at the same time. An application cannot send information if its peer is not ready to receive it.

Queued messaging is a form of asynchronous communications—the opposite of synchronous communications. In asynchronous communications an application can send information whenever it is ready to communicate. Since a queue is used to store messages temporarily, information is delivered when the peer application is ready to receive it. This form of communication does not assume or require any "coincidence in time" between communicating peers. An application might send a message even though the intended receiver is off line. By the time the receiving application obtains the message, the sender may have terminated.

A model of synchronous application processing is commonly confused with synchronous communications mechanisms. For example, an application using synchronous communications to send a request may be blocked from performing other work until it receives a response. This mechanism is in fact, an attribute of the programming interface provided by the communications facility, not of the underlying communications protocol.

When explaining the difference between synchronous and asynchronous communications to a nontechnical person, many people like to use a telephone analogy. A telephone call is a form of synchronous communications. In order for communication to succeed—at least in a synchronous manner—the person you are calling must be able to answer the call, respond to requests, acknowledge information received, and hang up only when the call is completed. If the call is terminated prematurely, the communication is left in an indeterminate state.

If only recovery of computer programs were as easy as recovery from inadvertently hanging up the phone! When a phone call is terminated prematurely, either party can call the other back and pick up the conversation where it ended. Reconnecting two applications in the middle of some work is much more difficult, frequently requiring costly manual intervention.

Voice mail is a form of asynchronous communications. A caller can leave a message while a person is out or engaged in another call, and the message will be delivered at a later time. If a problem occurs while a caller is leaving voice mail, he or she can always call back, enter voice mail, and leave the message again. When the person receives the first voice mail message, he or she can choose to ignore whether a second message is left, can respond with a negative acknowledgment, or can take another recovery action. Computer programs can take similar steps when asynchronous communications fail.

Open Database Connectivity (ODBC), remote procedure calls (RPC), and distributed object technologies, such as DCOM,[1] are examples of synchronous communications mechanisms. Each of these mechanisms assumes a client/server model. In the client/server paradigm the client creates a communications session with a server and then issues one or more requests before terminating the session. Control of communications never (or rarely) passes from the client to the server. Other forms of synchronous communications support a peer-to-peer relationship between communicating applications. Either peer can create a session, and control may pass between peers before the session is terminated.

Queued messaging is probably the most common form of asynchronous communications used today. Processes communicate through messages that are placed in and removed from queues. One process, a sender, places a message on a queue. Another process, the receiver, retrieves the message from the queue. Queue messaging is illustrated in Figure 1-1.

A queue is like a voice mailbox for messages that are waiting to be delivered, but the messages usually have special features. For example, messages can be assigned a range of priorities that affect ordering within a queue. Senders can specify a time-to-live attribute that determines when a message can be discarded if it is not delivered. MSMQ supports various classes of service, including guaranteed delivery.

We'll return to the differences between synchronous and asynchronous communications later in this chapter and when we discuss transaction processing. But now we'll look at queued messaging in more detail.

1.1.2 Queued Messaging Application Architectures

It makes sense to use synchronous communication facilities when you need to perform several pieces of work at the same time. But when would you use queued messaging in an application?

---

1. DCOM, or Distributed Component Object Model, is a version of COM that supports remote method invocation.

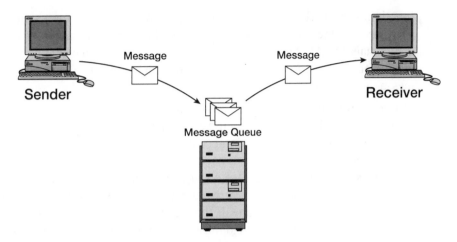

Figure 1-1   Queued messaging communications

Queued messaging is frequently used as a communications mechanism between applications because it offers some important properties.

- *Real-enough time.* In many larger applications a request for data or processing does not need to be serviced in real time. Customers are billed once a month rather than immediately following each credit card purchase. Car insurance renewal notices can be accumulated and printed at night. In business and commerce few applications require instantaneous communications between them: Real-enough time is acceptable.

- *Priorities.* Messages can be assigned priorities. As a message arrives at its target queue, it will be stored in the queue according to its priority. The message's priority also affects the order of routing through the network.

- *Reliability.* Queued messaging is more reliable than many synchronous communications facilities, because messages can be stored to disk. Information is exchanged directly between two applications when ODBC, RPC, and other synchronous mechanisms are used. If an application or the network fails during an exchange, information may be lost, and an outcome is often left in doubt.

- *Scalability.* Queues buffer requests and make it possible to tune the number of processes servicing requests during peak-load periods.

Queued messaging applications differ from on-line distributed applications in one fundamental respect—the degree of coupling between them. This difference manifests itself in two ways.

- *Coupling in time.* When two applications use synchronous communications, both applications must be on line, and the network between them must be functioning properly. There is no such requirement if queued messaging is used, because the applications communicate through an intermediary, a queue manager. All that is necessary is that a local queue manager be available when an application needs to send a message or wants to receive a message.

- *Coupling by identity.* In synchronous communications a request and its response are exchanged by a specific pair of processes. Process 1 sends a request to process 2, which responds back to process 1.

    In queued messaging any correspondence of identities is incidental. When process A places a message on a queue, it isn't addressed to a particular process. If processes Y and Z are ready to read messages from the queue, either might receive the message. If the receiver generates a second message in response to the first, the second message might be placed on a response queue or sent to an entirely different queue for servicing by another process. Even when the message is sent to a response queue, it isn't addressed to process A. If process C is ready to read a message from the response queue, process C, not process A, may receive the message.

Queued messaging is the communications mechanism of choice when work can be structured into a pipeline and when two or more existing applications need to be integrated.

1.1.2.1 Work Flow

In many industries several steps may need to occur in order to service a request. To implement this model of processing, a piece of work flows from one application to a second application, and then to another. This kind of structuring is common in the insurance, lending, and telecommunications industries, for example.

Figure 1-2 shows how several applications might implement a work flow. A work flow may be initiated as a result of an external or an internal event. A new customer calls in requesting an auto loan, or an insurance policy needs to be renewed. As it flows through a system of systems, work may be stored temporarily in a database pending other external events: Perhaps the customer must agree to the terms of a loan amount, or the results of a credit history check are needed. Eventually the work is restarted and completed. It frequently takes more than a month to process an insurance policy or to close a loan. Consequently the model pictured in Figure 1-2 is far more common than one might imagine.

1.1.2.2 Application Integration

Queued messaging is also used to integrate the services or processing of two or more existing systems. Two or more distinct systems developed to address different process-

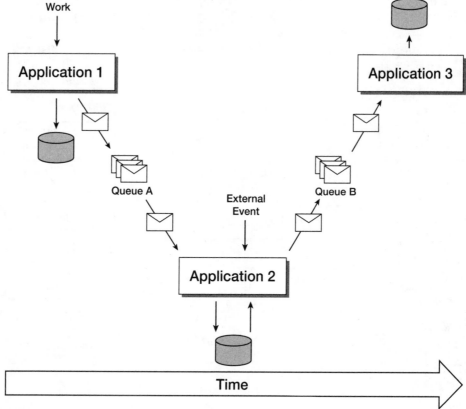

Figure 1-2 Applications cooperating to service a work flow request

ing requirements (potentially by different development organizations at different times) will be loosely coupled.

It's quite common that a company will decide to develop a new application that pulls data from one or two applications and to perhaps use processing from a third application. This form of integration architecture is pictured in Figure 1-3.

To integrate the existing systems with the new system, a processing agent is frequently implemented. The agent translates requests from the new system into operations that each existing system can perform. It is also typical to implement a process controller as part of the new system. The process controller interacts with the processing agents on behalf of front-end GUI (graphical user interface) applications. When a system is implemented with a process controller, the system adheres to the industry direction toward thin clients. A thin client supports a graphical user interface and may perform field validations, but does not support any business processing.

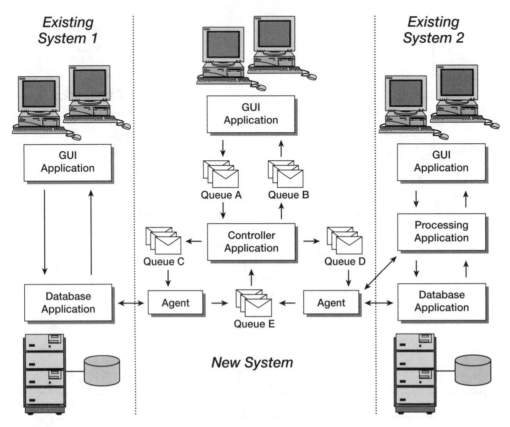

Figure 1-3   Using queued messaging to integrate two existing systems

In Figure 1-3 a user places a request for information into a message and sends it to the controller's input queue (Queue A). The controller picks up the message, examines it, and then translates it into a request for data from existing system 1 and a request for data and processing from existing system 2. Messages are placed in the input queues of each processing agent (Queue C and Queue D). The processing agents for each system obtain their messages and interact with their respective systems to satisfy the requests. Responses are placed in the controller's input queue (Queue E). The controller obtains both messages, perhaps mathematically calculates some result information or logically joins them, and returns the information in a message placed on the user's input queue (Queue B).

1.1.2.3   Requests and Responses versus Asynchronous Notifications

In Figure 1-3 the messages passed between applications are either requests or replies. The requests and replies adhere to loose coupling in time and loose coupling in identity. However, there are less tightly coupled forms of messaging.

In many cases a message can be a notification of an event. Perhaps the value of stock has changed and needs to be communicated to trading systems in Tokyo, Hong Kong, Singapore, and Bombay. Maybe the inventory of circuits in Golden, Colorado, has reached the 90 percent utilization rate, and a monitoring agent needs to notify the area manager to provision more circuits on the local telephone switch.

In these instances the receiving application has not requested the notification. There is no direct request-reply relationship between two applications. Rather the sending application simply knows to send a message when a particular event occurs, and the receiving application knows to perform a particular action if the message arrives. This is probably the loosest form of coupling between two applications.

It's worth noting that the asynchronous-notification model is rapidly gaining adherents in the distributed application design community. A growing number of vendors are beginning to provide technologies that implement a publication-subscription service, and users are embracing them. *Publish-subscribe,* or pub-sub as it is commonly called, is a model in which producer applications publish an ability to generate certain kinds of events. Consumer applications register, or subscribe, to particular kinds of events. Then as these applications execute, the producers asynchronously generate events that are consumed by subscribers. Today MSMQ enables asynchronous notifications. In the future pub-sub will layer over MSMQ.

1.2 Using MSMQ in Well-Known Distributed Application Architectures

Functional decomposition is a way of codifying distributed application designs. Any application or system can be decomposed into three general elements: presentation, processing, and data management. Presentation includes handling input from humans, displaying information, printing, faxing, and so on. Data management covers creation and access to files and database tables. Processing, in this context, relates to the reason that an application exists, such as scheduling appointments or clearing currency trades. This type of processing is sometimes described as "business processing" to emphasize the application's real purpose over incidental processing of inputs and outputs, reformatting of data, and so on. Let's examine how queued messaging and MSMQ might support various distributed application architectures.

1.2.1 Monolithic Systems

Historically departments have had total autonomy with respect to their information systems (IS) decisions, including complete control over the allocation of their IS budgets. Department heads could select from a range of hardware and software vendors, with little or no regard for budget allocations occurring elsewhere in the company, institution, organization, or university. Nearly all applications were designed and developed as monolithic, stand-alone systems. All user interactions, data management, and processing were implemented using a closed system design.

Two factors have forced more distributed designs on the industry. First, the need to share data and processing across systems became important. In certain industries—telecommunications, for example—the driving force was scalability. System vendors simply could not deliver mainframes that were powerful enough to support hundreds or thousands of users, to access data, and to perform the processing needed for complex operations. In almost all industries the same data might reside in multiple databases, and companies looked for a systematic way to manage the copies effectively. Second, the availability, functionality, and acceptance of client/server technologies have grown over the past 15 years.

Several standard application architectures have evolved to solve various technical problems. These distributed systems architectures are frequently described in terms of their number of tiers. Each tier implements a logical part of the overall system architecture. The focus on tiers has been unfortunate, however, since it draws attention to physical aspects of a system rather than to the services it provides.

1.2.2   Two-Tier Systems

A two-tier architecture usually supports departmental computing needs. Most application processing and the user interface run on user desktops. Common, data-oriented processing may be built into stored procedures that execute within the database system. However, the primary function of servers is to support access to data. A two-tier system is pictured in Figure 1-4.

Two-tier applications are usually developed specifically to support on-line user interactions.[2] The human user almost always generates the requests that flow from client to server, using a synchronous communications protocol. In a synchronous protocol the client issues a request and then waits for a response before proceeding with other work. If the server is not on line to service the request, the client will receive an error.

Two-tier applications are generally easy to develop. Another strength is that they work fine under low-volume requirements, such as small departmental systems or decision support.

Unfortunately two-tier applications do not scale well. For one thing, all on-line users contend for server system resources. Any system has limitations on the number

---

2. Automated injection of requests into the system is more prevalent in work-flow and three-tier applications.

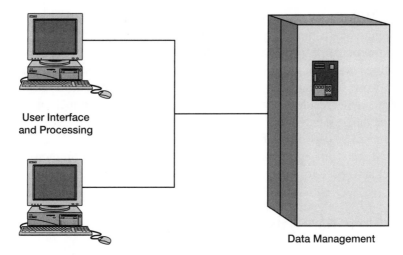

**User Interface
and Processing**

Data Management

Figure 1-4 Two-tier systems

of connections into a machine or a database, the size of swap space, the amount of virtual memory, and the amount of CPU cycles that are available. A rule of thumb is that most companies have trouble scaling two-tier applications to support more than 100 users. For better scalability many developers find that they need to reduce contention for system and application resources. To reduce contention it is often necessary to distribute data across several databases and to multiplex user requests across multiple processes and processors. In other words, additional application tiers are needed.

MSMQ is a great way to derive maximum scalability for a two-tier application. However, most two-tier application developers have come to explicitly or implicitly rely on specific features of synchronous data interfaces. These useful features are not available when using an MSMQ interface.

Clients in a two-tier application usually assume direct and synchronous communications with a server. With MSMQ a queue manager acts as an intermediary agent between the client and the server. The introduction of a queue manager has the effect of decoupling client/server interactions in two ways.

- An MSMQ-based server can return responses after an unpredictable interval. The response can even return after the user has exited the GUI. Thus you will need to design client applications to process responses returned no matter when they arrive.

- Although the application server may be off line, the queue manager will happily accept the request and place it in a queue. The client doesn't receive an error if the application server is off line.

In effect, MSMQ takes two-tier applications developers out of their comfort zone when developing interactions between the client and the server. My experience suggests that most companies will want to use MSMQ to integrate new and existing systems, including two-tier applications. For example, a new application that pulls data from one or two systems and that perhaps uses processing from a third system may be needed. The data that resides in two-tier systems may need to be transformed for processing by the third system. There may also be good reasons why data extraction and processing should be decoupled. For example, data may need to be collected throughout the day, whereas processing occurs after business hours. This common scenario is a perfect problem space for using MSMQ.

1.2.3 Three-Tier Systems

Many companies adopt a three-tier architecture to take a more enterprise approach to the definition of their infrastructure services and development of systems. The computing and communications infrastructure services are selected with the intent that many applications will share them. Scalability and availability of applications and the underlying support infrastructure are important. The failure of a system for even a short duration can cost a company in customer dissatisfaction and impact the productivity of thousands or tens of thousands of employees.

Ease of use for developers is a second important factor in technology selection. Many companies are facing extremely tough competition and need to change their business models/rules/practices frequently in order to stay competitive. The ability to create new applications from a substrate of basic services is often one of the prime motivating factors for going to a three-tier architecture.

Figure 1-5 illustrates a three-tier system. User interfaces, business processing, and database management are placed into separate processes and frequently execute on different computers in the system. The user interface typically is placed on low-end, single-user desktops. Databases may reside on mainframes, as well as on medium- or high-powered servers. The sizing of systems to support business processing depends on many factors. Each tier may even have its own hardware and software architecture.

Applications in each tier are expected to fulfill a particular role. Presentation services are designed for individual department requirements. Some departments may design special toolbars or other widgets to help their personnel work more effectively. Today many users are sophisticated enough to write Visual Basic programs to connect to Microsoft Word files, Excel spreadsheets, and Access databases. When a set of interfaces for business processing and data access are made available to users, they can reuse those interfaces to create their own applications. Thus users are able to meet current business needs without impacting the core business processing or data models within the company.

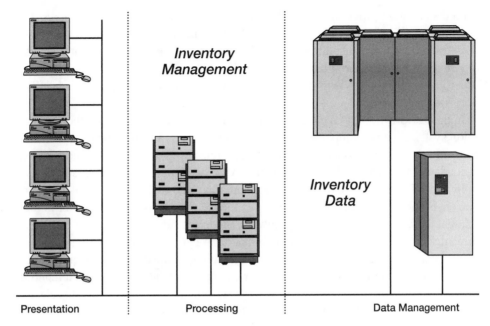

Figure 1-5   Three-tier systems

The business-processing tier reflects a company's structure, its important business functions, and the information flows between business units. Services within this tier may include shipping, inventory management, and billing and may in turn be subdivided into smaller, more reusable, or customized services. For example, in an inventory system separate applications might manage the inventory of parts and finished products.

Business processes apply business rules. Readers unfamiliar with three-tier concepts may ask what exactly a business rule is. For example, a bank offers automated telephone banking services and teller-assisted banking services. The bank charges customers a fee for requesting teller-assisted operations that could have been performed through automated services, such as a transfer between accounts. This charging rule can be considered a business rule.[3] A process in the business-processing tier would implement this rule (and others).

As companies try to build a system of systems and to automate the flow of information between systems, work flow becomes an increasingly important function

---

3. Ideally an object is invoked to perform the transfer regardless of whether the request comes from the automated telephone banking services system or through teller-assisted services. In order to apply the business rule correctly, the object needs to know the context of the operation. Context can be an extremely difficult problem if many business rules depend on it. We call your attention to this problem and note that several solutions are possible.

within the business-processing tier. The prescriptions governing work as it flows through a set of business applications are called business rules.

In three-tier systems an attempt is made to define data entities and relationships to support larger enterprise requirements instead of narrower departmental needs. Numerous departmental views of data may be woven together into a consolidated, enterprise data model.

In their efforts to organize and model the data used and produced by their information systems, some companies distinguish "private" data from "corporate" data. For example, temporary results from an interest rate computation may be considered private data if they are unlikely to be shared. All other data is a sharable resource. Applications in this tier are thought to "steward" the data on behalf of the corporation.

Consistency is a fundamental concern in the data tier. As we will see later in the book, databases support consistency, but data modelers define consistency. Some companies go so far as to talk about the semantic integrity of corporate data. That is, the data model must reflect a user's semantic meaning of the data, or expectation of what is to occur when a change is made. For example, the data model for a telephone company should not allow a customer with a residential telephone service to select business data services. Semantic-integrity rules are typically implemented within stored procedures. As more companies begin to provide access to corporate data through object interfaces, developers are likely to embed semantic-integrity rules within the object itself instead of using stored procedures.

Many companies take a more rigorous approach to management of three-tier applications and supporting infrastructures, partly because application processing is spread across more processes. As the number of processes increases, more points of failure are introduced. A second factor is that communications and other enabling services are more likely to be shared. More coordination and control are desirable as a result. However, the fundamental reason is that the complexity of networks, nodes, and applications makes automated monitoring and recovery a necessity.

Three-tier applications achieve greater scalability by reducing resource contention through distribution and replication. Data is logically partitioned and physically distributed across multiple databases on separate machines. User demand for other computing resources is multiplexed over processes replicated on many machines rather than on a single server.

The three-tier approach to distributed application development may sound great, but it suffers from at least two problems in practice. First, the three-tier model is viewed only in physical terms: graphical user interfaces on desktops, business processing on midrange servers, and data on high-end servers. Starting from a purely physical view, it is easy to come up with a closed application design that distributes presentation, business processing, and data elements of the application on separate machines. This kind of design does not facilitate sharing and reuse; the interfaces between tiers are narrowly defined rather than broadly usable.

Second, many companies do not successfully use a "top-down" approach to model their data and processes. Large companies' enterprise data and business-processing models can be very complex to develop, because the companies need to integrate numerous views of data and to accommodate a variety of processing alternatives. Capturing all data and processing rules can be a difficult and time-consuming effort, yet this exercise is required if companies expect to maximize sharing and reuse.

For a start, companies find it difficult or impossible to define requirements that enable processing and data tiers to be reusable by other applications. Frequently two development organizations resist working with each other. Even when diverse organizations want to work together, requirements are difficult to gather. Many companies don't go through the formal process of developing a business case for an application, deriving all requirements, and creating a well-specified and documented design before development begins.

Another problem is that requirements may change continually. The underlying technologies or client organizations that will use an application may change from week to week. A large application can impact a major segment of a business, and it is not unusual for these fluctuations to hinder progress. In such an environment it is quite difficult to derive stable requirements or to create detailed designs.

MSMQ technology facilitates implementing three-tier systems. Queuing has been used successfully for years to integrate systems and to facilitate the flow of work between applications. However, system designers need to be aware of two limitations when using MSMQ.

- MSMQ is available only on Windows platforms. Tools from other vendors address messaging in the non-Windows world, so this limitation isn't a show-stopper. Integration tools from Level 8 Systems and other vendors will be needed to access data and applications in other environments. We'll talk more in Chapter 2 about how to do this.

- MSMQ does not enable an application to perform on-line, distributed transactions.[4] This problem is addressed by using other Microsoft technologies. MSMQ can participate in distributed transactions controlled by Microsoft's Distributed Transaction Coordinator (DTC). The strengths and weaknesses of queued messaging and on-line transaction processing are discussed in great detail in Chapter 10. Chapter 11 demonstrates how MSMQ operations can be controlled by DTC.

---

4. On-line, distributed transactions enable two or more databases distributed across a network to be updated in a single transaction. This form of transaction processing has its own set of problems. Data and processing can be restructured to eliminate the need for a distributed transaction, as described later in the book. In some situations, however, performing a distributed transaction is required.

1.2.4 Web Applications

With the advent of the World Wide Web (WWW), user presentation has become distributed. A browser acts as the presentation device. Its main purpose is to paint screens that are described in the Hypertext Markup Language (HTML). The Web server handles much of the processing related to presentation. The server sends pages to the browser for display and interprets input entered by users from the browser. In many applications the server dynamically generates HTML based on criteria such as a user's profile or the input from a previous page.

A Web system is pictured in Figure 1-6. Some people describe Web applications as adding another tier to two- and three-tier architectures. This is correct from a physical point of view. The browser and the Web server usually reside on separate machines. Other people look at the Web as subdividing an existing tier. This argument also has merit, because the primary responsibility of the Web server remains presentation processing. Most Web servers deployed today do not assume a role of supporting business processing or maintenance of corporate data.

Web applications can, in fact, have a variety of architectures. Java and COM further complicate the architecture, because much more processing is possible within the

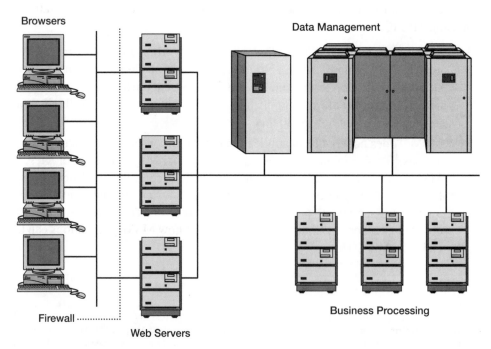

Figure 1-6 Web applications

browser environment. Both Java and COM enable the browser to become a vehicle for invoking business-processing services directly.

Two important benefits can be derived from the Web. First, Web front ends to applications make it very easy to develop and to update presentation processing. JavaScript or COM scripts can be downloaded to execute in browsers. Web servers can invoke other scripting languages to dynamically build pages of HTML. Compiling and linking are not needed. Second, Web servers also provide substantial support for integrating existing systems into a Web environment. The Common Gateway Interface (CGI), Microsoft's Internet Server API (ISAPI), or the Netscape Server API (NSAPI) make it possible to access processing and data managed by current systems.

Web applications can suffer from problems that plague two- and three-tier applications. For example, a single Web server does not scale to support thousands of concurrent users. If high levels of scalability are needed, several Web servers can act as front ends, or gateways, to an application. Each server interacts with browsers, using HTTP. Browser requests can be load balanced across all systems.

MSMQ services and applications developed with them can be accessed through COM, the Microsoft technology that enables interoperability. Within an Internet or intranet environment, MSMQ can be used directly through the COM interface or indirectly, by using custom *controls*.

COM controls are the architecture for developing programmable software components. Controls can be used in any COM-aware containers. A control container is simply the client software that knows how to use the control. Visual Basic programs are probably the most common kind of control container today, but there is tremendous growth in the use of controls within COM-aware Web browsers, such as Microsoft's Internet Explorer. Any COM control can be an Internet control that adds functionality to a Web page.

The COM interface to MSMQ defines a small framework of components that help COM applications use MSMQ services. These components make it easy to perform MSMQ operations. Just a small amount of code is needed to create and to open a queue, to construct a message and to send it, receive and process a response, or conclude queued messaging communication. We'll learn more about using the COM interface throughout this book.

1.3   The Future of MSMQ

As useful as MSMQ is today, Microsoft has lots of plans for MSMQ. MSMQ will become the transport for time-independent COM applications. In this architecture a client application will be able to invoke services of components even though they are not directly connected. The application will communicate with the component by using queued messages; however, developers will work within the COM distributed object framework when developing their applications and will make normal COM methods calls. Time-independent method calls will even be able to participate in transactions.

An effort to enhance COM, called COM+, will help to make time-independent programming easy. COM+ will handle all MSMQ details and will schedule applications. In fact, COM+ will allow components to be configured to serve on-line and time-independent operations; no changes to the components will be needed. Thus users will derive the benefits of an enhanced COM object model and the reliability and power of MSMQ!

Microsoft also plans to evolve MSMQ with Windows NT. In the current implementation of MSMQ, internal directory, security, and administrative services are provided. In MSMQ 2.0 these services will be migrated to Windows NT 5.0 directory, security, and administration services. MSMQ objects, such as queues, will be registered in Active Directory. NT security services will store keys that are used to authenticate, to encrypt, and to decrypt messages. And an MSMQ snap-in will be developed for the Microsoft Management Console (MMC). Farther into the future, we may see publish-subscribe and other services developed on top of MSMQ.

1.4 Conclusion

In this chapter we've started to see some of the important strengths of MSMQ and of queued messaging. MSMQ can be used in various distributed application architectures, and it is particularly well suited to integrating decoupled applications. In later chapters we'll talk about transaction processing. At that time we'll see that queued messaging is a terrific way to build high-performance, scalable transaction processing applications.

But now it's time to take a closer look at the features and functionality of MSMQ. After that we'll exercise our understanding of MSMQ features by developing a set of distributed applications. In Chapters 4 and 5 we'll learn the basics of sending and receiving messages. Then we'll work with advanced MSMQ features, including asynchronous notification, transactions, and security. Throughout the book we'll try to provide design tips that help you make the most of your applications.

1.5 Resources and References

Chappell, D. 1996. *Understanding ActiveX and OLE: Strategic Thinking about Applications for Windows and the Internet.* Redmond, WA: Microsoft Press.

Dickman, A. 1995. "Two-Tier versus Three-Tier Apps," *Information Week* (November 13): 74–80.

Gilman, L., and R. Schreiber. 1997. *Distributed Computing with IBM MQSeries.* New York: Wiley.

Mueller, J. P. 1997. *ActiveX from the Ground Up.* Berkeley, CA: Osborne McGraw-Hill.

Rogerson, D. 1997. *Inside COM.* Redmond, WA: Microsoft Press.

Sessions, R. 1998. *COM and DCOM: Microsoft's Vision for Distributed Objects.* New York: Wiley.

Umar, A. 1997. *Application (Re)Engineering: Building Web-Based Applications and Dealing with Legacies.* Upper Saddle River, NJ: Prentice Hall.

———. 1997. *Object-Oriented Client/Server Internet Environments.* Upper Saddle River, NJ: Prentice Hall.

2
Chapter

Overview of MSMQ

Architecture and Features

It's time to dive into MSMQ, the exciting new technology from Microsoft. In this chapter we'll survey the architecture of MSMQ and examine its features. This chapter is intended for IS managers and developers. Many distributed computing infrastructures support scalable applications, but administrative complexity increases significantly with the number of hosts in the messaging environment. The MSMQ architecture hides a lot of administrative complexity while offering surprising flexibility. This is an important reason for developers to use MSMQ.

MSMQ features are important because they are what make messaging such a flexible way for applications to communicate. Many companies have used messaging to develop new applications that integrate with existing applications in the enterprise. Messaging has done very well to service these needs, for three important reasons.

- Existing applications are by nature decoupled. They were not developed using a component architecture that supports standardized application interfaces. Most were engineered as self-contained systems that do not share data or processing with other systems. Messaging provides excellent support for integrating decoupled applications.

- New messaging applications are relatively easy to implement.

- Messaging products are available for all widely used operating systems and transaction processing environments.

Like previous messaging technologies, MSMQ supports decoupled application integration and provides simple-to-use communications. Thus it is relatively easy to implement new messaging applications that leverage existing decoupled applications.

MSMQ is available only for Windows environments and does not offer wide platform coverage. However, Level 8 Systems provides technologies to help you to integrate non-Windows applications and transaction processing systems into an MSMQ environment. You would deploy an MSMQ communications backbone on inexpensive (and, increasingly, scalable) Windows NT platforms. New and existing applications that are developed and deployed in other operating environments can be integrated into the MSMQ messaging backbone, using Level 8 Systems technologies. We look more closely at the Level 8 Systems technologies at the end of this chapter.

2.1   Selected Definitions

Let's begin to examine MSMQ by offering certain definitions. These definitions will be refined as we proceed through the chapter.

- A *message* is exchanged by MSMQ applications. A message can serve many purposes, such as a request or query, a notification, or a database update. The critical factor is that the sender and the receiver agree on how the message is interpreted. Each message has associated properties that define the message content.

- A *queue* stores messages passed between applications. Applications can send messages or retrieve messages from queues. Several kinds of queues are defined within the MSMQ architecture, including public and private queues. Queues have associated properties.

- A *queue manager* is the process that manages queues on a host.

- A *transaction,* a unit of work, comprises one or more operations that all succeed or all fail. A *transactional message* is one that is sent within a transaction.

- The *MSMQ Information Store* (MQIS) is a distributed database that maintains information about the MSMQ environment, including users, machines, public queues, the network configuration, and more. MQIS is accessed when creating, locating, or deleting queues and to get or set queue properties. MQIS does not store messages or perform queue management.

- *MSMQ servers* are machines that perform queue management and message routing tasks and that maintain MQIS information.

- *MSMQ independent clients* are machines that can perform many operations, such as sending and receiving messages and creating or destroying private queues. These tasks can even occur while the client machine is disconnected from the MSMQ environment (thus unable to communicate with any MSMQ server). However, selected operations, such as querying the MSMQ Information Store, can be performed only while an independent client is able to communicate with an MSMQ server.

- *MSMQ dependent clients* are machines that rely on an MSMQ server for all operations.

- A *source machine* is the MSMQ independent client or server from which a message is sent.

- A *target queue* is the queue to which a message is to be sent.

- A *destination machine* is the MSMQ independent client or server on which a message's target is maintained.

- A *sender* is an MSMQ application that places messages in a queue. A sender can execute on an MSMQ server, independent client, or dependent client machine. We also use the term sender for applications that receive a response message.

- A *receiver* is an MSMQ application that removes messages from a queue. A receiver can execute on an MSMQ server, independent client, or dependent client machine. We also use the term receiver for applications that send a response message.

- *Store-and-forward* is the general message processing protocol provided by MSMQ as a message is transferred between queue managers. On receiving a message, a queue manager stores it (in memory or to disk) and then attempts to forward the message to another queue manager. If the message can be forwarded successfully, it is removed from storage. Otherwise it remains in storage until later, when it can be forwarded successfully.

- *Message routing* is the process by which a message is sent from a source machine through one or more intermediate machines to a target queue on a destination machine.

Many of these concepts are illustrated in Figure 2-1.

At times, using the terms sender and receiver (or sending and receiving application) may seem confusing. Why not use client and server?

There are a couple of reasons why client and server are not used throughout the book. Perhaps you have already begun to see some differences between queued messaging and client/server applications. In the client/server model clients usually only send requests and receive responses. Servers receive requests, process them, and return responses. The request and the response are always correlated.

Messaging applications do not adhere to the roles typically associated with client/server applications. Queued messaging applications are coupled far more loosely.

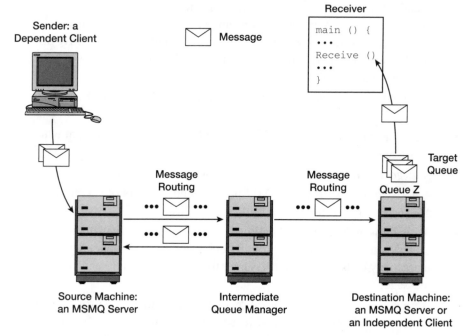

Figure 2-1 Selected messaging concepts

- Not all messages are requests, and many messages will have no direct response.

- A sender and a receiver do not have any direct interaction; messages flow through one or more queue managers.

- The role of an application at any given instance can change. One moment the application is sending messages. The next moment it is receiving messages.

In this book we'll label an application on the basis of its role in handling a message. You should be careful not to assign client/server role responsibilities to processes that send or receive messages.

2.2 Programming Interfaces

MSMQ is designed with many object-oriented characteristics. Key among these are the definition of several object classes. Two of these objects, messages and queues, are used in any MSMQ application. Messages and queues have several properties associated with them. Messaging and queue options are controlled by using these properties.

Programmers have a choice of two APIs when working with messages and queues.[1] The MSMQ API leverages the object-oriented design principles behind message and queue objects while making MSMQ features available through a C language interface. Developers who have been around transaction processing for years will feel at home using this interface. Message and queue properties can be examined and changed by using a defined set of data structures that are passed through MSMQ API function calls.

Developers who have worked with object-oriented design and programming languages will feel comfortable with the COM interface, which specifies a set of MSMQ components that enable developers to create applications very efficiently. The components have properties, methods, and events associated with them. ActiveX developers use the properties primarily of the `MSMQMessage`, `MSMQQueue`, and `MSMQQueueInfo` components to examine and to change message and queue properties. For example, a message label is passed as the value associated with the `MSMQMessage.Label` property.

In this book we use Visual Basic to demonstrate MSMQ COM solutions and C to show MSMQ API solutions. However, COM components can be used with C++ programs and Java applets.

The programming capabilities of each interface are nearly identical. Through the MSMQ API, developers have access to several properties that would be used in developing connector applications (discussed later in this chapter). COM components do not expose connector message properties. In addition, the MSMQ API supports a broader set of event notifications when receiving a message. However, nearly all developers will be able to derive the features they need from either API.

2.3   Messages and Message Queues

MSMQ message communications and queue options are controlled by using properties. Message and queue properties are discussed next and at length in Chapter 3.

2.3.1   Messages

Message properties are used to control several characteristics of message handling, sending, routing, and retrieval. These characteristics include message security, source and destination information, labeling, and time-to-live.

---

1. That MSMQ sports two interfaces is good for developers but hard on writers. It means that at times I will cover the same information twice—once for each interface.

MSMQ supports two kinds of message delivery handling: *express* and *recoverable*. Express messages are stored in memory until they can be delivered. Since express messages are not written to disk, they offer extremely high-speed communications. However, an express message is lost if a system is rebooted or an MSMQ queue manager fails while the message resides in queue manager memory.

Recoverable messages are not lost if a machine or a queue manager crashes, because they are stored in a backup file at each intermediate queue until delivered to the destination queue. The queue manager for the destination queue stores the message in its own backup file until it is received by an application. When using recoverable messages, you sacrifice communications speed but gain better failure protection.

MSMQ also supports transactional semantics when sending or receiving recoverable messages. A message can be placed in or removed from a queue as part of a transaction. Therefore MSMQ operations can be coordinated with other transactional operations.

Duplicate messages are possible when express or (nontransactional) recoverable messages are used. However, transactional properties guarantee that the messages are delivered. Exactly-once semantics apply to transactional messages: Duplicates are eliminated. All messages sent within a transaction arrive in order.

Table 2-1 makes use of a lot of information discussed later in this chapter and in other chapters. The table summarizes the strengths and weaknesses of express, recoverable, and transactional messages.

Table 2-1 Message Delivery

Message Delivery	Strengths	Weaknesses
Express Messages	Extremely fast communications (20,000 per second in my tests)	Lost during system failures Duplicate messages possible
Recoverable Messages	Fast communications (over 1000 per second in my tests) Not lost during system failures	Duplicate messages possible
Transactional Messages	Exactly-once semantics Guaranteed delivery Can be coordinated with updates to other resources (for example, data)	Lots of I/O overhead Degraded communications performance (100s per second)

2.3.2   Queues

Queue properties are used to designate and to control several characteristics of message queues. These characteristics include whether a queue is transactional and whether it supports only authenticated access, as well as its type, base priority, size, and label.

Two kinds of queues are defined in MSMQ: *application queues* and *system queues*. Application queues are used by MSMQ applications and can be created dynamically by messaging applications using either programming API, or administrators can set them up. Once created, applications can send messages to and receive messages from queues.

System queues are created by MSMQ. Only MSMQ can send or receive messages on system queues.

MSMQ treats transactional queues differently from nontransactional queues. Nontransactional sending and receiving is required when accessing nontransactional queues. However, messages can be placed on transactional queues only within a transaction. Retrieving a message from a transactional queue is allowed outside a transaction.

Public queues are registered in the MSMQ Information Store. Applications can locate public queues with its help. MSMQ also supports private queues; such queues are not registered with the MSMQ Information Store. *Private* queues are known only by the queue managers on the host on which they reside.

2.3.2.1   Application Queues

The MSMQ architecture defines three kinds of application queues: *message, administration,* and *response* queues. Each type of queue serves a special purpose for messaging applications.

- Application messages are sent to and read from message queues. A sender will place its requests on message queues, and receivers read the messages from these queues.

- Administration queues, perhaps a misnomer, are meant to store positive or negative acknowledgment messages generated by MSMQ on behalf of applications. To receive acknowledgments for a given message, an application must set up two properties. One specifies the kinds of acknowledgments it wants to receive in the message's acknowledgment property. The application must also place a special kind of name, a format name, for an administration queue into the message's administration queue property to indicate where acknowledgment messages should be sent. Then MSMQ will automatically generate acknowledgments and send them to the specified administration queue. By default no acknowledgment messages are generated.

- Response queues are where application response messages are placed. If a sender expects some information to be returned to it in reply to a message, the receiver creates a response message and places it on a response queue. The name of the response queue can be agreed to in advance by the sender and the receiver, or it may be passed in the response queue property of a request message.

Note that these are the designated purposes for each type of queue, but MSMQ does not enforce these rules on MSMQ applications. Nothing restricts applications from using the queues for other purposes. But it's not clear why an application designer would want to break this model. Violating this model could lead to debugging and maintenance problems.

2.3.2.2 System Queues

MSMQ also defines three kinds of system queues: *journal, dead letter,* and *report* queues.

- Journal queues are created automatically by MSMQ when a machine is added to the enterprise or when an application queue is created. MSMQ maintains a journal queue on every MSMQ server and independent client to track the messages it sends to other computers. An application can select to have a message placed in the source machine journal by setting its journal property. Message journaling at the source machine is not performed by default.

  MSMQ also creates a journal queue for every application queue to track messages removed from the application queue by message receivers. As a message is removed from application queues, MSMQ copies the message to the queue's journals if the queue's journal property is set. Message journaling at the target queue is not performed by default.

- Dead letter queues hold messages that cannot be delivered. A message might be undeliverable because it has expired or because the sender is not authorized to put messages in a queue, has not used authentication, has attempted to send a transactional message to a nontransactional queue, and so on.

  MSMQ maintains two dead letter queues on any given MSMQ server or independent client: one for transactional messages and one for nontransactional messages. MSMQ also handles transactional and nontransactional messages differently.

  MSMQ automatically forwards undeliverable transactional messages to the transactional dead letter queue of the source machine. By contrast, MSMQ does not automatically send undeliverable nontransactional messages to a dead letter queue. The sending application must indicate that this is desired. An application can set the journal message property to control forwarding of undeliverable nontransactional messages. When that is set, MSMQ stores these messages to the nontransaction dead letter queue on the machine where message delivery failed. The dead letter queue can reside on the source machine, destination machine, or on a machine in between the two.

- Report queues are used to track the progress of messages as they are transmitted through an enterprise. An application can set the trace message property if it wants report messages to be generated for an application message.

2.3.2.3 Public and Private Queues

When created, an application queue can be designated as a public queue or a private queue. Public and private queues follow naming conventions that are discussed in Chapter 3. Public queue information—its properties—is replicated throughout the enterprise, and any application can use MSMQ lookup functions to locate them. If an application creates a private queue for other applications to use, the location of the private queue must be distributed to them. For example, a response queue address can be passed in the message property defined for that purpose.

2.4 Sending and Receiving Messages

Messages are always sent asynchronously to a target queue. In other words, a sending application resumes execution immediately after a message is submitted. Asynchronous message sending improves application performance, because a target queue may be located across a network or may be inaccessible when the message is sent.

Applications can read messages synchronously or asynchronously. During a synchronous read, the application can wait (forever) until a message is available, or it can resume execution after a time interval of its choosing. In the latter case it specifies an interval, in milliseconds, that it is willing to wait.

The MSMQ API and COM components provide the ability to read messages asynchronously. COM components implement a simple event mechanism. The MSMQ API supports three asynchronous notification mechanisms.

- Developers can define a callback function that is called by MSMQ when a message arrives.

- The Windows event mechanism can be used to signal threads within a process that a message has arrived or that the receive call timed out.

- Processes within a Windows NT system can be notified that a message has arrived through a completion port.

2.4.1   Peeking at Messages

During a read operation, the receiving application has the option to remove the message from the queue or to inspect it while leaving the message in the queue. The act of removing a message from a queue is sometimes called a *destructive read.* The act of inspecting a message without removing it is sometimes described as a *peek* at the message or as performing a *nondestructive read.* Peeking at messages is particularly useful in a couple of situations.

- An application may need to correlate two or more messages sent to it. For example, an application may be performing work on behalf of a user. As part of that work, an application may send request messages to three other applications. The sending application would use a message property known as a *correlation ID* to correlate message acknowledgments or a response message with a request.

    Perhaps the application expects to receive three response messages. First, it will peek at messages in a response queue to see whether all responses are there. If three response messages are in the queue, they can be removed and processed. Otherwise the messages are left in the queue until all have arrived.

- Many companies have created administrative applications to monitor and manage their queued messaging infrastructure. A company may want to determine the number of messages on a queue without destroying all messages. If the number of messages in a queue exceeds a specified limit, this could indicate a problem, such as that a sender or a receiver has failed and needs to be restarted. Large numbers of messages in a machine journal may indicate that a network outage has occurred. The administrative applications could take corrective action, such as attempting to restart a sending or receiving application, troubleshooting a network problem by pinging routers and machines, or alerting the operations staff by pager. In fact, peeking at messages without removing them from a queue makes sense in thousands of application and administrative scenarios.

2.4.2   Transactional Messaging

MSMQ treats transactional messaging differently from ordinary recoverable messaging. First, messages can be transactionally enqueued or dequeued only from transactional queues. Second, MSMQ automatically forwards undeliverable transactional messages to the transactional dead letter queue on the source machine from which the message was sent.

Three kinds of transactions are supported: *external, internal,* and *XA.* MSMQ can participate in an external transaction involving other participants, including Microsoft Transaction Server (MTS) and SQL Server. Applications can also transactionally send and receive messages by using an internal transaction; here MSMQ can be the only resource manager. Finally, all Microsoft transactional technologies can participate in an XA transaction, one controlled by a third-party transaction manager.

2.4.2.1 External Transactions

The Distributed Transaction Coordinator (DTC) controls external transactions. It is the distributed transaction manager used by MTS, SQL Server, and MSMQ during external transactions. Figure 2-2 illustrates the relationship among DTC, MSMQ, MTS, and SQL Server. MSMQ and SQL Server, frequently described as resource managers, handle persistent state shared by transactions, such as databases and recoverable queues. MTS, often described as a communications manager and occasionally as a communications resource manager, does not manage persistent state.

Let's look more closely at how the applications, components, and technologies interact in Figure 2-2:

1. Application A creates a transaction by using the DTC.

2. Application A updates data in a local SQL Server database.

3. Application A sends a message with MSMQ.

4. Application A invokes the update method of transactional component XYZ by using MTS. Component XYZ resides on a remote machine.

5. Within the update method of transactional component XYZ on the remote machine, a database update is performed.

6. Component XYZ receives an MSMQ message.[2]

7. The component XYZ signals its ability to commit the transaction by calling the MTS `SetComplete` method. This returns control to application A.

8. Application A tells DTC to commit the transaction. DTC then invokes the two-phase commit protocol to commit all updates to resources on the local and remote machines.

The example as pictured in Figure 2-2 is in fact a little more complicated than what we have shown in the pseudocode. Application A uses a DTC *transaction dispenser*

---

2. Component XYZ is not receiving the message sent by application A. That message is not released to MSMQ until application A commits its transaction. Since component XYZ is executing under the control of application A's transaction, it can only receive a different message.

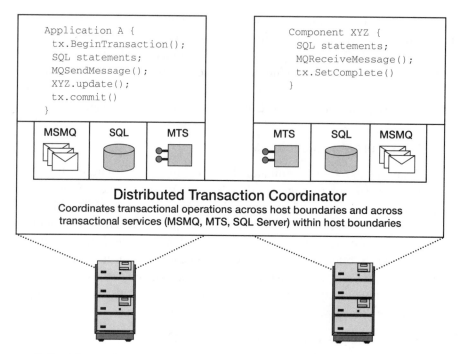

Figure 2-2 The relationship among DTC, MSMQ, MTS, and SQL Server

object to create transaction objects. Each transaction object represents a transaction. If an application wishes to work on more than one transaction at a time, it simply creates as many transaction objects as it needs. Transaction objects can then be used to control transactions composed of one or more MSMQ, MTS, and database operations. When work is completed, the transaction object is used to commit or to abort all work.

2.4.2.2 Internal Transactions

Only MSMQ can be used as a resource manager for an internal transaction. MTS and SQL Server cannot participate in the transaction. You can think of external transactions as general-purpose transactions, whereas internal transactions are MSMQ-specific transactions. As such, internal transactions have been optimized and provide better performance than do external transactions.

Aside from how internal transactions are created, their use by MSMQ remains unchanged. You can create an internal transaction by using `MQBeginTransaction()`, which is part of the MSMQ API, or `MSMQTransactionDispenser()`, which is an MSMQ COM component. One or more messages can be sent within an internal transaction, and the work is committed or aborted. In Chapter 11 we'll see how to implement transactional MSMQ applications.

2.4.2.3 XA Transactions

MSMQ, MTS, and SQL Server can also be used as part of an XA transaction.[3] Applications running under the control of a third-party TP monitor define transaction boundaries. The DTC accepts XA commands issued by third-party TP monitors and coordinates Microsoft transactional technologies and applications written for them. This model enables Microsoft applications and technologies to function like downstream transactional applications and resource managers when used within an XA transaction.

2.4.3 Message Security

MSMQ message security features are especially attractive. Message authentication and integrity, as well as encryption, are implemented for you.

2.4.3.1 Message Authentication and Integrity

One-way authentication is provided for messages sent to a receiving application. This form of authentication enables the receiving application to determine who sent a message. MSMQ also verifies that the message was not modified during transmission.[4] Best of all, MSMQ hides most of the mechanics of message authentication from application developers. Authentication is as easy as setting one or more message properties.

MSMQ uses an *asymmetric* key protocol based on internal or external certificates to sign each message. Certificates are issued by certificate authorities and are used to certify the identity of a sender or a receiver.

Asymmetric key protocols use a key pair during authentication. When a sending application selects message authentication, the MSMQ runtime retrieves the sending application's internal certificate, external certificate, or security context of the sender. Then MSMQ creates a digital signature, attaches the signature and certificate to the message, and sends the message to the target queue.

The target queue manager checks the integrity of the message and uses the sender's certificate to verify the identity of the sender. If the integrity of the message is

---

3. XA is a system-level interface, defined by X/Open, for controlling transactions. Most major TP monitors support this specification, but it does have limitations. For example, it assumes a single-threaded application processing model.

4. A more powerful form of authentication—two-way, or mutual authentication—enables the sender and the receiver to authenticate each other. That is, the sender can authenticate the identity of the receiver, and the receiver can authenticate the identity of the sender during an exchange. Two-way authentication, although stronger, adds significant overhead to message communications and is not implemented by MSMQ. It is worth noting that the identity of the receiver is authenticated to MSMQ, and access controls can be placed on the target queue to defend against unwanted accesses.

not compromised and if the sender's identity is valid, MSMQ sets the message's authenticated property to 1, thereby indicating to the receiving application that the message is safe to process. Unauthenticated messages are delivered to a receiving application with the authenticated property set to 0. If the hash values of the message suggest that the message was tampered with in transmission, the message is discarded. A negative acknowledgment is also returned, if the sending application requested one.

Internal certificates contain a public key written in the form of an X.509 certificate. They have no additional sender information that can be used to authenticate a user. Thus internal certificates are recommended when the receiving application wants only to authenticate the sender. If the receiver wants to examine other information contained in a certificate, an external certificate is needed.

Why would an application want to use external certificates? An application may wish to implement very stringent messaging security. For example, an application can validate other information within an external certificate. External certificates contain information about the certificate-issuing authority and the certificate authority's signature, in addition to a certified user identity and its public key.

Queues can be set to accept only authenticated messages. Unauthenticated messages are rejected when they are sent to these queues. MSMQ will also generate a negative acknowledgment, if requested by the sending application.

2.4.4 Message Encryption

The MSMQ runtime makes it possible to send a *private message* across the network. Application programmers do not need to encrypt or decrypt messages. The runtime does this on their behalf.

When a sending application sets the privacy property of a message, the source machine queue manager uses a shared private key and the destination machine queue manager's public key to encrypt the message before sending it out. The queue manager of a target queue decrypts a private message by using its private key and passes the message to the receiving application in clear text.

The privacy level of a target queue can be set to accept only private messages. Nonprivate messages are rejected when they are sent to queues that require private messages. MSMQ can generate a negative acknowledgment, if requested by the sending application. Alternatively the queue privacy–level property can be set to accept only nonprivate messages. By default queues accept both private and nonprivate messages.

Note that when an application on an MSMQ dependent client receives a message, it is being retransmitted from the MSMQ server to the dependent client across the network in clear text. If a company is highly concerned about security, applications should be deployed only on MSMQ server or independent client machines. Dependent clients should not be allowed to send and receive messages from MSMQ servers across unprotected networks, such as the Internet.

2.5 MSMQ Architecture

Several features play a vital role in enabling MSMQ to offer flexible messaging that will scale to thousands of deployed computers without overwhelming administrators with unnecessary complexity.

- Computers can be grouped into administrative units.
- Communications are organized around network connectivity rather than as a (potentially large) set of point-to-point connections.
- MSMQ automatically routes messages on the basis of administratively established costs and preferred routing patterns.
- Information about computers, networks, queues, and communications costs is maintained in a distributed database.

2.5.1 MSMQ Enterprise

All computers running MSMQ are part of an MSMQ *enterprise* and share a common, replicated database. The architecture of an MSMQ enterprise and the shared database make administering the MSMQ infrastructure simpler than many other distributed computing infrastructures.

Rather than having thousands of computers in a single unit or domain, most large companies like to organize computers into smaller domains. To facilitate this kind of organization, MSMQ allows an enterprise to be composed of one or more *sites,* or physical groupings of computers. You may want to align site boundaries with organizational boundaries or a physical location. Computers within a site do not have to use the same network protocol. The key assumption that MSMQ makes about sites is that communication between computers within a site is fast and inexpensive.

If an organization is dispersed over several physical locations that are linked by low-speed networks, each location should be defined as a separate site. The naming of queues or machines is unaffected, and access control can be administered by NT groups affiliation.

Sites are connected to other sites through *site links*. A site link is an abstract notion of the cost of routing messages across a particular network link to another site. Administrators assign the cost of a site link between two sites. MSMQ calculates the optimal message route between sites, based on the cost of each site link. A site link cost can range from 0 to 999,999. A value of 0 indicates that two sites are not connected. Lower values indicate lower site link costs. You'll need to experiment with settings to tune message routing in your environment.

MSMQ does not limit the number of servers that can be assigned as site links. Multiple site links provide load balancing and failure recovery.

Does it ever make sense to define more than one MSMQ enterprise in your company? Only under very special circumstances. It makes sense to define separate MSMQ enterprises where developers can develop and test unproven applications, do performance tuning, and train administrative personnel.

Most companies should create only one MSMQ deployment or production environment. A single MSMQ enterprise for deployed applications maximizes application sharing, interoperability, and integration. Isolation between sites and access or administrative controls can be enforced by using MSMQ security features.

A company that defines more than one MSMQ enterprise can still send messages between them. But doing so introduces unnecessary complexity.

A *primary enterprise controller* (PEC) is defined when an MSMQ enterprise is created. The PEC maintains information about the MSMQ enterprise configuration and certification keys that are used to authenticate messages between principals. The PEC also routes messages within and between sites.

A *primary site controller* (PSC) is installed at every site in an MSMQ enterprise. The PSC maintains the master copy of information about the computers and queues in its site. The primary enterprise controller functions as a PSC for its site.

A site can also have zero or more *backup site controllers* (BSC) installed. When one or more BSCs are configured into a site, MSMQ balances access to site information across the PSC and the BSCs. Having one or more BSCs also reduces the chance that a single point of failure (the PSC) will disable the entire site. The PSC and the BSCs also route messages within and between sites.

MSMQ allows administrators to define routing servers within a site. The servers support dynamic routing and intermediate store-and-forward message queuing. MSMQ routing servers also enable computers that use a variety of protocols to communicate. MSMQ routing servers do not hold a read-only replica of the PSC or the PEC database.

2.5.1.1 MSMQ Information Store

MSMQ servers use a distributed database called the *MSMQ Information Store* (MQIS) to maintain security credentials and to maintain routing information. Servers, workstations, and clients all have read access to the MQIS, but various servers within the enterprise maintain the master copy of data in the MQIS.

- The primary enterprise controller maintains enterprise information. This information includes the enterprise name, PEC name, list of sites and connected networks, default MQIS replication intervals, and user certificates.

- Each primary site controller manages its own site information. This information includes the list of computers within the site and public queues on each computer.

Changes in the enterprise topology are immediately replicated by the primary enterprise controller to other primary site controllers as they occur. Other changes to enterprise information are replicated to PSCs periodically.

Each primary site controller maintains the master copy of MQIS data describing its site. This information is replicated periodically to other primary site controllers. They also replicate MQIS information to backup site controllers in their site.

All data is replicated by using MSMQ messages and private queues. By default intrasite replication occurs every 2 seconds, and intersite replication occurs every 10 seconds. The difference in intervals reflects the architectural assumptions that communication is quicker and cheaper within sites than between sites. MQIS replication intervals can be adjusted from the MSMQ Explorer Administration interface.

2.5.1.2 MSMQ Servers, Independent Clients, and Dependent Clients

Three kinds of hosts are defined in the MSMQ architecture: *servers, independent clients,* and *dependent clients.* MSMQ servers have already been introduced. The PEC, PSCs, and BSCs are examples of MSMQ servers. These servers help to maintain the MSMQ Information Store, and they provide intermediate store-and-forward facilities when routing messages to target queues. An MSMQ server can also function as a "connector server." Connector servers allow MSMQ-based applications to communicate with foreign computers that use other messaging systems, such as Microsoft Exchange and IBM's MQSeries. Connector servers from Level 8 Systems also support MSMQ functions on non-Windows hardware.

MSMQ independent clients are able to create and modify queues locally and to send and receive messages. These clients also have the ability to store a message locally if a target queue is unavailable. However, independent clients do not have the intermediate store-and-forward capability of MSMQ routing servers and do not store information from the MSMQ Information Store.

Independent clients can operate while disconnected from the MSMQ environment and while mobile. In disconnected mode an independent client cannot access the MSMQ Information Store. If an application needs to execute while the independent client is disconnected, it must observe the following restrictions:

- Public queues can be created or deleted only while the machine is connected to the MSMQ environment.
- Queues cannot be located. The application must know the format name for a target queue.
- Machine and queue properties cannot be accessed.

- Security context information cannot be retrieved. Thus messages cannot use authentication.

- Queue security descriptors cannot be accessed or modified.

Applications on independent clients can still prepare messages and send them. The applications can also retrieve and process messages that arrived while the client was connected to a site.

Independent clients can also be configured to connect into multiple sites.[5] Because MSMQ provides automatic site recognition, a person who travels to several offices, for example, can have his or her laptop configured to work within various sites.

MSMQ dependent clients cannot function without access to the queue manager on an MSMQ server. These clients rely on an assigned queue manager to perform all functions on their behalf, such as queue creation and sending and receiving messages.

2.5.2 Connected Networks

The concept of *connected networks* helps to organize communications based on network connectivity. A connected network (CN) is composed of computers that can support the same network protocol and communicate directly with one another. In other words, any two computers on the same connected network can open a session between them.

All computers on a physical local area network and using the same protocol must belong to the same connected network. The reason is that computers on the same network will monitor the same broadcasts. Aside from this restriction, users have a lot of flexibility in how they overlay site organization on connected networks. For example, a connected network can be shared by more than one site (Figure 2-3a), or a site can be composed of two or more connected networks (Figure 2-3b).

Bridging two connected networks is easy. A computer can reside on multiple connected networks (one connected network per network interface). In order for two colocated connected networks to exchange messages, at least one MSMQ server must be placed on both connected networks. MSMQ supports connected networks that use IP or IPX as transport protocols.

2.5.3 Message Routing

MSMQ provides flexible routing of messages within and between sites. MSMQ assumes that intrasite routing is fast and inexpensive and that intersite routing is slow

---

5. An independent client can be within only one site at a time.

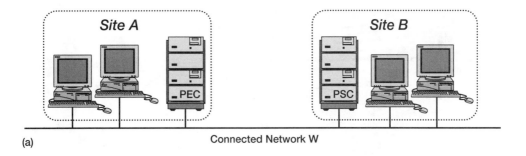

(a)

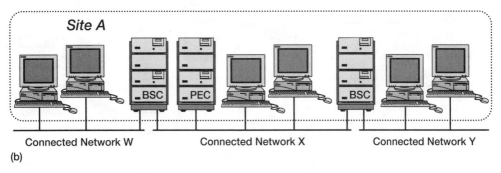

(b)

Figure 2-3   Connected networks and sites: (a) Two sites sharing a single connected network; (b) One site spanning three connected networks

and expensive. MSMQ always attempts to deliver a message directly to a target queue. Direct delivery will fail if a connection cannot be established between the source and destination machines or if administrators define special routing rules. Direct connections cannot be established when the source and destination machines do not share a common connected network. Network and machine failures can also make it impossible to establish a direct connection. Under these conditions MSMQ uses store-and-forward routing of messages through one or more intermediate servers to the target queue.

Session contention occurs in many client/server applications when too many clients attempt to establish sessions with a server machine. Session contention can be reduced by concentrating the message traffic (hence session establishment) within a set of routing servers. Administrators can define special message routing rules to minimize session contention on particular hosts. MSMQ uses these rules to route messages optimally through one or more routing servers. These concepts are illustrated in Figure 2-4.

Administrators can implement *intrasite session concentration* by defining routing servers for within a site. Between sites, administrators can direct messages across

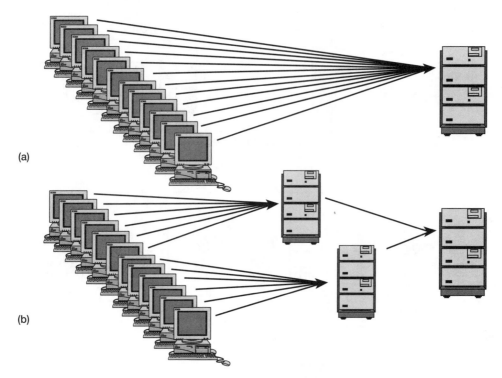

Figure 2-4 (a) Session contention; (b) Session concentration

specific network segments, using *intersite session concentration.* In both cases messages are funneled through routing servers to reduce the number of sessions to a given host.

2.5.3.1 Intrasite Routing

The process of routing messages to target queues within a site is called *intrasite routing.* MSMQ always chooses the shortest available path as measured by the number of servers a message must pass through to reach its destination.

Independent clients can be configured to use *in-routing servers* (InRSs) and *out-routing servers* (OutRSs). When an OutRS server is configured for an independent client, every outgoing message is sent by using store-and-forward through the OutRS to its target queue. When an InRS server is configured for an independent client, messages are routed through the InRS. The PEC, PSCs, BSCs, and routing servers can all be used as InRSs and OutRSs. By default independent clients are not configured to use InRSs or OutRSs.

Using InRSs or OutRSs adds one hop for each message sent. When considering routing within a site, a site administrator needs to balance the cost of adding hops against the benefits of using session concentration.

2.5.3.2 Intersite Routing

Intersite routing is the process of routing messages to target queues at other sites. MSMQ determines a message's optimal intersite route by computing the sum of the site link costs. As already described, administrators can set the cost of routing between sites. A *site gate* provides session concentration between sites. Zero or more site gates can be set up to route messages between two sites. Thus some sites may be connected twice, perhaps by low- and high-speed network links. Other sites may not be linked directly; messages sent between them will need to flow across one or more routing servers in intermediate sites.

2.5.4 Enterprise Security

MSMQ provides message authentication, integrity, and encryption. In addition, MSMQ provides access control of several MSMQ objects and auditing of security-related events.

2.5.4.1 Access Control

Operations on the enterprise, sites, connected networks, computers, and queues can be restricted. MSMQ access controls can be set by using the MSMQ Explorer. Queue access controls can also be set through either programming API.

- At the enterprise level it is possible to control the creation of sites and connected networks, registration of certificates, setting and viewing of enterprise properties and permissions, the ownership of an enterprise, and the deletion of the enterprise.

- Site operations that can be controlled include the privilege to install a backup site controller or routing server, to install a new machine, to set and view site properties and permissions, to take ownership of a site, and to delete a site.

- Access controls on connected networks include setting and viewing of CN properties and permissions, setting ownership of a connected network, and deleting a connected network.

- Controllable operations on computers include the ability to receive or view messages in a machine dead letter or journal queue, to create queues, to set and view computer properties and permissions, to take ownership of the computer, and to delete the computer.

- We've already seen that queues can be configured to accept only authenticated or private messages. It is also possible to restrict access to specific users or groups of users. Associated with each queue is a security descriptor that can be set when a queue is created and modified later. This descriptor controls who can create, open, read from, and delete a queue and also specifies who can modify the security descriptor itself. These access controls can be set programmatically. Using the MSMQ Explorer, one can control receiving and viewing messages in an application and system queues (or their corresponding journal queues), sending messages to the queue, setting and viewing queue properties and permissions, and deleting the queue.

MSMQ checks the security descriptor to determine whether a user has sufficient rights to perform an operation. All operations fail if the user does not have appropriate rights.

2.5.4.2 Auditing

MSMQ can audit access operations to an MSMQ enterprise, sites, connected networks, machines, and queues. Audit log messages are written to the event log on the server on which an operation is performed. A nearly infinite set of events can be audited. Auditing can be set up for the success, failure, or the success and failure of events.

2.6 Integration with non-MSMQ Messaging Environments

MSMQ defines an architecture for MSMQ applications to communicate with non-MSMQ environments. The architecture is based on connector servers. Connector servers enable *connector applications* to send and receive messages using other messaging systems.

MSMQ connector servers receive the messages from MSMQ on internal connector queues. A connector application exchanges messages with the foreign message system.

Through an MSMQ connector server, MSMQ applications can perform the same operations on *foreign queues* that they would typically perform on the queues within their enterprise. Connector applications make standard MSMQ API calls to move messages between foreign queues and ordinary MSMQ queues. When messages are exchanged between messaging systems, the connector application must translate between MSMQ message properties and the message format understood by the *foreign computer.* The connector application is also responsible for handling message acknowledgments. Message properties provide support for message authentication and encryption between MSMQ and foreign messaging environments.

Luckily Level 8 Systems has implemented technologies and connectors that enable integration of MSMQ with several non-MSMQ environments. And Microsoft has provided a connector that enables MSMQ applications to send and receive messages through Microsoft Exchange.

For companies interested in high-performance queued messaging across a wide range of operating systems, the technologies from Level 8 Systems are most important. Such companies will want to use MSMQ as a low-cost messaging backbone and will integrate existing TP applications and environments into the MSMQ environment.

Level 8 Systems offers two solutions to integrate existing TP applications and environments into the MSMQ environment. See Figure 2-5.

The FalconMQ Client enables applications on CICS, UNIX, IBM AS 400, DEC VMS, and Unisys platforms to interact with MSMQ in a way similar to dependent clients. These clients need to communicate with MSMQ through a server. Since the client cannot create MSMQ queues in the local environment, it creates queues on a server.

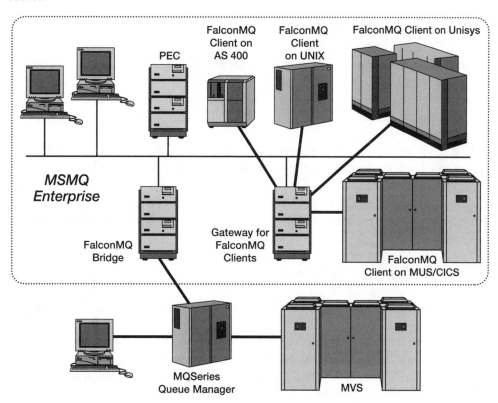

Figure 2-5   Level 8 Systems' FalconMQ Client and FalconMQ Bridge

The FalconMQ Bridge enables MSMQ and IBM MQSeries applications to exchange messages. Many companies have deployed MQSeries as a way to access mainframe applications and services. With Level 8's FalconMQ Bridge, the two messaging environments can be joined.

FalconMQ Client applications are like other applications that communicate through MSMQ. CICS client applications are provided with a COBOL/CICS interface. Other clients use a C language interface.

The FalconMQ Client interfaces differ in two ways from the MSMQ API. First, MSMQ relies on underlying Windows operating system security and event services when an MSMQ application creates a security context or asynchronously receives messages. These services are not implemented in non-Windows environments. Consequently client applications cannot use security descriptors or asynchronously receive messages. Asynchronous behavior can still be implemented by using native operating system threads. Other MSMQ features are supported. For example, FalconMQ Clients can transactionally send and receive messages.

Second, clients are provided with additional API functions that enable client applications to control what MSMQ Gateway server they use. All FalconMQ Clients are assigned to a default server. The first time a client application calls a Gateway API function, the client software will automatically establish a connection to the client's default Gateway server. However, the client can programmatically connect to other Gateway servers by using `MSMQGatewayOpen()`. If the application uses multiple threads, each thread can open a different Gateway server. However, a thread can open only one Gateway server at a time. Threads call `MSMQGatewayClose()` to disconnect from a Gateway server.

The ability to control server connections can be useful. Developers can implement failover capabilities or can improve performance by connecting directly to a server that other FalconMQ clients use.

Many companies use IBM's MQSeries as a messaging service. MQSeries integrates with most transaction processing environments and is available on a large number of platforms.

Level 8 Systems has implemented a bridge between the MQSeries and MSMQ messaging environments. The FalconMQ Bridge operates in the background. Messages sent by MQSeries applications using the `MQPUT()` API can be read by MSMQ applications using the MSMQ API or COM components. Messages sent by MSMQ applications using the native APIs can be read by `MQGET()`. The MSMQ connector architecture facilitates message exchange transparency on the MSMQ side.

A foreign queue must be defined to MSMQ before an MSMQ application can send messages to an MQSeries application. When the MSMQ application is ready, it opens the foreign queue and sends one or more messages. A message is stored temporarily on an MSMQ connector queue. The FalconMQ Bridge dequeues the message from the connector queue, converts the message properties to the MQSeries message descriptor, and transmits the message to the MQSeries destination queue for processing by a MQSeries application.

When it wants to send a message to an MSMQ application, an MQSeries application opens a remote queue representing the MSMQ destination queue and sends one or more messages. MQSeries stores the messages temporarily on an MQSeries queue manager's transmission queue. The FalconMQ Bridge removes the message from the transmission queue, converts the message structure to MSMQ message properties, and transmits the message to its MSMQ destination queue.

In MSMQ, a *foreign connected network* is used to represent the MQSeries network in MSMQ. A foreign computer is defined for each MQSeries queue manager. MQSeries queues are treated as foreign queues. In MQSeries, queue manager aliases and transmissions queues are defined to route messages to MSMQ.

Once the FalconMQ Bridge is installed and configured into each messaging environment, messages transfer can occur. MSMQ applications use an MQSeries queue manager name in place of an MSMQ machine name in pathnames. If a queue called `Billing` is managed by the MQSQM1 MQSeries queue manager, MSMQ applications would use a pathname of `MQSQM1\Billing` as the pathname for the queue; a call to `MQPathNameToFormatName` returns the appropriate format name for the MQSeries queue. The format name is then used to open the queue for sending or receiving messages.

When MSMQ and MQSeries share equivalent message properties, the FalconMQ Bridge translates properties directly. The Bridge also translates roughly equivalent property definitions. FalconMQ Bridge will ignore or assign default values to properties that have no equivalent definitions.

2.7 Conclusion

MSMQ is a powerful, easy-to-administer distributed messaging environment. Internal and external transaction support, message authentication and encryption, access control and auditing, automatic message acknowledgment, and other facilities combine to make MSMQ a feature-rich environment for developing distributed applications.

MSMQ also provides excellent cross-platform integration support. Applications in non-Windows environments can use MSMQ as a messaging backbone. Technologies from Level 8 Systems enable these applications to be integrated with MSMQ as FalconMQ Clients or through the FalconMQ Bridge. MSMQ can also exchange messages with e-mail users through the Exchange Connector, or developers can implement their own e-mail connectors, using MAPI.

Now that you understand the power of MSMQ, let's begin to learn more about developing MSMQ applications. In Chapter 3 we look closely at message properties and queue names.

2.8 Resources and References

Chappell, D. 1998. "Understanding MSMQ," *Microsoft Systems Journal* (July).

Dickman, A., and K. Walker. 1997. "Microsoft Delivers the Message," *Information Week* 639 (June 30): 51.

Level 8 Systems. 1997. *FalconMQ Bridge for MQSeries: System's Administrator's and Programmer's Guide.* New York: Level 8 Systems.

————. 1997. *MSMQ Gateway: System's Administrator's and Programmer's Guide.* New York: Level 8 Systems.

Microsoft Message Queue Explorer Administrator's Online Help.

Microsoft Message Queue Server Online Help.

Microsoft SQL Server Books Online.

Microsoft Transaction Server Online Help.

X/Open. 1991. *X/Open CAE Specification: Distributed Transaction Processing: The XA Specification.* Cambridge, MA: X/Open.

————. 1996. *X/Open Guide: Distributed Transaction Processing: Reference Model, Version 3.* Cambridge, MA: X/Open.

3 Chapter

Properties and
Queue Names

This chapter discusses queue and message properties and queue names at a level needed for you to develop MSMQ applications. It is intended for developers.

Before you play your first game of golf, it's useful to learn some fundamentals about the game, such as when to use various clubs and how to swing the club. The same is true in programming. Before we dive into some programming examples, let's cover two fundamental topics that you will need to understand in order to develop an MSMQ application.

In this chapter we'll examine queue and message properties and discuss queue naming. Chapters that follow will build on this information as they explain programming examples and techniques.

3.1 Properties

The design of MSMQ incorporates object-oriented characteristics. Key among these are the definition of several object classes, such as message, queue, and queue manager. Associated with each object class is a set of attributes, or properties. When an MSMQ enterprise is created and as it grows, instances of site, queue, queue manager, machine, and connected network objects are created.

In this chapter we are concerned with those objects that are most likely to be directly used in application programs: queues and messages. MSMQ applications will send or receive messages stored in queues. When applications begin to communicate, they create or use instances of queue and message object types.

MSMQ also defines queue manager properties that can be programmatically examined and updated. These properties may be of interest to administrative applications but are not discussed in this chapter.

Let's look at some of the ways queue and message properties can be used to customize communications between MSMQ applications. The idea in these sections is to introduce the various properties MSMQ offers. A reference of queue and message properties is presented in Appendix A.

3.1.1 Queue Properties

Queue properties help administrators and developers to define queue behavior and to control queue features. Properties can be examined and set programmatically or administratively. MSMQ automatically sets most properties to their designated default values, so creating a queue and configuring its properties is not a complex task.

When programming with the MSMQ API, you can use the following functions:

- `MQCreateQueue()`—Programmers can set queue properties when creating a queue.

- `MQGetQueueProperties()`—Once a queue is created, properties can be examined.

- `MQSetQueueProperties()`—Queue properties can be modified.

- `MQLocateBegin()`—A program stipulates search criteria to be used when it queries the MQIS to locate a queue. The search criteria are defined by a set of queue properties, values for the properties, and relationships between each property and the specified value, such as equal to, not equal to, less than, and greater than.

ActiveX programmers will use queue properties with the following MSMQ components:

- `MSMQQueueInfo`—You create an instance of an `MSMQQueueInfo` component to get and set queue property values. If you are creating a queue, all properties associated with the `MSMQQueueInfo` are set to their default values. A programmer can override the default property values by assigning new values to the component instance. Then the developer can call `MSMQQueueInfo.Create()` to create the queue.

If a queue already exists, you can create an instance of `MSMQQueueInfo` and call `MSMQQueueInfo.Refresh()` to retrieve its current property values, which can be examined and modified. You need to call `MSMQQueueInfo.Update()` to make modifications permanent.

- `MSMQQuery`—When a program needs to locate one or more queues, it creates an instance of `MSMQQuery`, which is used to query the MQIS. As described previously, a program stipulates search criteria to be used for the query. The set of queues that meet the search criteria are returned as an `MSMQQueueInfos` object.

- `MSMQQueueInfos`—This is a collection of `MSMQQueueInfo` objects. Following a query, a program can iterate through the collection and select the queue it wants.

Administrators can create and set queue properties by using the MSMQ Explorer. Most queue properties are optional. If the programmer or administrator does not specify their values to MSMQ, default values are assigned. All MSMQ API queue properties begin with `PROPID_Q`. Most queue properties are defined as attributes of the `MSMQQueueInfo` component. Keep the following rules in mind.

- `PROPID_Q_PATHNAME` (or its COM equivalent, `MSMQQueueInfo.Pathname`) is required for creating a queue and cannot be reset after the queue is created.

- By default queues are not transactional when they are created. This property cannot be changed once the queue is created. If a queue needs to be transactional, its `PROPID_Q_TRANSACTION` property must be set to `MQ_TRANSACTIONAL` when the MSMQ API is used. In COM you stipulate whether a queue is transactional by setting the `IsTransactional` parameter of `MSMQQueueInfo.Create()` to `TRUE`.

Most applications will use a small number of queue properties for creating message queues, administration queues, or response queues. On the other hand, administrative applications may use a large number of these properties. Whether you are developing a typical application or an administrative application, it's important to understand how queue and message properties can help you.

Table 3-1 briefly describes each queue property. An expanded version of this table is given in Appendix A. The properties are presented in alphabetical order, since few queue properties are interrelated. We'll present selected scenarios that demonstrate how to use these queue properties later in the chapter and throughout the book.

Visual Basic automatically converts the times returned by `MSMQQueueInfo.CreateTime` and `MSMQQueueInfo.ModifyTime` to the local system time and system date. In C `ctime()` converts the time and date for display.

Table 3-1 Queue Properties

Queue Property	COM Equivalent	Description
PROPID_Q_ AUTHENTICATE	MSMQQueueInfo. Authenticate	Indicates whether a queue accepts nonauthenticated messages or only authenticated messages.
PROPID_Q_ BASEPRIORITY	MSMQQueueInfo. BasePriority	The base priority for the queue. A queue's base priority is used for routing messages over the network. Messages addressed to a queue with a higher priority are sent before messages addressed to queues with a lower base priority.
PROPID_Q_ CREATE_TIME	MSMQQueueInfo. CreateTime	A read-only property indicating the time and date when the queue was created. The time returned is the number of seconds elapsed since midnight (00:00:00), January 1, 1970 (Coordinated Universal time).
PROPID_Q_ INSTANCE	MSMQQueueInfo. QueueGuid	Uniquely identifies a *public* queue instance. Set by MSMQ when a queue is created, the queue identifier can be used to obtain a format name.
PROPID_Q_ JOURNAL	MSMQQueueInfo. Journal	Indicates whether messages will be copied to a queue journal when they are retrieved from a queue. MSMQ creates a queue journal when a queue is created.
PROPID_Q_ JOURNAL_QUOTA	MSMQQueueInfo. JournalQuota	The size in kilobytes of a target journal queue. The default is INFINITE.

3.1.2 Message Properties

Message properties help define the characteristics of a message, informing MSMQ how to handle a message—for example, to make it recoverable or not. Message properties also indicate information to the sender or receiver, such as where to send a response message. Message properties are established programmatically.

All MSMQ API message properties begin with PROPID_M. Using the MSMQ API, programmers set message properties before they send or receive a message. MQSendMessage() is called to send the message, and MQReceiveMessage() is called to receive a message.

Queue Property	COM Equivalent	Description
PROPID_Q_LABEL	MSMQQueueInfo. Label	A queue label; a user-friendly way to identify the queue.
PROPID_Q_ MODIFY_TIME	MSMQQueueInfo. ModifyTime	A read-only property indicating the last time the properties of a queue were modified. The time returned is the number of seconds elapsed since midnight (00:00:00), January 1, 1970 (Coordinated Universal time).
PROPID_Q_ PATHNAME	MSMQQueueInfo. PathName	Specifies the queue's MSMQ pathname, which includes the name of the machine on which the queue's messages are stored, whether the queue is public or private, and the name of the queue. This property is required when a queue is created.
PROPID_Q_ PRIV_LEVEL	MSMQQueueInfo. PrivLevel	The queue's required privacy level, which determines how the queue handles encrypted messages.
PROPID_Q_QUOTA	MSMQQueueInfo. Quota	The size in kilobytes of the queue storage. The default is INFINITE.
PROPID_Q_ TRANSACTION	MSMQQueueInfo. IsTransactional	Specifies whether the queue is transactional or nontransactional. This property cannot be reset once the queue is created.
PROPID_Q_TYPE	MSMQQueueInfo. ServiceTypeGuid	The type of service, such as manufacturer or inventory, that is associated with messages sent to and retrieved from the queue.

In COM message properties are defined as attributes of the MSMQMessage class. When programmers create an MSMQMessage instance, all properties are set to their default values. Programmers can override the default values by assigning new values to the component properties. MSMQMessage.Send() sends the message. Message properties are also set when a message is received.

Message properties are organized around specific topic areas. Four categories of message properties are described in this chapter: basic messaging; acknowledgment, journal, and reports messages; security; and additional message-handling properties. A fifth category of message properties relates to connector applications. These properties are not presented here. However, all message properties, including connector message properties, are described in detail in Appendix A.

Table 3-2 **Basic Messaging Properties**

Basic Messaging Property	COM Equivalent	Description
PROPID_M_BODY	MSMQMessage.Body	The body of the message. Any type of information can be placed into a message body. The sending and receiving applications are responsible for understanding the type of information in the message.
PROPID_M_BODY_SIZE	MSMQMessage.BodyLength	The length of a message body in bytes.
PROPID_M_BODY_TYPE	No COM equivalent.	The data type of a message body (string, array of bytes, or object). COM automatically assigns and interprets types for MSMQMessage.Body.
PROPID_M_CLASS	MSMQMessage.Class	Indicates whether a message is a normal MSMQ message, one of several positive or negative acknowledgments, or a report. MSMQ typically sets this property.
PROPID_M_CORRELATIONID	MSMQMessage.CorrelationId	An application-defined identifier that enables a sending application to correlate messages. To facilitate correlation of request and response messages, a responding application will set the correlation ID of a response message to the message ID of a request message. MSMQ automatically does this for acknowledgment and report messages. The sending application can examine the correlation ID to match the response message to a request.

3.1.2.1   Basic Messaging Properties

Some properties that control basic messaging are listed in Table 3-2. A sender can use basic message properties to

- Define the body of a message and identify the type of data contained in the body
- Give the message a user-friendly label

Basic Messaging Property	COM Equivalent	Description
PROPID_M_ DELIVERY	MSMQMessage. Delivery	A property used by a sending application to indicate to MSMQ how to handle message delivery: either *recoverable* (stored to disk) or *express* (stored in memory).
PROPID_M_LABEL	MSMQMessage.Label	An application-specific, user-friendly message label assigned by the message creator.
PROPID_M_LABEL_ LEN	No COM equivalent.	The length of the message label in characters.
PROPID_M_MSGID	MSMQMessage.Id	A unique, read-only message identifier generated by MSMQ when a message is sent. The sending application will read the message ID if it needs to correlate the message with other messages. The receiver application may assign a message ID as the correlation ID of a response.
PROPID_M_ PRIORITY	MSMQMessage. Priority	The priority assigned to a message by the sender. The priority affects message placement in a queue.
PROPID_M_ RESP_QUEUE	MSMQMessage. ResponseQueueInfo	The format name of the queue to which response messages can be sent by the receiving application. A sending application sets this property.
PROPID_M_RESP_ QUEUE_LEN	No COM equivalent.	The character length of the format name for the response queue.
PROPID_M_SRC_ MACHINE_ID	MSMQMessage. SourceMachineGuid	A read-only property attached to a message by MSMQ to indicate the computer from which a message originated.

- Specify whether a message should be recoverable
- Assign a priority that determines where a message is placed within a destination queue
- Designate a queue to which response messages are to be sent
- Examine message identifiers and correlation identifiers that enable two messages to be correlated

Table 3-3 Acknowledgment, Journal, and Report Message Properties

Message Acknowledgment, Journal, and Report Property	COM Equivalent	Description
PROPID_M_ ACKNOWLEDGE	MSMQMessage.Ack	Used by a sending application to indicate the type of acknowledgment message, if any, that MSMQ should return to an administrative queue.
PROPID_M_ ADMIN_QUEUE	MSMQMessage. AdminQueueInfo	Set by a sending application, the format name of the queue to which an acknowledgment message is sent when requested by the sending application.
PROPID_M_ADMIN_ QUEUE_LEN	No COM equivalent.	The character length of the format name for the administration queue.
PROPID_M_DEST_ QUEUE	MSMQMessage. DestinationQueueInfo	A read-only property attached to a message by MSMQ to indicate the queue to which the message is to be sent. This property would typically be used by an application that inspects messages in a machine journal or a dead letter queue.

A receiver can use basic message properties to

- Choose one message over another for removal from a queue. Selection criteria can be made by using a message label, correlation ID, body content, or other properties. MSMQ does not limit the search criteria.

- Create a response to a request message. The request message's identifier value is placed in the correlation ID of the response message.

- Send a message to the correct response queue. A format name is extracted from the response queue message property, and the response queue is opened with the format name.

3.1.2.2 Acknowledgment, Journal, and Report Message Properties

Table 3-3 (see also Appendix A) provides a brief description of message properties that control the maintenance of message journals and the generation of acknowledgments and reports. These properties allow a message sender to

Message Acknowledgment, Journal, and Report Property	COM Equivalent	Description
PROPID_M_DEST_QUEUE_LEN	No COM equivalent.	The character length of the format name for the destination queue.
PROPID_M_JOURNAL	MSMQMessage.Journal	Used by a sending application to indicate whether MSMQ should send a copy of a message to the machine journal of the source machine, to a dead letter queue, or to neither. MSMQ automatically sends transactional messages to the transactional dead letter queue (DEADXACT) on the source machine if the message is not delivered.
PROPID_M_TRACE	MSMQMessage.Trace	Used by the sender to indicate whether to trace the store-and-forward route of a message to its destination queue. An administrator must have defined a report queue of the source machine, or this property is ignored.

- Request various kinds of positive or negative acknowledgment and to designate an administrative queue to which MSMQ sends acknowledgements
- Control whether messages are placed in journal queues during transmission
- Stipulate whether report messages should be generated as an application message is forwarded through queues to its target queue

3.1.2.3 Message Security Properties

Security-related message properties enable a sender to

- Select authentication of a sender to the receiver and define a preferred hash function for creating a digital signature
- Specify whether internal or external certificates should be used during the authentication process
- Elect to send private messages and to select a preferred encryption algorithm

Table 3-4 **Message Security Properties**

Message Security Property	COM Equivalent	Description
PROPID_M_ AUTH_LEVEL	MSMQMessage. AuthLevel	Determines whether a message should be authenticated. An internal certificate is used to sign the message unless external certificates are supplied.
PROPID_M_ AUTHENTICATED	MSMQMessage. IsAuthenticated	Indicates whether MSMQ could authenticate the message. This property is used only by the receiving application when receiving the message.
PROPID_M_ HASH_ALG	MSMQMessage. HashAlgorithm	Determines the hash algorithm used when authenticating messages.
PROPID_M_ SECURITY_ CONTEXT	MSMQMessage. SecurityContext	Used by a sending application when it wants to reuse an external certificate to send several messages. The security context includes the user's external security certificate and is represented as an opaque handle. When the handle is copied into this property, MSMQ uses it to authenticate the message. If an external certificate will be used only once, the application should set MSMQMessage.SenderCertificate or PROPID_M_SENDER_CERT.

A receiver can determine whether MSMQ has authenticated a message and may derive the identification of the sender. Table 3-4 lists some of the security-related message properties. For more information, see Appendix A.

3.1.2.4 Additional Message-Handling Properties

Table 3-5 covers some additional message properties that applications may find of use. Many of these properties have to do with the *life* of a message. A sending application can specify how long a message has to live before it is discarded. A receiving application can determine when a message was sent or arrived on the target queue. These properties merit a quick review.

Message Security Property	COM Equivalent	Description
PROPID_M_ SENDER_CERT	MSMQMessage. SenderCertificate	Used when a sending application will use an external certificate once to send a message. Otherwise the application should set MSMQMessage.SecurityContext or PROPID_M_SECURITY_CONTEXT.
PROPID_M_ SENDER_CERT_LEN	No COM equivalent.	The character length of the sender certificate buffer.
PROPID_M_ PRIV_LEVEL	MSMQMessage. PrivLevel	Defines whether a private (encrypted) message should be sent. When privacy is indicated, the source queue manager encrypts the body of the message, and the target queue manager decrypts the message body.
PROPID_M_ ENCRYPTION_ALG	MSMQMessage. EncryptAlgorithm	Allows a sender to determine the encryption algorithm to use when sending private messages.
PROPID_M_ SENDERID	MSMQMessage. SenderId	The identity of the message sender.
PROPID_M_ SENDERID_LEN	No COM equivalent.	The length in bytes of the sender ID.
PROPID_M_ SENDERID_TYPE	MSMQMessage. SenderIdType	The data type of the sender identifier found in PROPID_M_SENDERID or MSMQMessage.SenderIdType. MSMQ handles only a SID, or security identifier.

Visual Basic automatically converts the times returned by MSMQMessage.ArrivedTime and MSMQMessage.SentTime to the local system time and system date. In C ctime() converts the time and date for display.

MSMQ uses two message timers: *time-to-reach-queue* and *time-to-be-received.* If either timer expires before the message reaches its target queue, MSMQ discards the message or sends it to the dead letter queue; the act is determined by the value assigned to PROPID_M_JOURNAL or MSMQMessage.Journal. The time-to-be-received timer takes precedence over the time-to-reach-queue timer when it is set to a lesser value.

Table 3-5 Additional Message-Handling Properties

Additional Message-Handling Property	COM Equivalent	Description
PROPID_M_ APPSPECIFIC	MSMQMessage. AppSpecific	An application-specific index value that a receiving application can use to customize methods for sorting messages.
PROPID_M_ ARRIVEDTIME	MSMQMessage. ArrivedTime	A read-only property indicating when the message arrived at the queue. The time returned is the number of seconds elapsed since midnight (00:00:00), January 1, 1970 (Coordinated Universal time).
PROPID_M_ SENTTIME	MSMQMessage. SentTime	A read-only property indicating when the message was sent. The time returned is the number of seconds elapsed since midnight (00:00:00), January 1, 1970 (Coordinated Universal time).
PROPID_M_TIME_ TO_BE_RECEIVED	MSMQMessage. MaxTimeToReceive	The total time (in seconds) that the message is allowed to live. This time interval includes the time needed by the message to get to its destination queue, plus the wait time before it is retrieved by an application. By default this property value is INFINITE.
PROPID_M_TIME_ TO_REACH_QUEUE	MSMQMessage. MaxTimeToReachQueue	The total time (in seconds) that the message is allowed before it reaches its destination queue. MSMQ always gives the message one chance to reach its destination if the queue is waiting for the message. If the queue is local, the message always reaches the queue.
PROPID_M_VERSION	No COM equivalent.	A read-only property indicating the version of MSMQ used to send the message.

3.2 Queue Naming

In modern distributed infrastructures naming services are fairly important. They enable users and applications to associate user-friendly or logical names for entities in their networks. Logical names help facilitate location independence; the entity can be moved around the network with no impact on users and applications. Naming services support location independence by associating one or more physical attributes about the entity, such as the IP address of the machine on which the entities exist and a port number, with a logical name.

In an MSMQ environment several entities might be addressed by using logical names, including the MSMQ enterprise, sites, connected networks, computers, and queues. The MSMQ Explorer enables users to locate these entities in either of two ways.

- Traverse through a hierarchy of objects to find an entity. One hierarchy consists of the enterprise, sites, machines, queues, and messages. Each object is represented by a logical name.

- Use the Explorer search capability. From the toolbar you select the Tools menu. Use the Find option to search for a Computer or a Queue. When you enter a logical name for a computer or a queue, Explorer locates it for you. If you search by type for a computer or queue, Explorer locates all instances of that type.

But what kinds of names are used in MSMQ applications? And how are they used? Two kinds of queue names are used: a pathname and a format name. Each is important, and each will be discussed in the following sections.

3.2.1 Pathnames

The pathname for a queue is similar to a file name. The pathname describes where a queue is located and defines whether the queue is public or private.

Why should you care about a pathname? When you use the MSMQ API or COM components to create a queue, the pathname is a required property. It can also be used to derive a format name, which is needed when an application opens a queue.

A pathname consists of the name of the computer on which a queue is located, followed by the name of queue. For public queues a backslash character (\ ) separates the computer and queue names. For private queues the computer and queue names are separated by \$private\. To indicate queues on the local machine " . " can be substituted for the name of the local machine. On dependent clients " . " refers to the client's designated server.

Private queues can be created only on the local machine. However, applications can use the pathname of a remote private queue to obtain a format name.
The following are some examples of pathnames:

```
"PSWTech\myQueue"
    // a public queue named "myQueue" on the machine PSWTech
".\myTransactionQueue" // a public queue on the local machine
"HStern\$private\parts"
    // a private queue on machine HStern
".\$PRIVATE\myPrivateResponseQueue"
    // a private queue on the local machine
```

Keep the following restrictions in mind:

- All computers in your MSMQ network must have a unique name, even if they are on separate, nonconnected networks. Computer names, defined when you install the operating system, cannot be changed. The name space for computers is flat (as opposed to hierarchical).

- All queues on a computer must have a unique name. MSMQ will return MQ_ERROR_QUEUE_EXISTS if you attempt to create a queue with the name of an existing queue.

- A pathname is represented as a string of Unicode characters. The maximum length of a pathname is 124 Unicode characters.

What Is Unicode?

Unicode is a character-encoding scheme that uses 2 bytes, not 1 byte, for every character. Unicode is an International Standards Organization (ISO) standard that defines character and symbols for almost all languages. The Component Object Model (COM) supports Unicode on all 32-bit Windows systems.

3.2.2 Format Names

A queue format name is nothing more than a unique name for the queue. MSMQ generates a format name when the queue is created and later when it is needed by an application. MQIS does not store format names; they are generated when requested.

Applications can store format names for future reference. Why is this interesting? For example, you may want to develop an application for independent clients that are mobile and periodically disconnected from the MSMQ enterprise. In order to send a message, your application must open a queue first. The client machine doesn't need to be connected to the MSMQ enterprise to open a queue, but the queue's format name is required! A format name cannot be derived using a pathname when the client is disconnected because the MQIS isn't able to be accessed. You could write your application to access a configuration file when disconnected from the network. The format name for a target queue could be placed in the configuration file.

Format names differ from pathnames in several respects. For example, format names are not user-friendly. Format names and pathnames are also used in different situations. A pathname is used primarily to create a queue. Format names are used to

- Open a queue by using `MQOpenQueue`.[1]
- Get or set a queue's properties. Developers can call `MQGetQueueProperties` or `MQSetQueueProperties`.
- Get and set security attributes. Developers can call `MQGetQueueSecurity` or `MQSetQueueSecurity`.
- Delete the queue by using `MQDeleteQueue`.[2]

When `MQCreateQueue()` of the MSMQ API is used, a queue format name is returned when a queue is created. A format name can also be derived from the MSMQ API calls `MQHandleToFormatName()`, `MQInstanceToFormatName()`, and `MQPathNameToFormatName()`. ActiveX developers can use `MSMQQueueInfo.FormatName` to derive a format name once the property has been set by MSMQ—after creating a queue or when selecting an `MSMQQueueInfo` instance during an `MSMQQuery` queue lookup.[3]

MSMQ defines five kinds of format names:

- *Public* format names are associated with application queues registered in the MQIS.
- *Private* format names identify private queues that are created and managed locally by the queue manager on the local computer.
- *Machine* format names address machine journal and dead letter queues maintained on a machine.
- *Direct* format names enable MSMQ applications to open queues that are not in your enterprise, or to send messages directly, that is, without using store-and-forward, to a queue.

---

1. Internally COM translates a pathname to a format name before opening a queue. Thus a user doesn't have to set the format name to open a queue.

2. Format names are not required to delete a queue.

3. Careful readers may detect a difference within the MSMQ and COM APIs. Format names are properties of `MSMQQueueInfo` components, but a format name is *not* a queue property in the MSMQ API.

- *Connector* format names address foreign queues. (We don't discuss these kinds of format names in this chapter.)

Most MSMQ applications will use public or private format names. Let's look briefly at public, private, machine, and direct format names next.

3.2.2.1 Public Queue Format Names

Public queues are registered in the MQIS. The format name of a public queue can be derived by using MQIS or can be manually generated. When a public queue format name is used, MSMQ uses MQIS to determine where the computer is located, and so on.

Global Unique Identifiers (GUIDs)

Selected properties use a global unique identifier (GUID), a type used widely in the Windows environment. A GUID is a 128-bit value guaranteed to be unique across space and time. To guarantee uniqueness across space, a GUID includes a 48-bit value unique to the computer on which it was generated. The value is usually derived from the address of a network card. A 60-bit time stamp guarantees uniqueness across time (or at least for another thousand years). Additional random bits are included in a GUID. A GUID can be generated by using the uuidgen or guidgen programs.

Format names for public queues have the following structure:

```
"PUBLIC=QueueGUID"
```

The structure begins with the string "PUBLIC=" and is followed by the queue identifier. The queue instance identifier is a GUID, represented as a Unicode string, generated by MSMQ when the queue was created.

You can use the MSMQ Explorer to determine a public format name. First, locate the public queue and right click on its icon to bring up an option menu; select Properties. The queue's GUID (or ID) is displayed under the General tab. A sample general information tab for a queue appears in Figure 3-1.

Note that the queue's location is not part of the format name. There's a real virtue to this, as message operations will succeed regardless of the queue location. In a future release of MSMQ it will be possible to use a public queue format even after a queue has been relocated to another machine.

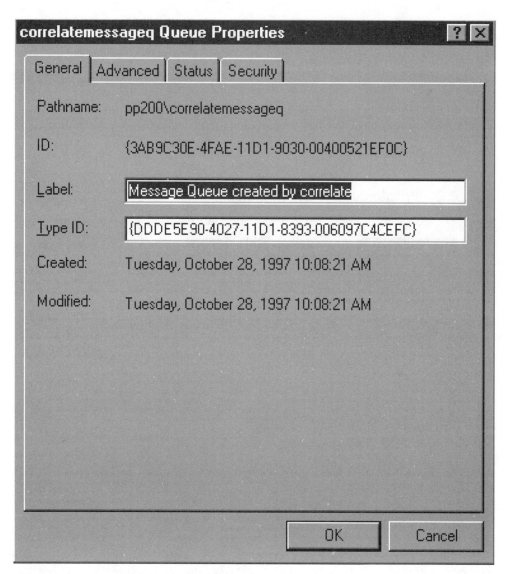

Figure 3-1 General information tab for a queue

A public format name is defined in the following MSMQ API example:

```
// Set a format name into a string
Lpwstr publicFormatName =
        L"PUBLIC=78EB3B11-36B5-11d1-9015-00400521EF0C";
```

Next, the format name is defined, using the `MSMQQueueInfo` COM component:

```
Dim pubQInfo as New MSMQQueueInfo
pubQInfo.FormatName = "PUBLIC=78EB3B11-36B5-11d1-9015-00400521EF0C"
```

To specify a journal associated with a public queue, you would append `";JOURNAL"` to the public format name. The format name for a public queue's journal queue is:

```
"PUBLIC=QueueGUID;JOURNAL".
```

3.2.2.2 Private Queue Format Names

A private queue is never registered in the MQIS. Only the local queue manager on the computer on which it resides is aware of a private queue.

Format names for private queues have the following structure:

```
"PRIVATE= MachineGUID\QueueNumber"
```

The private format name of the queue includes the string `"PRIVATE ="`. The GUID of the computer on which the private queue is located, a hexadecimal number that identifies the queue, follows this string. A backslash separates the machine GUID and queue number.

A private format name is defined in the following MSMQ example:

```
Lpwstr privateFormatName =
        L"PRIVATE=EE21B650-36BE-11d1-9015-00400521EF0C\00000015";
```

Next, the format name is defined, using the `MSMQQueueInfo` COM component:

```
Dim privQInfo as New MSMQQueueInfo
privQInfo.FormatName = _
        "PRIVATE=EE21B650-36BE-11d1-9015-00400521EF0C\00000015"
```

To specify a journal associated with a private queue, append `";JOURNAL"` to the private format name. The format name for a private queue's journal queue is:

```
PRIVATE=MachineGUID\QueueNumber;JOURNAL
```

3.2.2.3 Machine Format Names

Every server and independent client has a computer journal and two dead letter queues. To specify a machine queue associated with a computer, begin the format name with `"MACHINE="`, followed by a machine GUID. One of three designations follows this construct to define which queue is being addressed.

To derive the machine GUID for a computer, you can use the MSMQ Explorer. First, locate the computer and right click on its icon to bring up an option menu; select Properties. The computer's machine GUID (or ID) is displayed under the General tab. A sample general information tab for a computer appears in Figure 3-2.

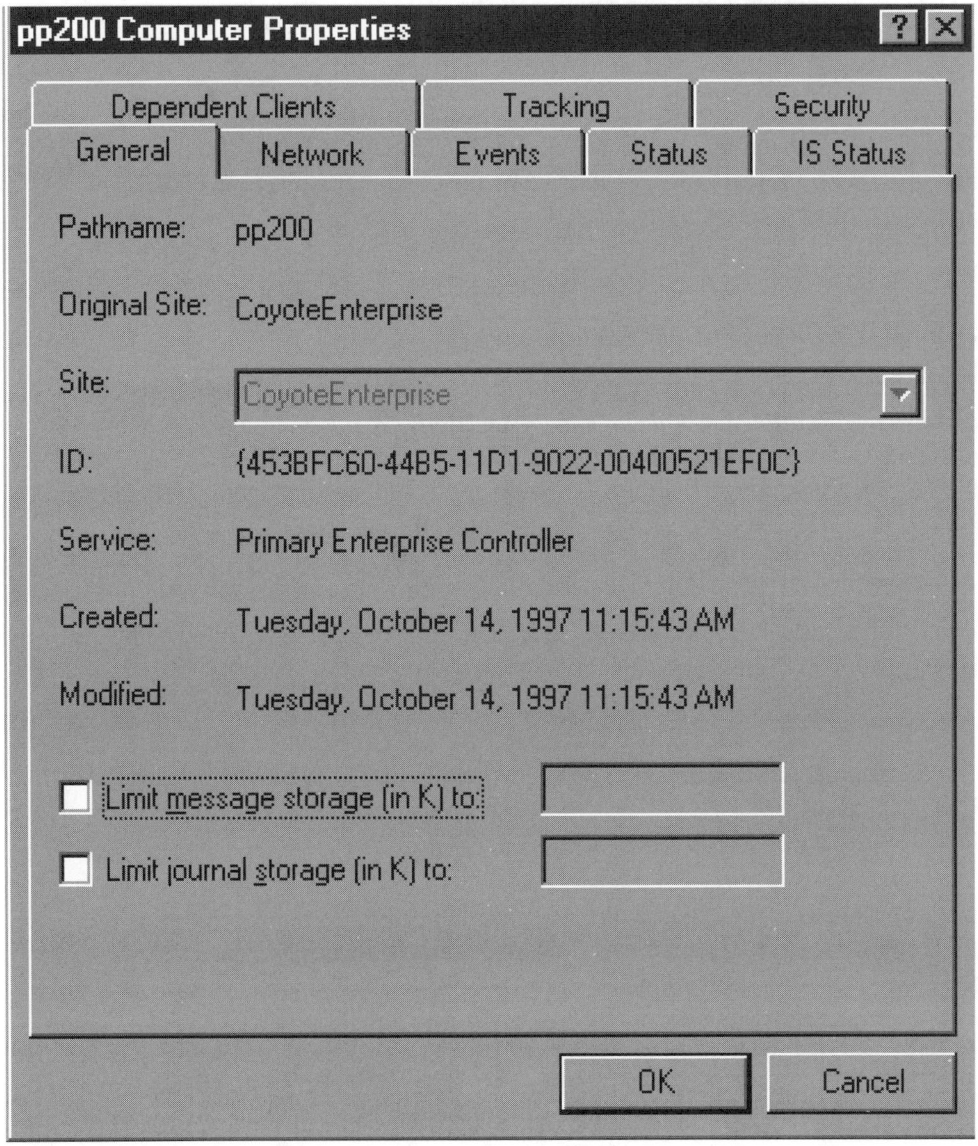

Figure 3-2   General information tab for a computer

Append " ;JOURNAL" to the computer's machine GUID to define the format name for the public machine journal:

```
MACHINE=MachineGUID;JOURNAL
```

Every server and independent client has a nontransactional and a transactional dead letter queue. To specify a nontransactional dead letter queue associated with a computer, begin the format name with "MACHINE=", followed by the computer's machine GUID and ending with ";DEADLETTER":

```
MACHINE=MachineGUID; DEADLETTER
```

To specify a transactional dead letter queue associated with a machine, begin the format name with "MACHINE=", followed by the computer's machine GUID, and append ";DEADXACT":

```
MACHINE=MachineGUID; DEADXACT
```

3.2.2.4 Direct Format Names

Direct format names begin with "DIRECT=" and have two additional parts: an *address specification* and a *queue name.* The address specification can be defined by using a network address for the target machine or its computer name. MSMQ supports the TCP and SPX network protocols. To specify a TCP network address, begin the address specification with "TCP:", followed by the computer's IP address:

```
TCP:IP_address
```

For SPX networks begin the address specification with "SPX:", followed by the network number, a colon, and host number of a computer:

```
SPX:network_number:host_number
```

A computer name address specification begins with "OS:" and is followed by a UNC or DNS name:

```
OS:host_name
```

A queue name is at the end of a direct format name.

Some direct format names specified in C are as follows:

- ```
  // A TCP network address and public queue name
  Lpwstr directFormatName1 =
          L"DIRECT=TCP:202.23.37.1\PSW_MSMQ_QUERIES";
  ```
- ```
  // A DNS computer name and private queue
  Lpwstr directFormatName2 =
          L"DIRECT=OS:accounting.pswtech.com\$private\TimeSheets";
  ```

Next, the format name is defined, using the `MSMQQueueInfo` COM component:

```
Dim dirQInfo1 as New MSMQQueueInfo
Dim dirQInfo2 as New MSMQQueueInfo
' A DNS computer name and public queue
DirQInfo2.FormatName = "DIRECT=OS:PSWAcademy\SimpleQueue1"
' A SPX network address and private queue
DirQInfo2.FormatName = _
            "DIRECT=SPX: 00000008:00A0315E3636\\$private\rateQuote"
```

3.3 Conclusion

In this chapter we've covered two fundamental topics that you will need when developing MSMQ applications using COM components or the MSMQ API. We've reviewed the properties that will help us to create customized queue and messaging strategies. We've learned how pathnames and format names are used, their structure, and how to create them. Now we are now ready to begin to develop applications using MSMQ. We'll learn how to develop two simple applications for exchanging requests and responses through queues. In the next chapter we'll work with MSMQ COM components and Visual Basic. In Chapter 5 we'll demonstrate the use of the MSMQ API.

3.4 Resources and References

Microsoft Message Queue Explorer Administrator's Online Help.

Microsoft Message Queue Server Online Help.

4
Chapter

An MSMQ Application Using the COM Components

This chapter, intended primarily for developers, provides a complete MSMQ example application implemented in Visual Basic, using COM components. Developers who would use COM with other languages will also find this chapter useful. C language users who will use the MSMQ API to develop applications should skip to Chapter 5. Managers may want to read the introductory paragraphs of each major section.

MSMQ defines nine components that conform to COM, Microsoft's Component Object Model. The components can be created and manipulated like any other COM objects. Applications that are developed in Visual Basic, Java, and Visual C++ can use them.

COM components can be used in Web and normal object-oriented applications. In a Web environment Visual Basic scripts, Java applets, and Internet Information Server (IIS) can access MSMQ COM components. Within an HTML page that is displayed by Internet Explorer, MSMQ COM components can be referenced by using the <OBJECT> tag in VBScript. Internet Explorer also can execute Java applets. MSMQ applets can create instances of MSMQ components that facilitate communications. When VBScript or Java run within Internet Explorer, MSMQ needs to be installed on the client desktop.

Active server pages (ASP) make it possible for browsers to access MSMQ services through IIS. IIS interacts with MSMQ COM components by using active server pages written in VBScript. Browsers can send and receive messages through normal HTML pages. Using IIS, MSMQ needs to be installed only on the machines running

IIS. Best of all, C++ programs, ASP scripts, and applets can use the COM examples in this book with few changes.

In normal, object-oriented applications, you can use COM to create and work with instances of MSMQ objects. Visual Basic hides a lot of the mechanics of COM. For this reason I prefer it as a language for illustrating the features of MSMQ.

In this chapter we'll develop a distributed version of the well-known Hello World program in Visual Basic. Hello World is fairly simple in comparison with most applications that will use MSMQ. However, that simplicity allows us to demonstrate several basic features of MSMQ while ignoring other, extraneous matters. We'll use the Hello World example to learn about

- Creating a queue, using the MSMQ Explorer
- Creating a queue, using the COM components
- Looking up queues in MQIS
- Creating and examining message contents
- Sending and receiving messages
- Closing a queue

4.1   Overview of Hello World

In this section we'll briefly describe two programs created in Visual Basic by using MSMQ COM components. The programs, sender and receiver applications, exchange messages.[1] From the standpoint of using MSMQ, little distinguishes the sender and receiver applications in the Hello World example. Both programs create queues, locate queues, open queues, send and receive messages, and close queues.

Both programs are clients of MSMQ. We adopt the convention of consistently calling one program the sending application, or sender, and calling the other program the receiving application, or receiver. Although the sender receives messages and the receiver sends responses, these names describe the general role of each program in exchanging messages.

The queues used in this example can be created programmatically or by administrators before the programs first execute. Each method is demonstrated later in this chapter.

A type identifier can be assigned to a queue. The type identifier, a GUID, can represent a kind of service (for example, inventory management) provided by applications that read messages from the queue. The MQIS helps you to locate queues in the enterprise by its type identifier.

---

1. Source code for this example is available at http://www.psw.com/msmq.

We'll assign type identifiers to the queues used in this example. A Hello World request queue has a type value of

```
{711A7B92-20BA-11d1-8379-006097C4CEFC}
```

A response queue has a type value of

```
{E8EA7B81-215C-11d1-837A-006097C4CEFC}
```

Both the sender and the receiver use these queues. It sometimes helps to have a rule governing queue creation by applications. An application can locate or create the queue from which it receives messages. But the application only locates the queue to which it sends messages. This is a rule I like, but you're free to construct other rules to suit your purposes.

When the sender starts up, it attempts to locate an existing response message queue by using its queue type as an MQIS search criterion. If an existing response queue cannot be located, the sender creates one. The sender never creates a request queue. Rather it locates request queues through MQIS and opens the first queue instance returned.

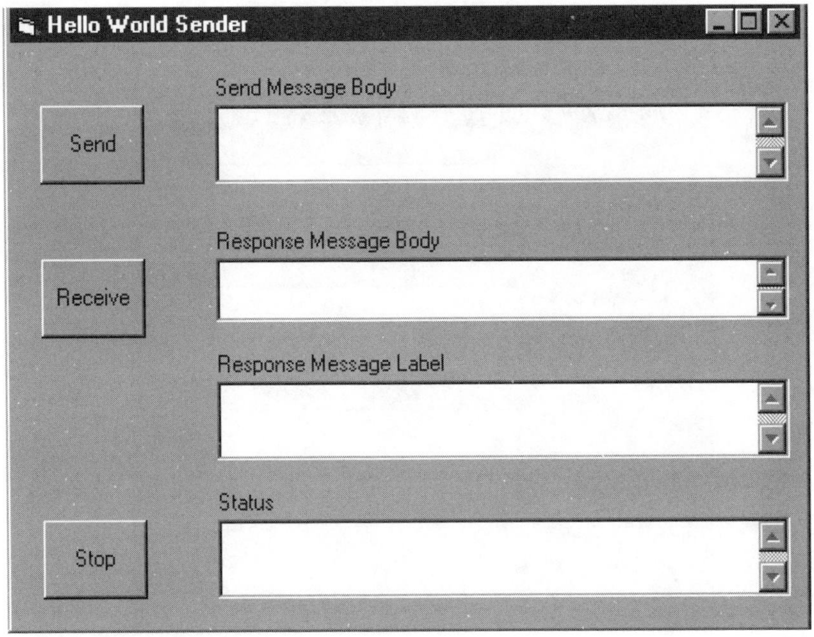

Figure 4-1   Sender window

While the sender program is running, a user works with the window shown in Figure 4-1. A message is placed in the request queue when the Send button is clicked. The sender attempts to receive a response message when the Receive button is clicked. If a message is received, its body and label values are displayed in text windows. The Stop button is clicked to quit.

A user running the sender program can send requests and receive responses in any order. When a request is sent, text from the Send Message Body text box is copied into the message body. A label of "Hello World" and a response queue property are also assigned. The message is sent to the request queue. When a response message is to be received, the sender program waits for a message to arrive and removes it from the response queue. The message body and the label are printed.

The receiver program window is shown in Figure 4-2. The receiver attempts to receive a request message when the Receive Message button is clicked. If a message is available, the receiver prepares a response and sends it to the response queue. The Stop button is clicked to quit. The receiver program could be implemented with no user interface. I've included one to help you experiment with sender and receiver interactions.

When the receiver program starts up, it attempts to locate an existing request queue by using its queue type as an MQIS search criterion. The receiver opens the first queue instance returned. If a request queue cannot be located, the receiver creates one. Then the receiver reads messages synchronously. When a message is removed

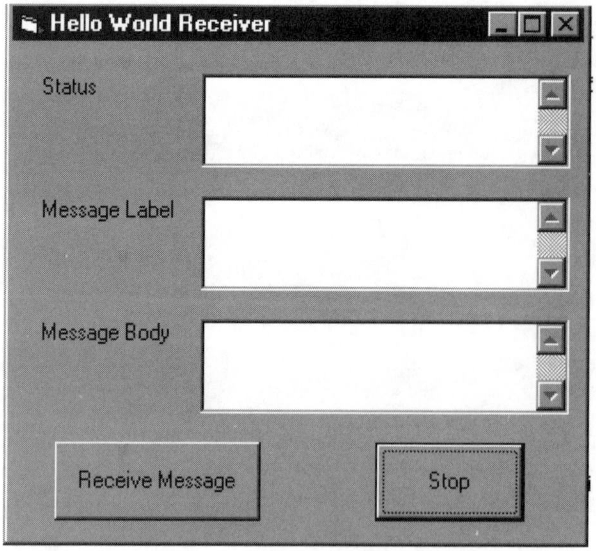

Figure 4-2   Receiver window

from the request queue, the receiver prints the message body, the label, and the response queue format name and then prepares a response message, opens the response queue (using the response queue property), sends the response message, and closes the response queue. The response message has the label `"Response Label to ::"` and is followed by the request message label. The message body begins with `"Response Message to ::"` and is followed by the request message body.

Several senders and receivers can be executing at the same time, even on the same machine. However, you will notice some messaging anomalies when several senders or receivers share the same queues. We briefly discuss these anomalies in Chapter 6.

4.2   MSMQ COM Components

Nine COM components are defined for MSMQ. In this chapter we use five of them. Other components support transaction processing and enable messages arriving in a queue to be treated as events. We'll demonstrate the use of these components in Chapters 7 and 11. Appendix A contains a reference for all MSMQ COM components.

4.2.1   MSMQQueueInfo

This component represents information about an MSMQ message queue. You use `MSMSQueueInfo` to create, to open, and to delete a queue. (A queue is closed by using its `MSMQQueue` component instance.) `MSMSQueueInfo` instances can also set or return most queue properties.

`MSMQQueueInfo` properties are outlined in Chapter 3. Five methods are available.

- `Create`—Create a queue with default or selected property values.
- `Delete`—Delete an existing queue. The `MSMQQueueInfo` component must be destroyed separately.
- `Open`—Open an existing queue. This method returns an `MSMQQueue` component that can be used to send or receive messages and to close the queue.
- `Refresh`—Refresh the property values for a queue. The values for public queues are retrieved from MQIS. Private queue values are obtained from the local queue manager.
- `Update`—Update property values in the MQIS or on the local computer.

4.2.2 MSMQQueue

This component represents an MSMQ message queue instance. You use MSMQQueue to read messages from a queue and to close the queue. (An instance of MSMQMessage is used to send a message.)

MSMSQueue properties enable you to determine whether the queue is open, as well as the access and sharing attributes used to open the queue; and to obtain an MSMQQueueInfo component that contains its queue properties. Each MSMQQueue instance maintains an internal cursor into the queue.

Eight MSMQQueue methods are available.

- Close—Close an instance of the queue. A queue is closed implicitly when an MSMQQueue instance goes out of scope.
- EnableNotification—Start event notification for asynchronously reading messages from a queue.
- Peek—Read the first message in a queue without removing the message from the queue (a *nondestructive* read).
- PeekCurrent—Read the message under the current cursor position from the queue without removing the message.
- PeekNext—Read the message after the current cursor position from the queue without removing the message.
- Receive—Read and remove the first message in the queue (a *destructive* read).
- ReceiveCurrent—Read and remove the message under the current cursor.
- Reset—Reset the current cursor to point at the start of the queue.

4.2.3 MSMQMessage

This component represents an MSMQ message instance and is used to set message properties and to send the message. A message can be set into an MSMQMessage instance by using any of the MSMQQueue read methods.

MSMQMessage properties are described in Chapter 3. One method, Send, is defined. This method sends the message to a queue represented by an MSMQQueue instance.

4.2.4 MSMQQuery

This component enables you to look up existing public queues in the MQIS. This simple component has no properties and only one method, LookupQueue. This method searches MQIS for queues that meet specified search criteria and returns queue information in an instance of `MSMQQueueInfos`. An MQIS query can filter queue information, based on its instance identifier, service type, label, and creation and modification times.

4.2.5 `MSMQQueueInfos`

This component contains a collection of queue information. An `MSMQQueueInfos` instance is set when `MSMQQuery.LookupQueue()` is called. Each `MSMQQueueInfos` instance maintains an internal cursor into a collection of `MSMQQueueInfo` components. Using `MSMQQueueInfos` instances, a program can scroll through the collection and extract queue information into `MSMQQueueInfo` instances.

`MSMQQueueInfos` has no properties and two methods.

- `Next`—Return the next `MSMQQueueInfo` object in the collection.
- `Reset`—Place an `MSMQQueueInfo` cursor at the start of a collection.

4.3 Queue Creation

In this section we'll demonstrate how to create queues administratively, using the MSMQ Explorer, and programmatically, using COM components. A basic design issue is whether queries should be created by administrators or by programmers.

In any environment and in any software system, some failures are controllable and some are not. I come from a background in which production environments are tightly controlled in an effort to minimize failures and down time. The dollar cost of down time across all industries is staggering: an average of $300,000 per incident, by one estimate. In addition, there are other exposures due to failures: A business can suffer the loss of customers, money, or even an operating license.

In an effort to minimize risks and audit events, many companies institute a variety of controls. Some companies follow change and configuration processes. Others subscribe to the use of "quality gates" that encompass design, development, testing, as well as a range of day-to-day operations issues.

As a result of my background, I've come to favor designs that offer control and simplified error recovery over other design criteria. Administrative queue creation clearly offers better control over an MSMQ configuration.

- Administrators know how many queues are being used and can size the system to meet demand. If queues are created and destroyed programmatically, widely varying and unpredictable demands may be placed on a system. In addition, peak-load requirements may be more difficult to ascertain.

• When queue configuration is managed by administrators, queue properties can be controlled centrally. For example, configuration of security properties can be based on the policy of "least trust." This means that only selected users or groups can send or receive messages from a queue and that fewer users or groups can modify queue properties, including access controls.

However, creating queues administratively has one important negative aspect. In the event of a system failure, it may be necessary to move a set of applications to a new system. Then recovery is slowed down because administrators need to manually regenerate the queue environment, including access controls. Human error is also a possibility when queues are manually regenerated. But if applications are responsible for creating their own queues, administrators don't need to perform any MSMQ configuration. Queues are rebuilt by the applications as they start up.

One final thought: If you choose to implement administrative queue creation, be sure to keep MSMQ queue configuration records up to date. If maintaining accurate records is not a common practice in your operations environment, seriously consider creating your queues programmatically.

4.3.1 Using MSMQ Explorer

Two queues need to be created for Hello World: a request queue and a response queue. Each queue must be assigned its correct type in order for senders and receivers to function properly. In this section we will use MSMQ Explorer to set up a request queue. The steps to set up a response queue are nearly identical. The only difference is that a response queue uses a different GUID.

Begin by starting up the MSMQ Explorer. To do this, click the Start button at the bottom of your desktop, bring up the pop-up menu of Programs and then the Microsoft Message Queue pop-up menu, and select Explorer.[2] An Explorer window appears, as shown in Figure 4-3. The Explorer window has two parts. On the left an MSMQ enterprise is represented as a tree structure. When you highlight an object in the left panel, the objects directly under it are displayed on the right. Initially the top level of the enterprise, containing folders for sites, connected networks, and enterprise servers, is displayed.

Now open the site folder, choose a site, and select a computer within that site on which the queue is to be created. With a computer highlighted, right click on it to get an options menu. From the options menu place the mouse pointer over New. Doing so

---

2. Some versions of MSMQ place Explorer under different pop-up menus. You may need to experiment to locate it.

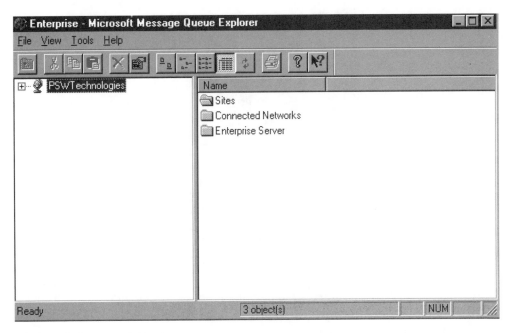

Figure 4-3   MSMQ Explorer

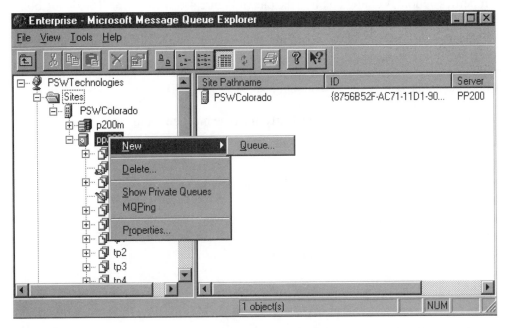

Figure 4-4   Choosing the site and computer on which a request queue is to be created

Figure 4-5 Defining the request queue name

will bring up a menu with one entry in it, Queue (Figure 4-4). Click on the Queue option.

A new window appears; you name the queue and define it as transactional or not. You should enter a queue name; by default Hello World uses "HelloWorldMessageQ". Do not select the transactional option, which Hello World cannot use. A sample entry is pictured in Figure 4-5. Click on OK. If you click on the View pull-down menu on the Explorer toolbar and click on Refresh, the new queue will appear in the right-hand list of queues.

Now we need to set the type identifier for the queue. Click on the new queue to highlight it, and then right click to display a pop-up menu of options. Click on the Properties option. A dialog box like the one in Figure 4-6 will appear. The dialog box has four tabs. On the General tab you see a text box labeled Type ID, which contains the queue's current type value. When the queue is created, MSMQ assigns it the default type GUID

```
{00000000-0000-0000-0000-000000000000}
```

In order for Hello World to work properly, the type must be set to

```
{711A7B92-20BA-11d1-8379-006097C4CEFC}
```

Replace the default type identifier with the Hello World request type identifier, and click OK.

You can repeat this process to create a Hello World response queue. Assign a reasonable name to the queue (for example, "HelloWorld Response Q"). The response queue should be given a type identifier of

```
{E8EA7B81-215C-11d1-837A-006097C4CEFC}
```

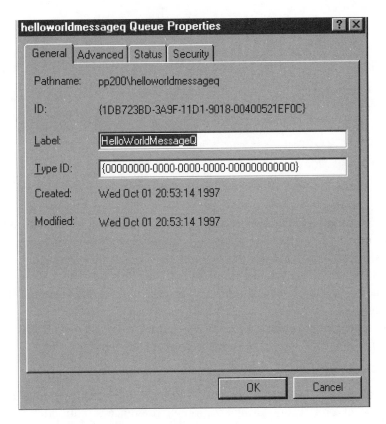

Figure 4-6   The Queue Properties dialog box

4.3.2   Using COM

In the Hello World sample applications, we develop a function called `createQueue`. It can be called when a program needs to create a new queue. We will demonstrate how to use `createQueue` in Section 4.6. This function is fairly reusable, and you can easily modify it to suit your needs. The function follows, along with notes.

```
Function createQueue(QPath, QLabel, QGuid) As MSMQQueueInfo
    Dim queue As New MSMQQueueInfo
    ' Set up queue properties
    queue.PathName = QPath

    queue.Label = QLabel
    queue.ServiceTypeGuid = QGuid
    ' Create queue
    On Error GoTo createErrorHandler
```

②
```
     queue.Create
     Set createQueue = queue
Exit Function

' Handle errors
createErrorHandler:
     StatusText.Text = "createErrorHandler :: Error: " _
         + Str$(Err.Number) + " :: " + "Reason: " + Err.Description
     Set createQueue = Nothing
End Function
```

① The function accepts a pathname, a character string describing the queue, and a type identifier (or NULL). A pathname, QPath, is required when a queue is created. The character string QLabel enables the program to associate an administrator-friendly label with the queue. The type identifier QGuid may be used to assign a specific type to the queue as it is created. The queue label and the type identifier are not strictly required and could be declared *Optional* in the Visual Basic code.

The function passes a reference to an MSMQQueueInfo object back to the caller. Thus the first statement within the function creates a new instance of an MSMQQueueInfo component.

② A queue is created. If the created operation succeeds, an MSMQQueueInfo reference is returned. If an error occurs during creation, no reference is returned. Instead, the function jumps to statements below the createErrorHandler label. This error-handling code pops up a Visual Basic message box that displays the error value and its description.

When a queue is created using default permissions, any user can send messages to a queue, but only the owner or creator is given read or receive permission. If we wanted to make a queue readable by others, we could have created it by including

```
queue.Create IsWorldReadable := True
```

By default nontransactional queues are created. If we wanted to make the queue transactional, we could have created it by including

```
queue.Create IsTransactional := True
```

4.4 Locating Queues

In this section we demonstrate how to locate a public queue through the MQIS. You locate a queue by specifying search criteria and issuing a query. MSMQ returns the set of public queues that satisfy your search criteria.

Certain kinds of search criteria will serve you better than others when locating a queue. I recommend using queue properties that do not assume a particular location. Location independence is important because a queue may move from one machine to another. Why should your applications assume that the queue is at a specific location if they don't have to?

Queue labels or type identifiers satisfy this requirement. Consider using them when performing a search.

In Hello World senders and receivers always search for queues by using a type value. The use of type identifiers gives your programs a more object-oriented flavor. A receiver will create a request message queue if none is located. A sender will create a response message queue if none is located.

Hello World defines a general-purpose lookup function, `locateQueueByType`, which accepts a type identifier (or `NULL`) and returns a reference to an `MSMQQueueInfo` instance. In Section 4.6, we show how a program might use `locateQueueByType`.

```
Function locateQueueByType(QGuid) As MSMQQueueInfo
    Dim qQuery As New MSMQQuery
    Dim messageQs As New MSMQQueueInfos
    Dim messageQ As MSMQQueueInfo

    On Error GoTo locateErrorHandler
    ' Set up query
    Set messageQs = qQuery.LookupQueue(ServiceTypeGuid:=QGuid)
    messageQs.Reset
    ' Select the first queue returned
    Set messageQ = messageQs.Next

    If messageQ Is Nothing Then
        GoTo locateErrorHandler
    Else
        Set locateQueueByType = messageQ
    End If
Exit Function

locateErrorHandler:
    StatusText.Text = "locateErrorHandler :: Error: " _
        + Str$(Err.Number) + " :: " + "Reason: " + Err.Description
```

```
      Set locateQueueByType = Nothing
End Function
```

① A queue type identifier or NULL is passed to `locateQueueByType`. In order to locate a queue, we need to create an instance of `MSMQQuery`, `MSMQQueueInfos`, and `MSMQQueueInfo`.

② The `MSMQQuery` component has one method, `LookupQueue()`, which returns a collection of queues that satisfy one or more lookup restrictions. We stipulate that queues must have a `ServiceTypeGuid` equal to the GUID passed to `locateQueueByType`. A collection of `MSMQQueueInfo` instances is returned as an `MSMQQueueInfos` instance.

③ The `LookupQueue` method allows developers to search for queues by using the following five optional properties:

- `QueueGuid`—A queue identifier
- `ServiceTypeGuid`—A queue service type
- `Label`—A queue label
- `CreateTime`—A creation time
- `ModifyTime`—A last-modification time

A program can use any, all, or none of these properties in a search.

`QueueGuid` is a unique queue identifier value. When you search by `QueueGuid`, you are looking for a specific queue. No two queues in the MSMQ enterprise can have the same `QueueGuid` value.

If `ServiceTypeGuid`, `Label`, `CreateTime`, or `ModifyTime` is specified in a search, programmers can also specify an optional relationship operator for them. MSMQ applies the relationship operators to each property during a search and returns queue information that satisfies all search criteria. The optional relationship arguments for `ServiceTypeGuid`, `Label`, `CreateTime`, and `ModifyTime` are `RelServiceTypeGuid`, `RelLabel`, `RelCreateTime`, and `RelModifyTime`. The following seven search relationships can be specified for each property:

- `REL_EQ`—A queue's property must equal the value passed to `LookupQueue()`. By default a search uses `REL_EQ` if no relationship operator is specified.

- `REL_NEQ`—A queue's property must not equal the value passed to `LookupQueue()`.

- `REL_LT`—A queue's property must be less than the value passed to `LookupQueue()`.

- REL_LE—A queue's property must be less than or equal to the value passed to LookupQueue().
- REL_GT—A queue's property must be greater than the value passed to LookupQueue().
- REL_GE—A queue's property must be greater than or equal to the value passed to LookupQueue().
- REL_NOP—MSMQ ignores the queue property value passed to LookupQueue().

Suppose that you wanted to search for a queue with an identifier of

{23D981B0-47BC-11d1-9029-00400521EF0C}

You could do this with the following code:

```
Dim messageQs As MSMQQueueInfos
Set messageQs = qQuery.LookupQueue _
    (QueueGuid := "{23D981B0-47BC-11d1-9029-00400521EF0C}")
```

Here's a second example. We'll search for a queue that was created on or before September 3, 1997, and with a ServiceTypeGuid of

{23D981B1-47BC-11d1-9029-00400521EF0C}

You could do this with the following code:

```
Dim messageQs As MSMQQueueInfos
Dim CreationDate

' Assign last date of interest during search and lookup results
CreationDate = #September 3, 1997#
messageQs = qQuery.LookupQueue ( _
    ServiceTypeGuid := "{23D981B1-47BC-11d1-9029-00400521EF0C}", _
    CreateTime := CreationDate, RelCreateTime := REL_LE )
```

In this example MSMQ assumes that RelServiceTypeGuid, the relationship operator for ServiceTypeGuid, is REL_EQ.

4 We set the collection cursor to the first element in the collection. Then we extract a queue from the collection into an MSMQQueueInfo instance.

5 Since an MSMQQueueInfos collection will be empty if no queues meet the stipulated lookup restrictions, we test the MSMQQueueInfo instance to see whether it is set. If it is not, we do not return a reference and instead jump to the error handler, which pops up a message box with an error message. Otherwise the instance is good, and we return a reference to it.

4.5 Creating the Hello World Sender Form

This section briefly outlines how the Hello World Sender application is set up. We outline the controls that are used and specify the global variables.

As you saw in Figure 4-1, three command buttons, four text windows, and four labels are placed on the program's only form. To create the Hello World Sender form, drag the command buttons, text windows, and labels from the toolbox to the form, and place the visual controls as you see them in that figure.

Figure 4-7   The Visual Basic Property Window

Table 4-1	Visual Control Property Settings for the Hello World Sender	
Control	**Property**	**Setting**
Label1	Caption	Send Message Body
Label2	Caption	Response Message Body
Label3	Caption	Response Message Label
Label4	Caption	Status
Command Button 1	Name	SendMessage
	Caption	Send
Command Button 2	Name	ReceiveMessage
	Caption	Receive
Command Button 3	Name	StopButton
	Caption	Stop
Text Box 1	Name	ReqBodyText
	MultiLine	True
	ScrollBars	Vertical
	Text	(empty)
Text Box 2	Name	ResBodyText
	Locked	True
	MultiLine	True
	ScrollBars	Vertical
	Text	(empty)
Text Box 3	Name	ResLblText
	Locked	True
	MultiLine	True
	ScrollBars	Vertical
	Text	(empty)
Text Box 4	Name	StatusText
	Locked	True
	MultiLine	True
	ScrollBars	Vertical
	Text	(empty)

Next, you will need to set the properties of each visual control on the form. To set properties, you will use the Property Window (see Figure 4-7).

First, click on a visual control. Visual Basic loads properties for that control into the Property Window. Property titles are listed in the left column of the window, and settings are listed in the right column. As you scroll through the list of properties, you can edit the settings. Table 4-1 lists the property setting for each control on the form.

The following example code shows how we use text box names to place status information into the status text box:

```
StatusText.Text = _
    "SendMessage_Click :: success :: response queue created"
```

Similar assignments are used to populate the response message body and to label text boxes.

Finally, we define several variables and components at the module level of the form, to be accessed in various functions and procedures. Two constants are set to the request and response message queue types. The next two constants contain a pathname that is used if a response queue needs to be created and a label to be assigned to that queue. The final constant is used as a request message label. Two references to MSMQQueueInfo components are defined that enable a request and a response queue to be located through the MQIS. Finally, two references to MSMQQueue components are defined that allow the application to interact with the request and response queues.

```
Const RequestGUID = "{711A7B92-20BA-11d1-8379-006097C4CEFC}"
Const ResponseGUID = "{E8EA7B81-215C-11d1-837A-006097C4CEFC}"
Const ResponseQPath = ".\HelloWorldResponseQ"
Const ResponseQLabel = "Message Queue created by Hello World Sender"
Const RequestLabel = "HelloWorld"
Dim requestQ As MSMQQueueInfo
Dim responseQ As MSMQQueueInfo
Dim openRequestQ As MSMQQueue
Dim openResponseQ As MSMQQueue
```

4.6   Opening Queues and Sending Messages

A request message is sent after a user enters a message body and clicks the Send button. A private procedure, SendMessage_Click(), is invoked by Visual Basic when the button is clicked.

```
Private Sub SendMessage_Click()
    Dim ReqMsg As New MSMQMessage
    Dim Where As String
    On Error GoTo ErrorHandler
```

```
        Where = "Locating or creating response queue"
❸   If responseQ Is Nothing Then
            Set responseQ = locateQueueByType(ResponseGUID)
            If responseQ Is Nothing Then
                Set responseQ = createQueue(ResponseQPath, ResponseQLabel, _
                    ResponseGUID)
            End If
            If Not responseQ Is Nothing Then
                StatusText.Text = _
                    "SendMessage_Click :: success :: response queue's " _
                    + "format name is: " + responseQ.FormatName
            Else
                StatusText.Text = "SendMessage_Click :: failure :: " _
                    + "could not locate or create response queue"
            Exit Sub
            End If
        End If

❹   Where = "Locate request queue"
        If requestQ Is Nothing Then
            Set requestQ = locateQueueByType(RequestGUID)
            ' Set requestQ = locateQueueByType(ResponseGUID)
            If Not requestQ Is Nothing Then
                StatusText.Text = "SendMessage_Click :: success :: " _
                    + "request queue's format name is: " + requestQ.FormatName
            Else
                StatusText.Text =  "SendMessage_Click :: failure :: _
                    + "could not locate request queue"
            Exit Sub
            End If
        End If

❺   Where = "Opening request queue"
        If openRequestQ Is Nothing Then
            Set openRequestQ = requestQ.Open(Access:=MQ_SEND_ACCESS, _
                ShareMode:=MQ_DENY_NONE)
        End If

❻   Where = "Preparing request message body and label"
        ReqMsg.Body = ReqBodyText.Text
        ReqMsg.Label = RequestLabel
        Where = "Setting response queue"
        Set ReqMsg.ResponseQueueInfo = responseQ
```

(7)
```
      Where = "Sending request message"
      ReqMsg.Send openRequestQ
Exit Sub
```

(2)
```
ErrorHandler:
      StatusText.Text = "SendMessage_Click :: "
          + Where + " :: Error: " _
          + Str$(Err.Number) + " :: " + "Reason: " + Err.Description
End Sub
```

(1) Within this procedure we declare an MSMQMessage instance that is used to send a request message. A second string variable, Where, is used to track execution progress during debugging and to provide status to the user.

(2) We tell Visual Basic to jump to the ErrorHandler instructions if an error is detected. Under ErrorHandler the status box is populated with an error number and explanatory text about where in the SendMessage_Click() procedure the error occurred. ErrorHandler is placed at the bottom of the procedure.

(3) Since SendMessage_Click() can be executed repeatedly, we first test to see whether responseQ, a component representing the response queue, is set. If responseQ is not set, we attempt to locate a queue, using the locateQueueByType() procedure defined in a previous section. Should locateQueueByType() fail to find a queue with a service type equal to ResponseGUID, it returns an unset reference to an MSMQQueueInfo instance. In that case a queue is created. If a queue cannot be created, we pop up a message body containing error information. Otherwise the status is placed in the status text box.

(4) A request message queue is located if a queue was not located during a previous execution of this procedure. The code to locate a request queue is nearly identical to the code in **(3)** . The difference is that we do not ever create a request queue if one is not located through the MQIS. In Hello World only a receiver creates a request queue.

Notice that there are two lines that could set requestQ, the MSMQQueueInfo reference variable:

```
Set requestQ = locateQueueByType(RequestGUID)
' Set requestQ = locateQueueByType(ResponseGUID)
```

The second line is included as a comment. If the first line were commented out and the second line were used to locate a request queue, you could send messages to and receive messages from the response queue without having the Hello World receiver also running.

⑤ An MSMQQueueInfo component containing request queue information, requestQ, is used to open the request queue. An argument, Access, indicates how the queue should be opened. The argument has three options.

- MQ_PEEK_ACCESS—Your program can examine messages in the queue but cannot remove messages from the queue.

- MQ_SEND_ACCESS—Your program can place messages in the queue.

- MQ_RECEIVE_ACCESS—Your program can peek at messages and can remove them from the queue.

The Hello World Sender specifies MQ_SEND_ACCESS. When opening a response queue, Sender will use MQ_RECEIVE_ACCESS.

A second parameter, ShareMode, indicates whether a program wants exclusive access or shared access to the queue. Two values are allowed.

- MQ_DENY_NONE indicates that your program can allow other programs to access the queue. This setting must be specified when MQ_SEND_ACCESS or MQ_PEEK_ACCESS is used as the second parameter.

- MQ_DENY_RECEIVE_SHARE specifies that your program wants exclusive receive access to the queue. If MQ_DENY_RECEIVE_SHARE is selected MQ_RECEIVE_ACCESS must be used as the Access parameter value.

    If another program has already opened the queue with MQ_RECEIVE_ACCESS, MSMQ returns an error value of MQ_ERROR_SHARING_VIOLATION. From the moment your program opens a queue by using MQ_DENY_RECEIVE_SHARE, no other programs can read messages from the queue.

MQIS Propagation

MQIS is a distributed database of site, connected network, computer, and queue information. There is a lag from the time a public queue is created in one site until that information has been dispensed throughout an enterprise. Thus it is possible that a program can create a queue and then obtain an error when looking up information about it or opening it.

Using the MSMQ Explorer, you can adjust MQIS propagation intervals within a site and between sites to minimize this problem. For production applications you should consider coding your program to retry an MSMQQueueInfo.Open() or MSMQQuery.LookupQueue() call after 10 or 15 seconds if you obtain an unset component instance.

Since `SendMessage_Click()` can be executed repeatedly, we first test to see whether `openRequestQ` is set. If it is not, the request queue is opened for sending messages with shared access.

The character string from the Send Message Body text box is assigned to the `Body` property of the message. A global constant is used for the `Label` property. We copy
(6) response queue information to the `ResponseQueueInfo` property.

The message is sent. `MSMQMessage.Send` has two parameters. The first is an `MSMQQueue` instance. The queue it represents must be open prior to using the
(7) instance to send a message.

The second parameter, `pTransaction`, allows the send operation to be controlled within a transaction. An `MSMQTransaction` object can be passed, or one of four constants can be used. `MQ_MTS_TRANSACTION` indicates that the call is part of the current MTS transaction. `MQ_NO_TRANSACTION` specifies that the call is not transactional. `MQ_XA_TRANSACTION` is used if the call is part of an external XA-compliant transaction. `MQ_SINGLE_MESSAGE` is used to send a single transactional message. We will discuss the use of these constants in Chapter 11.

This application may use the request message queue to send several messages. Therefore the queue is not closed at the end of the procedure. This design improves application performance.

4.7   Receiving Responses

Now let's demonstrate how to read a response message from a queue. The Hello World Sender program attempts to read a reply from the response queue when a user clicks the Receive Message button. Visual Basic invokes the `ReceiveMessage_Click()` procedure.

(1)
```
Private Sub ReceiveMessage_Click()
    Dim ResMsg As MSMQMessage
    Dim Where As String
```

(2)
```
    On Error GoTo ErrorHandler
    StatusText.Text = ""
    ResBodyText.Text = ""
    ResLblText.Text = ""
```

(3)

```
Where = "Locating or create response queue"
If responseQ Is Nothing Then
    Set responseQ = locateQueueByType(ResponseGUID)
    If responseQ Is Nothing Then
        Set responseQ = createQueue(ResponseQPath, ResponseQLabel, _
            ResponseGUID)
    End If
    If Not responseQ Is Nothing Then
        StatusText.Text = "ReceiveMessage_Click :: success :: " _
            + "response queue's format name is: " + responseQ.FormatName
    Else
        StatusText.Text = "ReceiveMessage_Click :: failure :: " _
            + "could not locate or create response queue"
    Exit Sub
    End If
End If
```

(4)

```
Where = "Opening response queue"
If openResponseQ Is Nothing Then
    Set openResponseQ = responseQ.Open(Access:=MQ_RECEIVE_ACCESS, _
        ShareMode:=MQ_DENY_NONE)
End If
```

(5)

```
Where = "Receiving response message"
Set ResMsg = openResponseQ.Receive(ReceiveTimeout:=1000)
If Not ResMsg Is Nothing Then
    ResBodyText.Text = ResMsg.Body
    ResLblText.Text = ResMsg.Label
Else
    StatusText.Text = "ReceiveMessage_Click :: " + Where _
        + " :: No message was available to receive."
End If
ReqBodyText.Text = ""
Exit Sub
```

(2)

```
ErrorHandler:
    StatusText.Text = "ReceiveMessage_Click :: " _
        + Where + " :: Error: " _
        + Str$(Err.Number) + " :: " + "Reason: " + Err.Description
End Sub
```

① The declarations and instructions within ReceiveMessage_Click() are very similar to SendMessage_Click(), which we discussed in the previous section. An MSMQMessage instance is declared. Where tracks the execution progress during debugging and provides status to the user.

② Visual Basic jumps to the ErrorHandler instructions if an error is detected. Under ErrorHandler the status box is populated with an error number and explanatory text about where in the ReceiveMessage_Click() procedure the error occurred. ErrorHandler is placed at the bottom of the procedure.

③ Since ReceiveMessage_Click() can be executed repeatedly, we first test to see whether responseQ is set. If it is not set, we attempt to locate a queue by invoking the locateQueueByType procedure defined in a previous section. Should locateQueueByType fail to find a queue with a service type equal to ResponseGUID, it returns an unset reference to an MSMQQueueInfo instance. If a public response message queue doesn't exist, we create one locally for use by programs in the future.

You may be curious about why we locate or create a response queue in this procedure. Didn't we locate or create the response queue in SendMessage_Click()? The idea is that a user may start the program to drain a queue of messages. There's no guarantee that the user will ever send a message. Consequently we need to have code to locate a response queue in both procedures.

④ Since ReceiveMessage_Click() can be executed repeatedly, we first test to see whether openResponseQ is set. If it is not, the response message queue is opened for receiving messages with shared access.

⑤ The Receive method is called on openResponseQ, an MSMQQueue instance, to place a response message into ResMsg, an MSMQMessage instance. The Receive method can take four optional arguments.

- ReceiveTimeout controls the maximum length of time, in milliseconds, that a calling program will wait to receive a message. If a message is sitting in the queue, the call returns immediately. When a value for ReceiveTimeout is not specified, it is assumed to be INFINITE, and the calling program waits indefinitely. I recommend using a value of 500 or 1,000 (a half-second or a second). Longer wait times may be unacceptable to users of a visual application.

- The optional pTransaction argument allows the receive operation to be controlled within a transaction. An MSMQTransaction object can be passed, or one of three constants can be used. MQ_MTS_TRANSACTION

indicates that the call is part of the current MTS transaction.
`MQ_NO_TRANSACTION` specifies that the call is not transactional.
`MQ_XA_TRANSACTION` is used if the call is part of an external
XA-compliant transaction. We will discuss the use of these constants in
Chapter 11.

- `WantBody` can be set to `TRUE` or `FALSE`, depending on whether the program wants the message body copied to the `MSMQMessage` component. A value of `FALSE` improves application-processing speed. `WantBody` is `TRUE` by default.

- `WantDestinationQueue` can be set to `TRUE` or `FALSE`, depending on whether your program needs to explicitly know the destination queue to which a message was sent. This argument is typically not used unless a program is reading messages in a machine journal or a dead letter queue. By default `WantDestinationQueue` is assumed to be `FALSE`.

If a message was received in our program, MSMQ has populated `ResMsg` with its properties. We copy the message body and label into the appropriate text boxes. Otherwise we write status information in the status text box. Before exiting, we clear the Send Message Body text box.

4.8   Closing Queues

When the user clicks on the Stop button, the application closes any open queues and then exits. The `Close` method of each `MSMQQueue` instance is called.

```
Private Sub StopButton_Click()
    openRequestQ.Close
    openResponseQ.Close
    End
End Sub
```

COM implicitly closes any open queue and destroys the `MSMQQueue` instance when it goes out of scope. In this program `MSMQQueue` instances are globally declared, and we are able to maintain open connections to the queues for the duration of the program. If the `MSMQQueue` instances had been placed within `SendMessage_Click()` and `ReceiveMessage_Click()`, you would need to open (and close) a queue every time those procedures executed. This would slow down program execution.

Table 4-2 Visual Control Property Settings for the Hello World Receiver

Control	Property	Setting
Label1	Caption	Status
Label2	Caption	Message Label
Label3	Caption	Message Body
Command Button 1	Name	RecMsgButton
	Caption	Receive Message
Command Button 3	Name	StopButton
	Caption	Stop
Text Box 1	Name	StatusText
	Locked	True
	MultiLine	True
	ScrollBars	Vertical
	Text	(empty)
Text Box 2	Name	LabelText
	Locked	True
	MultiLine	True
	ScrollBars	Vertical
	Text	(empty)
Text Box 3	Name	BodyText
	Locked	True
	MultiLine	True
	ScrollBars	Vertical
	Text	(empty)

4.9   The Hello World Receiver

So far we have talked about how Hello World sender functions. The receiver procedures are nearly identical.

To create the Hello World Receiver form, drag the command buttons, text windows, and labels from the toolbox to the form, and place the visual controls as you see them in Figure 4-2. Table 4-2 lists the property setting for each control on the Receiver form.

In the Hello World Receiver, the following declarations are placed at the module level so that they can be accessed repeatedly by program functions.

```
Const RequestGUID = "{711A7B92-20BA-11d1-8379-006097C4CEFC}"
Const ResponseQPath = ".\HelloWorldMessageQ"
Const ResponseQLabel = "Message Queue created by Hello World Receiver"
Dim requestQ As MSMQQueueInfo
Dim openRequestQ As MSMQQueue
Dim openResponseQ As MSMQQueue
```

Visual Basic starts up `RecMsgButton_Click()` when the user clicks the
Receive Message button. That procedure reads a message from a request queue.

The first time the button is clicked, `RecMsgButton_Click()` attempts to
locate an existing request queue by calling `locateQueueByType()`. If none is
found, it creates a request queue by using `createQueue()`. Then the request queue
is opened. These steps are bypassed in subsequent calls.

Next, `RecMsgButton_Click()` waits up to 1 second to read a message
from the request queue. If a message is copied to the `ReqMsg`, an instance of
`MSMQMessage`, the body and the label are displayed in text boxes, and a response
message, `ResMsg`, is prepared. When the message is ready to send, the response
queue is opened, using the queue indicated by the `ResponseQueueInfo` property
of `ReqMsg`. `ResMsg` is sent and the queue is closed.

```
Private Sub RecMsgButton_Click()
    Dim ReqMsg As New MSMQMessage
    Dim ResMsg As New MSMQMessage
    Dim Where As String
    On Error GoTo ErrorHandler
    BodyText.Text = "" 'Clear text boxes
    LabelText.Text = ""
    StatusText.Text = ""

    Where = "Locating or creating request queue"
    If requestQ Is Nothing Then
        Set requestQ = locateQueueByType(RequestGUID)
        If requestQ Is Nothing Then
            Set requestQ = createQueue(RequestQPath, RequestQLabel, _
        RequestGUID)
        End If
        If Not requestQ Is Nothing Then
            StatusText.Text = _
                "RecMsgButton_Click :: success :: " _
                + "request queue's format name is :: " _
                + requestQ.FormatName
        Else
```

```
            StatusText.Text = "ReceiverForm_Load :: failure :: " + _
                "could not locate or create request queue"
            Exit Sub
        End If
    End If


Where = "Opening request queue"
    If openRequestQ is Nothing Then
        Set openRequestQ = _
        requestQ.Open(Access:=MQ_RECEIVE_ACCESS, _
        ShareMode:=MQ_DENY_NONE)
    End If


    Where = "Receiving request message"
    Set ReqMsg = openRequestQ.Receive(ReceiveTimeout:=1000)
    If Not ReqMsg Is Nothing Then
        BodyText.Text = ReqMsg.Body
        LabelText.Text = ReqMsg.Label
    Else
        StatusText.Text = "RecMsgButton_Click :: " + Where _
            + " :: No message was available to receive."
        Exit Sub
    End If


    Where = "Preparing response"
    ResMsg.Body = "Response Message to:: " + BodyText.Text
    ResMsg.Label = "Response Label to:: " + LabelText.Text


    Where = "Opening response queue"
    If ReqMsg.ResponseQueueInfo Is Nothing Then
        StatusText.Text = _
            "Opening response queue — Response queue information not set"
        Exit Sub
    Else
        Set openResponseQ = _
        ReqMsg.ResponseQueueInfo.Open(Access:=MQ_SEND_ACCESS, _
            ShareMode:=MQ_DENY_NONE)
    End If


    Where = "Sending request message"
    ResMsg.Send openResponseQ
```

```
    Where = "Closing response queue"
    openResponseQ.Close

    Exit Sub

ErrorHandler:
StatusText.Text = "ReceiverForm_Click :: " + Where + _
    " :: Error: " + Str$(Err.Number) + " :: " + "Reason: " + _
    Err.Description
End Sub
```

4.10 Summary

Very little code is required to develop the sender and receiver programs in Visual
Basic, using the MSMQ COM components. Visual Basic deserves a lot of credit. It is
a powerful language with an excellent development environment. The MSMQ components are also nicely designed. As intuitive objects, the MSMQ components enable
applications to be developed with an economy of program statements and method
arguments.

In the next chapter we develop the Hello World application with the MSMQ API.
Unless you are very interested in that exercise, I suggest that you skip to Chapter 6,
which discusses the fundamental issue of defining a queue and message architecture
that satisfies your needs. After Chapter 6 things get really interesting. We'll solve
some messaging problems, examine MSMQ message tracing and recovery facilities,
secure our communications, and exercise the transaction processing features of
MSMQ.

4.11 Resources and References

Microsoft Corporation. 1997. *Microsoft Visual Basic 5.0 Language Reference.* Redmond, WA: Microsoft Press.

———. 1997. *Microsoft Visual Basic 5.0 Programmer's Guide.* Redmond, WA:
Microsoft Press.

Microsoft Message Queue Explorer Administrator's Online Help.

Microsoft Message Queue Server Online Help.

5
Chapter

An MSMQ Application

Using the MSMQ API

This chapter, intended primarily for developers, provides a complete MSMQ example application implemented in C, using the MSMQ API. Managers may want to read the introductory paragraphs of each major section.

In this chapter we'll develop a sample application by using the MSMQ C language API. This application, like the one in Chapter 4, is very loosely based on the first program many programmers learn—Hello World. The program we develop in this chapter is a distributed version of that program.

We begin this chapter by discussing several data structures that are used by MSMQ API applications. Then we'll demonstrate how to

- Create a queue, using the MSMQ API
- Look up queues in MQIS
- Inspect queue properties, using the MSMQ Explorer
- Create and examine message contents
- Send and receive messages
- Close a queue
- Delete a queue, using the MSMQ API

By the end of this chapter we will have developed a couple of reusable support functions and will have created a full example program, using the MSMQ API.

5.1   Overview of Hello World

The program we develop, `hello.exe`, can act as a sending or a receiving application. The sender and the receiver exchange messages. A sender's request message is nothing more than a request for a response.

For now we'll assume that a single sender and receiver exchange messages. This is a simplifying assumption, one of many. In fact, several senders and receivers can be executing at the same time, even on the same machine. However, the communication semantics are different under one-to-one, one-to-many, many-to-one, and many-to-many relationships. First, let's consider the simple case of one sender and one receiver, the situation pictured in Figure 5-1.

The program is invoked from a Command Prompt window by typing **hello**. If the program is started with a −s or a −r switch, the program becomes a sender or a receiver, respectively. If no switches are entered, the program displays the following syntax message:

```
hello Syntax::
    hello -r [-c] :: Hello World receiver  [w/ queue creation]
    hello -s [-c] :: Hello World sender    [w/ queue creation]
```

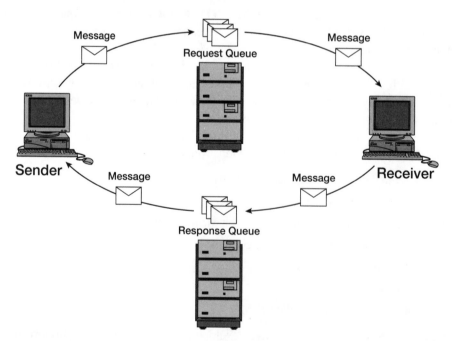

Figure 5-1 Hello World with one sender and one receiver

In this application the sender is not implemented as an event-driven program. That is, the sender places a message on the request queue and then waits for a response message. Some programs like to treat a message arriving on a queue as an event. When the event occurs, the program wakes up and processes the message. (We demonstrate this in Chapter 7.) Since we have a lot of information to cover in this chapter, however, we'll keep the Hello World program as simple as possible.

Message queues must be created before a sender and a receiver can exchange messages. Two options are possible.

- The sender and the receiver can create their own queues by using -c, an optional program switch. The switch tells the Hello program to create a message queue for itself. A receiver creates a public request message queue for receiving requests on its system. A sender creates a public response queue on the local system for receiving response messages. If the -c switch is not supplied, the program searches the MQIS for existing message queues to use. The program reports an error if none can be found.

- The alternative is to have an administrator create the request and response queues. The steps to create queues with the MSMQ Explorer are described in Chapter 4.

It is possible to associate a type identifier with every queue. A type identifier can be used to indicate a service that is provided when applications send messages to a queue. A type identifier is a programmatic way to distinguish one queue from another and to lend an object-oriented flavor to queued messaging communications.

This program assumes that a request queue has the following type:

```
// Hello Request Queue Type = {711A7B92-20BA-11d1-8379-006097C4CEFC}
static CLSID msgQueueType = { 0x711a7b92, 0x20ba, 0x11d1,
    { 0x83, 0x79, 0x0, 0x60, 0x97, 0xc4, 0xce, 0xfc } };
```

A response queue has the following type:

```
// Hello Response Queue Type = {E8EA7B81-215C-11d1-837A-006097C4CEFC}
static CLSID rspQueueType = { 0xe8ea7b81, 0x215c, 0x11d1,
    { 0x83, 0x7a, 0x0, 0x60, 0x97, 0xc4, 0xce, 0xfc } };
```

When the sender starts up, it creates a response message queue or opens an existing queue. Existing response queues are located by using `msgQueueType` as the MQIS search criterion. The sender always locates request queues through MQIS and opens the first queue instance returned. Then the sender repeatedly prompts the user for text to be copied into the message body. The label `"Hello World"` and a response queue property are also created as message properties. The message is sent to a request queue. Then the sender waits for a response message to arrive and removes it from the response queue. The response message body and the label are printed.

When the receiver starts up, it creates a request message queue or opens an existing queue. Existing request queues are located by using `rspQueueType` as the MQIS search criterion. The receiver opens the first queue instance returned and then receives messages synchronously. When a message is removed from the request queue, the receiver prints the message body, the label, and the response queue format name. The receiver then prepares a response message, opens the response queue (using the format name contained in the response queue message property), sends the response message, and closes the response queue. The response message has the label `"Hello World response label"`. The message body begins with `"Response to message :: "` and is followed by the request message body.

If the user gives the sender a message body of `"quit"`, the sender and the receiver shut down after the message exchange. If it created its own queue, the sender or the receiver deletes the queue before terminating.

5.2   Working with Properties in the MSMQ API

The MSMQ API defines a set of standard structures for representing queue and message properties. In fact, developers use identical structures for queue and message properties in several API calls.

MSMQ defines a total of 13 queue properties and 49 message properties. Values for one or more of those properties can be accessed and assigned through MSMQ API calls. Developers will use the `MQQUEUEPROPS` structure when working with queue properties. Most developers will use the `MQMSGPROPS` structure when working with message properties. Both `MQQUEUEPROPS` and `MQMSGPROPS` contain an array of `MQPROPVARIANT` structures. An `MQPROPVARIANT` structure is used to assign or to receive a single property value. Two other arrays are used to identify properties and to pass status information. A developer builds these structures and passes them to MSMQ through API calls. The general relationship between these structures is illustrated in Figure 5-2.

5.2.1   Using `MQQUEUEPROPS` to Represent Queue Properties

`MQQUEUEPROPS` is used to hold properties when creating a queue and when getting or setting queue properties. `MQQUEUEPROPS` is defined as follows:

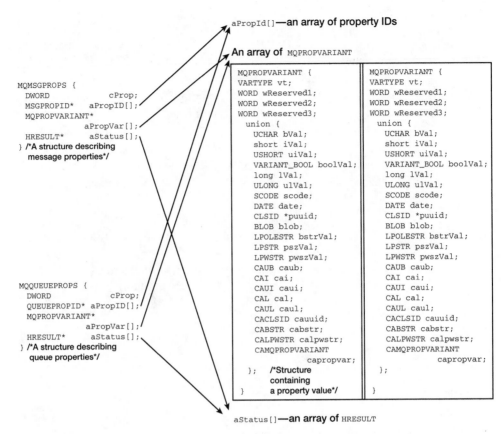

Figure 5-2 Relationship between MSMQ API property structures

```
typedef struct tagMQQUEUEPROPS {
    DWORD               cProp;      // Property counter
    QUEUEPROPID*        aPropID;    // Array of property identifiers
    MQPROPVARIANT*      aPropVar;   // Array of typed property values
    HRESULT*            aStatus;    // Array of status values
} MQQUEUEPROPS;
```

- cProp is a 32-bit integer that tells MSMQ how many properties the program wants to assign or access and indicates to MSMQ the length of each array in the MQQUEUEPROPS structure.

- aPropID is a pointer to an array of property identifiers. An example of a queue property identifier is PROPID_Q_LABEL. All elements of the array are of the QUEUEPROPID data type.

- aPropVar is a pointer to an array of MQPROPVARIANT structures. Each variant structure stores a tagged property value. That is, the variant structure

HRESULT

If real men don't eat quiche, do real developers check status codes? In distributed applications, they had better check those status codes, because a lot of errors that occur are beyond their control!

In the 32-bit Windows environment the HRESULT data type is used to report errors and status to developers. An HRESULT is a value divided into four fields that are described in the Win32 header file WINERROR.H. The MSMQ header file MQ.H also describes HRESULT and documents all values related to MSMQ.

In MSMQ success is reported by setting an HRESULT variable to a constant, such as MQ_OK. The value of MQ_OK is the same as the standard Win32 success constant, S_OK.

Most programmers are in the habit of comparing a status result with a constant value, such as S_OK or MQ_OK. Their code might look like the following code:

```
HRESULT hResult;
hResult = MQSendMessage(…);
If (hResult != MQ_OK) {
   // perform failure handling
} else {
   // perform success handling
}
```

In general, this is not a good practice in the Windows environment, since a call can return multiple success codes, in addition to multiple error codes. Rather it is recommended that programmers use the SUCCEEDED, FAILED, or IS_ERROR macros that are defined in WINERROR.H.

includes a value and a tag indicating the type of the value passed within the structure. The MQPROPVARIANT structure is discussed later.

- aStatus is optional. It is a pointer to an array of HRESULT elements that indicate the status of properties to be set.

The *n*th elements of each array are always related. Suppose that you are creating a queue with a base priority of 10. If you assign PROPID_Q_BASEPRIORITY to the third element of the PROPID array, MSMQ expects that the third element in the MQPROPVARIANT array contains a value for the queue's base priority. If a status

```
If (SUCCEEDED(hResult)) {
    // perform success handling
}
If (FAILED(hResult)) {
    // perform failure handling
}
If (IS_ERROR(hResult)) {
    // perform error handling
}
```

I like to use the following two constants and a macro to check and report errors:

```
#define ABORT 1   // Abort processing
#define RESUME 0  // Resume processing
#define PRINTERROR(S, HR, A) \
{ if (FAILED(HR)) \
      printf("PrintError: %s (0x%X)\n", S, HR); \
  if (FAILED(HR) && A) \
      exit(1); \
}
#endif
```

PRINTERROR accepts a user-friendly string describing the circumstances under which an error may have occurred, an HRESULT, and an indication of whether to abort the program or to resume processing. Examples in which PRINTERROR is used appear throughout this book.

Note that the PRINTERROR macro does not distinguish between errors. In some cases this is OK: An error is an error. In other cases you may want to construct finer-grained error handling.

array is defined, MSMQ will return status information about its ability to set the base priority in the third element. Later in this chapter we'll show how to use this structure in combination with MQPROPVARIANT and selected queue properties.

5.2.2 Using MQMSGPROPS to Represent Message Properties

When applications send or receive messages, developers will use the MQMSGPROPS structure to hold message properties. MQMSGPROPS is defined as follows:

```
typedef struct tagMQMSGPROPS {
    DWORD              cProp;      // Property counter
    MSGPROPID*         aPropID;    // Array of property identifiers
    MQPROPVARIANT*     aPropVar;   // Array of typed property values
    HRESULT*           aStatus;    // Array of status values
} MQMSGPROPS;
```

As you can see, it is similar to MQQUEUEPROPS, and each element in the structure is used in an identical way. Once you understand how to compose an MQQUEUEPROPS structure, you know how to compose an MQMSGPROPS structure.

5.2.3 Using MQPROPVARIANT to Represent Property Values

MQQUEUEPROPS and MQMSGPROPS always include a pointer to an array of MQPROPVARIANT structures. Each MQPROPVARIANT structure includes a value field and a tag field. The value field is a union of different types. The union type you use depends on the property value to be stored. The tag indicates the data type of a property value represented by the union. Programmers need to set the tag when they store a property in an MQPROPVARIANT structure.

The MQPROPVARIANT structure contains five elements. The vt field is used to indicate the type of the value contained within the MQPROPVARIANT structure. The last element in the structure is a union of all possible property value types. The union element you use to access or to assign property values depends on which property is being represented.

Table 5-1 Reference Information for PROPID_Q_AUTHENTICATE

Queue Property	COM Equivalent	Description
PROPID_Q_ AUTHENTICATE	MSMQQueueInfo. Authenticate	Determines whether a queue accepts non-authenticated messages. This property can take one of the following values:
• Data Type: VT_UI1		• MQ_AUTHENTICATE_NONE—The default. Authenticated and nonauthenticated messages are accepted
• MQPROPVARIANT: bVal		• MQ_AUTHENTICATE—Only authenticated messages are accepted.

```
struct tagMQPROPVARIANT {

    VARTYPE vt;

    WORD wReserved1;
    WORD wReserved2;
    WORD wReserved3;
        union {
            UCHAR               bVal;
            short               iVal;
            USHORT              uiVal;
            VARIANT_BOOL        boolVal;
            long                lVal;
            ULONG               ulVal;
            SCODE               scode;
            DATE                date;
            CLSID               *puuid;
            BLOB                blob;
            LPOLESTR            bstrVal;
            LPSTR               pszVal;
            LPWSTR              pwszVal;
            CAUB                caub;
            CAI                 cai;
            CAUI                caui;
            CAL                 cal;
            CAUL                caul;
            CACLSID             cauuid;
            CABSTR              cabstr;
            CALPWSTR            calpwstr;
            CAMQPROPVARIANT     capropvar;
        };
    };
};
typedef struct MQtagPROPVARIANT MQPROPVARIANT;
```

Consider the table entry of reference information for PROPID_Q_AUTHENTI-CATE, shown in Table 5-1. The first column contains information describing the data type for this property and the field within the union where property values are accessed or assigned. The entry for PROPID_Q_AUTHENTICATE indicates that this property has a data type of VT_UI1 and that values are stored in the bVal field of the structure's union.

Suppose that you want to store a PROPID_Q_AUTHENTICATE property value in the first element in an array of MQPROPVARIANT structures. The property value to be stored is MQ_AUTHENTICATE. You could set up the MQPROPVARIANT structure by using the following code sample:

```
MQPROPVARIANT propVar[1];       // Array of queue property variants
PropVar[0].vt = VT_UI1;         // Set the property type tag
PropVar[0].bVal = MQ_AUTHENTICATE; // Assign the property value
```

5.2.4 Scenarios Using MQQUEUEPROPS, MQMSGPROPS, and MQPROPVARIANT

Let's look at how you might use the MQQUEUEPROPS, MQMSGPROPS, and MQPROPVARIANT structures to set some queue and message properties. All examples use the following data definitions:

```
/* Data definitions */
#DEFINE PROPERTIES 10
#DEFINE NAME_LENGTH 100
MQPROPVARIANT propVar[PROPERTIES];    // Array of queue property
                                      // variants
QUEUEPROPID propId[PROPERTIES];       // Array of queue property IDs
HRESULT stats[PROPERTIES];            // Array of status indicators
MQMSGPROPS mProps;                    // Structure of message property
                                      // IDs and values
MQQUEUEPROPS qProps;                  // Structure of queue property
                                      // IDs and values
DWORD nProps = 0;                     // Property counter
WCHAR FormatName[NAME_LENGTH];        // Queue format name
DWORD formatLength = NAME_LENGTH;     // Format name length
WCHAR PathName[NAME_LENGTH];          // Queue pathname
QUEUEHANDLE mQHandle;                 // Handle to a message queue
WCHAR mBuffer[] = L"Sample message"; // Message body
HRESULT hResult;                      // A status variable
```

5.2.4.1 Create a Transactional Queue with a Pathname and a Label

In this example we create a transactional queue by sequentially performing the following actions:

- Initialize the property counter.
- Define the queue to be created as transactional and increment the property counter.
- Assign a pathname for the queue of PSW_200\queueName and increment the property counter.

- Give the queue a label of `"Transactional message queue"` and increment the property counter.
- Construct the `MQQUEUEPROPS` structure.
- Create the queue.

```
nProps = 0;                                  // Initialize the property
                                             // counter
propId[nProps] = PROPID_Q_TRANSACTION;       // Make the queue
                                             // transactional
propVar[nProps].vt = VT_UI1;
propVar[nProps].bVal = MQ_TRANSACTIONAL;
nProps++;

propId[nProps] = PROPID_Q_PATHNAME;          // Set PathName for queue
                                             // creation
propVar[nProps].vt = VT_LPWSTR;
propVar[nProps].pwszVal = L"PSW_200\\queueName";
nProps++;

propId[nProps] = PROPID_Q_LABEL;             // Set a descriptive queue
                                             // label
propVar[nProps].vt = VT_LPWSTR;
propVar[nProps].pwszVal = L"Transactional message queue";
nProps++;

qProps.cProp = nProps;                       // Construct the MQQUEUEPROPS
                                             // structure
qProps.aPropID = propId;
qProps.aPropVar = propVar;
qProps.aStatus = NULL;

hResult = MQCreateQueue(                     // Create the queue
        NULL,                                // Default security
        &qProps,                             // Queue properties
        FormatName,                          // Format name
        &formatLength);                      // Format name length
if (IS_ERROR(hResult)) {
    return();
}
```

MSMQ automatically uses default values for other queue properties.

5.2.4.2 Send an Authenticated Message Containing a Message Body and a Label

In this example we sequentially perform the following actions:

- Initialize the property counter.
- Define the message body and increment the property counter.
- Assign a message label and increment the property counter.
- Request authentication and increment the property counter.
- Construct the MQMSGPROPS structure.
- Send the message.

```
nProps = 0;
propId[nProps] = PROPID_M_BODY;            // Set the message body
                                           // property
propVar[nProps].vt = VT_UI1 | VT_VECTOR;
propVar[nProps].caub.cElems = sizeof (WCHAR *) (wstrlen(mBuffer) + 1);
propVar[nProps].caub.pElems = mBuffer;
nProps++;

propId[nProps] = PROPID_M_LABEL;           // Set the message label
                                           // property
propVar[nProps].vt = VT_LPWSTR;
propVar[nProps].pwszVal = L"Sample message label";
nProps++;

propId[nProps] = PROPID_M_AUTH_LEVEL;   // Set the authentication
                                        // property
propVar[nProps].vt = VT_UI4;
propVar[nProps].ulVal = MQMSG_AUTH_LEVEL_ALWAYS;
nProps++;

mProps.cProp = nProps;                      // Construct the MSGPROPS
                                           // structure
mProps.aPropID = propId;
mProps.aPropVar = propVar;
mProps.aStatus = NULL;                      // Status values are ignored

// Derive mQHandle - a handle to a message queue
```

```
hResult = MQSendMessage(          // Send the message
        mQHandle,                 // Message queue handle
        &mProps,                  // Message properties
        NULL);                    // Sending is not
                                  // transactional

if (FAILED(hResult)) {
    return();
}
```

This example does not include code to create or to open the message queue to which the message is sent. The queue handle, mQHandle, would be set when the queue is opened.

MSMQ automatically uses default values for other message properties. For example, the message is authenticated by using a digital signature created by using the default hash algorithm, MQMSG_CALG_MD5.

5.3 Creating Queues

In Chapter 4 we demonstrated how to create queues administratively, using the MSMQ Explorer. We also discussed the merits of creating queues administratively and programmatically. C programmers, for whom Chapter 4 was not relevant, are encouraged to read those sections.

The following definitions are used throughout the chapter:

```
// Programmatic Constants
#define PROPERTIES     10     // Maximum # of queue and message
                              // variants
#define BUFFER_LENGTH  100    // Maximum message length
#define DESC_LENGTH    100    // Maximum queue descriptor length
#define NAME_LENGTH    100    // Maximum name length for queues, etc.
#define ABORT          1      // Abort processing
#define RESUME         0      // Resume processing

// Macros
#ifndef PRINTERROR
#define PRINTERROR(S, HR, A) \
{ if (FAILED(HR)) \
    printf("PrintError: %s (0x%X)\n", S, HR); \
```

```
    if ((FAILED (HR)) && A)\
        exit(1); \
}
#endif

// Variables, etc.
WCHAR qPathName[NAME_LENGTH + 1];
```

Let's develop a reusable procedure, createQueue(), to create queues for MSMQ API applications.

❶
```
HRESULT createQueue(WCHAR * qPathName, CLSID *type, char * qLabel,
        WCHAR *formatName) {
    MQQUEUEPROPS    qProps;                        // Structure of queue
                                                   // property IDs and
                                                   // values

    MQPROPVARIANT propVar[PROPERTIES];             // Array of queue
                                                   // property values
    QUEUEPROPID    propId[PROPERTIES];             // Array of queue
                                                   // property IDs
    DWORD          nProps = 0;                     // Property counter
    DWORD          formatLength = NAME_LENGTH;     // Format name length
    WCHAR          wqLabel[NAME_LENGTH];           // Queue label
    HRESULT        hResult;                        // Standard Windows
                                                   // status

    printf("createQueue >>\n");
    printf("createQueue :: setting up queue properties...\n");
```

❷
```
    propId[nProps]          = PROPID_Q_PATHNAME; // Set PathName
    propVar[nProps].vt      = VT_LPWSTR;
    propVar[nProps].pwszVal = qPathName;
    nProps++;

    propId[nProps]          = PROPID_Q_TYPE; // Set queue type
    propVar[nProps].vt      = VT_CLSID;
    propVar[nProps].puuid   = type;
    nProps++;
```

❸
```
    swprintf(qDescriptor, L"%S", qLabel); // Set queue label
    propId[nProps]          = PROPID_Q_LABEL;
    propVar[nProps].vt      = VT_LPWSTR;
```

```
        propVar[nProps].pwszVal   = wqLabel;
        nProps++;

        qProps.cProp      = nProps;    // Construct the MQQUEUEPROPS
                                       // structure
        qProps.aPropID    = propId;
        qProps.aPropVar   = propVar;
        qProps.aStatus    = NULL;      // Do not inspect status values

        printf("createQueue :: calling MQCreateQueue...\n");
```

④
```
        hResult = MQCreateQueue(        // Create the queue
             NULL,                      // Default security
             &qProps,                   // Queue properties
             formatName,                // Format name
             &formatLength);            // Format name length
        PRINTERROR("createQueue :: Queue already exists",
             hResult, RESUME);
```

⑤
```
        if (hResult == MQ_ERROR_QUEUE_EXISTS) {
            // Queue already exist — get its format name
            printf("createQueue :: calling MQPathNameToFormatName...\n");
            hResult = MQPathNameToFormatName(
                 qPathName,             // Queue pathname
                 formatName,            // Format name
                 &formatLength);        // Format name length
            PRINTERROR(
                 "createQueue :: Cannot retrieve format name",
                 hResult, ABORT);
        }
        printf("createQueue <<\n");
        return (hResult);
    }
```

① A pathname is required when a queue is created. Here qPathName represents the pathname. In createQueue, qType is used to assign a specific type identifier to queues. In addition, it is always a good idea to assign an administrator-friendly label to a queue; qLabel satisfies this purpose. MQCreateQueue(), the MSMQ API call that creates a queue, returns a format name, formatName, which is needed to open the queue.

(2) Arrays of QUEUEPROPID values and MQPROPVARIANT tags/value pairs are constructed. A pathname, a queue type identifier, and a label are assigned to the arrays.
Then we construct the MQQUEUEPROPS structure.

(3) The MSMQ API uses Unicode characters. (The Unicode character set is described in
Section 3.2.1.) We use a standard Windows C function, swprintf(), to convert the
label string from ASCII characters to Unicode characters before setting the queue
label into an MQPROPVARIANT structure.

(4) A queue is created. The MQCreateQueue() call accepts a security descriptor, a
set of queue properties, a buffer to contain the newly created queue's format name,
and the length of the buffer. MQCreateQueue() returns a status result to
hResult, places the format name into the buffer, and returns the length of the
format name.

  In this call we could have constructed a security descriptor by using the Microsoft
SDK to set access controls for the queue. We have elected to have MSMQ set up a
default security descriptor.

(5) MQCreateQueue() can fail for a variety of reasons. Through a debugging process,
several errors have been eliminated. In this example we are concerned that a Hello
World queue may already exist. When the queue already exists, we attempt to obtain
its format name. If the format name cannot be retrieved or if other errors occur, we
abort the program after printing an error message. Otherwise createQueue returns
with a successful completion status code and the queue's format name.

5.4 Locating Queues

In this section we demonstrate how to locate a public queue through the MQIS. The
MSMQ API provides three calls for this purpose: MQLocateBegin(),
MQLocateNext(), and MQLocateEnd(). MQLocateBegin() sets up a query
context that includes search criteria. MQLocateNext() returns a search result and
can be called repeatedly until search results are exhausted. MQLocateEnd()
destroys the query context and releases most resources. You will need to call
MQFreeMemory() to release program memory.

  You can think of the MQIS as storing information about queues in a table. Each
queue entry is represented as a row in the table. Columns contain their queue property.

  Programs need to define two kinds of information before locating queues in
MQIS: search *restrictions* (or filters) and the queue properties to be returned. Search
restrictions help MQIS to eliminate queues that are not of interest to the program. One

or more restrictions can be used. A *column set* is used to specify which properties to return. MSMQ returns only the queue properties that are requested. See Figure 5-3.

In Hello World, type identifiers are used to locate queues in the following example. A reusable procedure, `locateQueueByType()`, accepts a type identifier (or NULL). The procedure returns the format name for a queue and its Unicode character length. The procedure follows.

```
HRESULT locateQueueByType(CLSID *qType, WCHAR *formatName,
    DWORD *formatLength){
    DWORD nProps = 0;                          // Property counter
    MQPROPVARIANT propVar[PROPERTIES];         // Property variants
    QUEUEPROPID   propId[PROPERTIES];          // Array of queue
                                               // property identifiers

    MQPROPERTYRESTRICTION propRestriction;     // Array of row search
                                               // restrictions

    MQRESTRICTION     restriction;             // Structure for search
                                               // restrictions

    MQCOLUMNSET       column;                  // MQIS column
                                               // information returned

    HRESULT           hResult;                 // Standard Windows
                                               // status

    HANDLE            hEnum;                    // Handle to locate
                                               // query info

    printf("locateQueueByType >>\n");

    // Prepare lookup restrictions - only return queues of a given
    // type
    propRestriction.prop = PROPID_Q_TYPE;
    propRestriction.prval.vt = VT_CLSID;
    propRestriction.prval.puuid = qType;
    propRestriction.rel = PREQ;
    restriction.cRes = 1; ;
    restriction.paPropRes = &propRestriction;

    // Prepare queue column set to retrieve pathname
    propId[0] = PROPID_Q_PATHNAME; ;
    column.cCol = 1;
    column.aCol = propId;

    // Locate query context
    printf("locateQueueByType :: calling MQLocateBegin\n");
```

(5)
```
    hResult = MQLocateBegin(
        NULL,                //Start search at the top
        &restriction,        //Restriction
        &column,             //ColumnSet
        NULL,                //No sort order
        &hEnum);             //Enumeration Handle
    PRINTERROR("locateQueueByType :: MQLocateBegin", hResult, ABORT);

    printf("locateQueueByType :: calling MQLocateNext\n");
    // Select the first queue instance
    nProps = PROPERTIES;
```
(6)
```
    hResult = MQLocateNext(
        hEnum,               // Handle to locate query return info
        &nProps,             // Number of properties retrieved
        propVar);            // Properties of the located queue
    PRINTERROR("locateQueueByType :: MQLocateNext", hResult, ABORT);
```
(7)
```
    hResult = MQPathNameToFormatName(propVar[0].pwszVal, formatName,
            formatLength);
    PRINTERROR(
        "locateQueueByType :: Cannot retrieve format name",
        hResult, ABORT);
    printf("locateQueueByType :: Formatted Name :: %S\n", formatName);
```
(8)
```
    MQFreeMemory(propVar[0].pwszVal);   // Clean up MSMQ allocated memory
    printf("locateQueueByType :: calling MQLocateEnd\n");
    hResult = MQLocateEnd(hEnum);    // Destroy locate query context
    printf("locateQueueByType <<\n");
    return(hResult);
}
```

(1) Several new data types are used in searches for a queue. MQRESTRICTION describes a set of MQIS query restrictions. A single restriction is defined, using an MQPROPERTYRESTRICTION structure. An array of MQPROPERTYRESTRICTION elements can be used to define more than one restriction. MQCOLUMNSET specifies the set of queue properties that should be returned with each search result. The queue properties are represented by an array of PROPID values. A HANDLE is an opaque pointer to a query context. The relationship between these data structures is illustrated in Figure 5-3.

(2) Let's look at how a search restriction is constructed. The definition of the MQPROPERTYRESTRICTION structure, shown previously, contains three elements.

Property Restrictions

```
MQRESTRICTION {
  ULONG cRes;
  MQPROPERTYRESTRICTION
        *paPropRes;  ─────────────────────────▶
  //pointer to array of
  //property restrictions
}/*A structure describing property
  restrictions for locating queues*/
```

```
MQPROPERTYRESTRICTION{
  ULONG rel;
  //PRLT, PRLE, PREQ,
  //PRNE, PRGE, or PRGT
  PROPID prop;
  //Queue prop id
  MQPROPVARIANT prval;
  //Comparison value
}/*A structure defining a
  query property restriction*/
```

Column Sets

```
MQCOLUMNSET {
  ULONG        cCol;
  //number of props
  PROPID       *aCol;  ─────────────────────────▶  aPropId[]—an array of PROPIDs
  //pointer to array
  //of prop ids
}/*A structure describing
  properties to be returned
  by an MQIS queue lookup*/
```

Figure 5-3 Relationship between property restriction and column set structures

PROPID defines the kind of queue property to be used as a restriction, or filter. MQPROPVARIANT indicates a property value that is used in the search. A search relationship operator is specified in the rel element. The following six relationship operators are defined:

- PREQ—MSMQ returns a result only if a queue's property equals the value placed in the MQPROPVARIANT structure.

- PRNE—MSMQ returns a result only if a queue's property does not equal the value placed in the MQPROPVARIANT structure.

- PRLT—MSMQ returns a result only if a queue's property is less than the value placed in the MQPROPVARIANT structure.

- PRLE—MSMQ returns a result only if a queue's property is less than or equal to the value placed in the MQPROPVARIANT structure.

- PRGT—MSMQ returns a result only if a queue's property is greater than the value placed in the MQPROPVARIANT structure.

- PRGE—MSMQ returns a result only if a queue's property is greater than or equal to the value placed in the MQPROPVARIANT structure.

The search restrictions and the relationship operators can be used in a variety of ways. For example, you could search for queues with a label of "Hello World", a quota less than or equal to 3MB, or a modification date later than September 30, 1997. Indeed, you could look for queues that satisfy all those restrictions.

Our Hello World senders and receivers place only one restriction on the lookup process. A queue must have the right type identifier.

③ Variables of the MQRESTRICTION type have two elements: cRes tells MSMQ how many restrictions are defined, and paPropRes points to an array of property restriction structures. In Hello World the propRestriction structure contains our single lookup restriction.

④ The properties to be returned from a query are defined by using an MQCOLUMNSET structure.[1] The structure has two elements. The first element, cCol, indicates how many properties should be returned with a query result. The second element, aCol, points to a PROPID array containing property identifiers.

Our goal is to obtain a format name so that a queue can be opened. Recall that a format name is not a queue property; hence it must be constructed. MSMQ API functions allow you to derive a format name from a pathname. We specify the pathname property in the column set.

The MQCOLUMNSET structure specifies one or more property values that we want returned as part of a lookup. But how does MSMQ return the property values? Property values will be returned in an array of MQPROPVARIANT, when MQLocateNext() is called.

⑤ MQLocateBegin() initiates an MQIS query. Search restrictions are passed as the second parameter. The third parameter is our column set. If we wanted MSMQ to sort results, we could specify sort criteria as the fourth parameter. MQLocateBegin() returns a query context handle as the last parameter. The handle is used in subsequent calls to MQLocateNext() and to MQLocateEnd().

⑥ In the Hello World application we use the first result returned. Thus we call MQLocateNext() once to get a queue pathname.

MQLocateNext() uses the query handle derived from MQLocateBegin(). MQLocateNext() returns the number of properties in the second parameter and the property values in the third parameter, an array of MQPROPVARIANT structures.

---

1. Note that the property values specified as restrictions and the properties returned from a search are completely independent. In our procedure we specify a search restriction based on queue type and ask for a pathname to be returned.

7 From the pathname we call `MQPathNameToFormatName()` to derive a format name.

8 At the end of a procedure, you should always clean up. An `MQPROPVARIANT` structure often points to other data structures. When `MQLocateNext()` returns queue properties, it frequently allocates memory to hold them. This includes different kinds of strings and GUIDs. To clean up, we release the memory allocated to hold the queue pathname and destroy our query context.

5.5 Opening, Closing, and Deleting Queues

To demonstrate opening, closing, and deleting a queue, let's look at the steps used by a Hello World receiver application.[2]

1
```
void receiver(int args, char ** argv) {
    HRESULT hResult;                    // Standard Windows result
                                        // indicator
    char qLabel[DESC_LENGTH +1];        // Optional queue descriptor
    WCHAR formatName[NAME_LENGTH];      // Holds the formatted name of a
                                        // queue
    DWORD formatLength = NAME_LENGTH;   // Format name length
    QUEUEHANDLE mQHandle;               // Queue handle

    printf("receiver >>\n");
    // Create message queue pathname
    swprintf(qPathName, L"pswtech\\HelloWorldMessageQ");
    printf("Hello World Message Queue PathName :: %S\n", qPathName);
```

2
```
if (args > 1) { // Create message queue or get formatName
    sprintf(qLabel, "Message Queue created by %s", argv[0]);
    printf("calling createQueue\n");
    hResult = createQueue(qPathName, &msgQueueType, qLabel,
        formatName);
```

---

2. The code for a Hello World sender application is nearly identical. The basic difference is that the sender opens the request and response queues. Why? The sender always sends a request to the same request queue and always receives a response on the same response queue. The receiver makes no assumption that it will always send responses to the same queue. There may be several senders, and each could use its own response queue. Every time a receiver removes a message from the request queue, it opens a response queue, using the format name contained in the `PROPID_M_RESP_QUEUE` message property.

```
    if (hResult == MQ_ERROR_QUEUE_EXISTS)
        PRINTERROR("receiver :: Cannot create queue — queue already exists",
            hResult, ABORT);
    } else {
        hResult = locateQueueByType(&msgQueueType, formatName,
            &formatLength);
        PRINTERROR(
            "receiver :: Cannot get formatname — Q may not exist!",
            hResult, ABORT);
    }

    printf("Formatted Name :: %S\n", formatName);
    printf("receiver opening message queue :: calling MQOpenQueue\n");
    hResult = MQOpenQueue(        // Open message queue
            formatName,           // Queue format name
            MQ_RECEIVE_ACCESS,    // Will receive responses on this queue
            MQ_DENY_NONE,         // Queue can be shared
            &mQHandle);           // Queue handle
    receiveMessages(mQHandle); // Receive messages

    MQCloseQueue(mQHandle);
    // Delete message queue
    if (args > 1) {
        hResult = MQDeleteQueue(formatName);
        PRINTERROR("receiver :: Cannot delete queue", hResult, RESUME);
    }
    printf("receiver <<\n");
}
```

❶ Several variables are declared, and most should be familiar by now. One data type is new: QUEUEHANDLE. When a queue is opened, MSMQ returns an opaque handle, representing a connection with a queue.

❷ Hello World sets the value of args based on program switches used. If −r is used, args is an even number. If −s is used, args is an odd number. When −c accompanies −r or −s, args is equal to or greater than 2. This indicates to create a queue. To create a queue, the procedure calls the createQueue() procedure described earlier. Otherwise it locates the queue by using locateQueueByType(). The format name returned by these procedures is used to open a queue.

3 A queue is opened. MQOpenQueue() expects a format name as the first parameter. The second parameter indicates how the queue will be accessed. Applications have three options:

- MQ_PEEK_ACCESS—A program can examine messages in the queue but cannot place messages in or remove messages from the queue.
- MQ_SEND_ACCESS—A program can place messages in the queue.
- MQ_RECEIVE_ACCESS—A program can peek at messages and can remove them from the queue.

The Hello World receiver uses MQ_RECEIVE_ACCESS to open the request message queue; the sender uses MQ_SEND_ACCESS. When opening a response message queue, the receiver uses MQ_SEND_ACCESS; the sender uses MQ_RECEIVE_ACCESS.

The third parameter of MQOpenQueue() indicates whether a program wants exclusive receive access or shared access to the queue. Two values are allowed:

- MQ_DENY_NONE indicates that a program will allow other programs to access the queue while it has the queue open. MQ_DENY_NONE must be specified when MQ_SEND_ACCESS or MQ_PEEK_ACCESS is used as the second parameter.
- MQ_DENY_RECEIVE_SHARE specifies that the program wants exclusive receive access to the queue (MQ_RECEIVE_ACCESS must be used as the second parameter value).
  If a program attempts to open a queue with MQ_DENY_RECEIVE_SHARE but another program already has the queue open with MQ_RECEIVE_ACCESS, MSMQ returns an error value of MQ_ERROR_SHARING_VIOLATION. Once a program opens a queue by using MQ_DENY_RECEIVE_SHARE, no other programs can read messages from the queue.

A queue handle is returned as the fourth parameter of MQOpenQueue().

4 The Hello World receiver begins to exchange messages. Hello World implements another procedure, receiveMessages(), for this purpose. We'll look at this procedure in the next section.

5 When the receiver is finished exchanging messages, it closes the request queue, using the QUEUEHANDLE variable returned by MQOpenQueue().

6 If a request queue is created at the beginning of the program, it is deleted, using its format name.

5.6 Receiving Messages and Sending a Response

In this section we'll look further at the Hello World receiver application. After establishing and opening a queue for reading requests, the receiver application calls `receiveMessages()`. Within that procedure messages are received and responses are sent. There may be several senders, and each sender may use a different response queue. The receiver does not assume that all responses should be sent to the same response queue. Rather every time it removes a message from the request queue, a receiver uses the queue whose format name is contained in the `PROPID_M_RESP_QUEUE` message property. The content of that property is used to open a queue and to send a response to it.

The `receiveMessages()` procedure uses a `QUEUEHANDLE` variable passed to it. The procedure is as follows.

```
void receiveMessages(QUEUEHANDLE mQHandle) {
    MQMSGPROPS mProps;                          // Structure of msg prop IDs
                                                // and values

    MQPROPVARIANT propVar[PROPERTIES];          // Array of message property
                                                // values

    MSGPROPID propId[PROPERTIES];               // Array of message property
                                                // identifiers

    DWORD nProps = 0;                           // Property counter
    char mBuffer[BUFFER_LENGTH];                // Message buffer
    char rMBuffer[BUFFER_LENGTH];               // Response message buffer
    WCHAR msgLabel[BUFFER_LENGTH];              // Message label
    WCHAR rMsgLabel[BUFFER_LENGTH];             // Response message label
    HRESULT hResult;                            // Standard Windows result
                                                // indicator

    WCHAR rFormatName[BUFFER_LENGTH];           // Response queue format name
    QUEUEHANDLE rQHandle;                       // Response queue handle

    printf("receiveMessages >>\n");
    while (1) {
        // Prepare properties of message to receive
        nProps = 0;
        propId[nProps] = PROPID_M_BODY; // Get the message body property
        propVar[nProps].vt = VT_UI1 | VT_VECTOR;
        propVar[nProps].caub.cElems = sizeof(mBuffer);
        propVar[nProps].caub.pElems = (unsigned char *) mBuffer;
        nProps++;
```

```
propId[nProps] = PROPID_M_LABEL; // Get the message label
propVar[nProps].vt = VT_LPWSTR;
propVar[nProps].pwszVal = msgLabel;
nProps++;

propId[nProps] = PROPID_M_LABEL_LEN; // Get the message label
length
propVar[nProps].vt = VT_UI4;
propVar[nProps].ulVal = BUFFER_LENGTH;
nProps++;

propId[nProps] = PROPID_M_RESP_QUEUE; // Get the response queue
propVar[nProps].vt = VT_LPWSTR;
propVar[nProps].pwszVal = rFormatName;
nProps++;

propId[nProps] = PROPID_M_RESP_QUEUE_LEN; // Get the response
queue length
propVar[nProps].vt = VT_UI4;
propVar[nProps].ulVal = BUFFER_LENGTH;
nProps++;

mProps.cProp = nProps; // Create a MSGPROPS structure
mProps.aPropID = propId;
mProps.aPropVar = propVar;
mProps.aStatus = NULL;
```

4
```
hResult = MQReceiveMessage(        // Receive a message
    mQHandle,             // Message handle
    INFINITE,             // Wait a long time for a message
    MQ_ACTION_RECEIVE,    // Receive, don't peek
    &mProps,              // Message properties
    NULL, NULL, NULL,     // Synchronous receives
    NULL,                 // Queue cursor
    MQ_NO_TRANSACTION);   // Nontransactional
```

5
```
if (FAILED(hResult)) {
        PRINTERROR("receiveMessages :: Cannot receive response message!",
            hResult, RESUME);
} else {
```

```
        printf("receiveMessages :: Received message body :: %s\n", mBuffer);
        printf("receiveMessages :: Received message label :: %S\n", msgLabel);
        printf("receiveMessages :: Response queue :: %S\n", rFormatName);
```

6
```
        hResult = MQOpenQueue( // Open response queue
            rFormatName,          // Queue format name
            MQ_SEND_ACCESS,       // Will receive responses on this queue
            MQ_DENY_NONE,         // Queue can be shared
            &rQHandle);           // Queue handle
        PRINTERROR("sender :: Cannot open response queue!", hResult, ABORT);
```

7
```
        // Assign a message body
        sprintf(rMBuffer, "Response to message :: %s",mBuffer);
        // Assign a message label
        swprintf(rMsgLabel, L"%s response label", msgLabel);

        nProps = 0;
        propId[nProps] = PROPID_M_BODY; // Set the message body
        propVar[nProps].vt = VT_UI1 | VT_VECTOR;
        propVar[nProps].caub.cElems = sizeof(rMBuffer);
        propVar[nProps].caub.pElems = (unsigned char *)rMBuffer;
        nProps++;

        propId[nProps] = PROPID_M_LABEL; // Set message label
        propVar[nProps].vt = VT_LPWSTR;
        propVar[nProps].pwszVal = rMsgLabel;
        nProps++;

        mProps.cProp    = nProps; // Create a MSGPROPS structure
        mProps.aPropID  = propId;
        mProps.aPropVar = propVar;
        mProps.aStatus  = NULL;
```

8
```
        hResult = MQSendMessage(  // Send the message
            rQHandle,             // Response queue handle
            &mProps,              // Response message
            MQ_NO_TRANSACTION);   // Sending is not transactional
        PRINTERROR("receiveMessages :: Cannot send message!", hResult, RESUME);
```

(9)
```
            MQCloseQueue(rQHandle);
        }
```

(10)
```
        if (strcmp(mBuffer, "quit") == 0) // Should we terminate?
            break;
    } /* while (1) */
    printf("receiveMessages <<\n");
}
```

(1) The `MQMSGPROPS`, `MQPROPVARIANT`, and `MSGPROPID` types, discussed in previous sections, are used to obtain and to assign message property values. A counter variable, `nProps`, is used throughout Hello World to count the number of elements in MSMQ arrays and to indicate that information to MSMQ. Several ASCII and Unicode character buffers are defined for request and response message labels and message bodies and to hold the response queue format name. Since we will be opening and closing a response queue, we need a variable of type `QUEUEHANDLE`.

(2) The Hello World receiver is going to loop repeatedly, receiving a message and sending a reply within the loop.

(3) We construct an `MQMSGPROPS` structure that is used when receiving a message. Through this structure we request the message body, its label, and the format name of a queue to which a response should be sent. Note that the `PROPID_M_LABEL_LEN` message property is required when `PROPID_M_LABEL` is retrieved with a message.

(4) To receive a message, we call `MQReceiveMessage()`. The first parameter is a queue handle representing a connection to a queue manager. `MQReceiveMessage()` will return immediately when a message is in the queue, or it will wait the number of milliseconds indicated by the second parameter. If `INFINITE` is specified, `MQReceiveMessage()` will wait indefinitely.

Let's talk about the third and seventh parameters together. It is possible to peek at a message in a queue or to remove it from the queue. An application can even remove messages out of sequence from the queue if it creates a queue cursor. Using the cursor, an application can peek sequentially at the messages in the queue, beginning with the first message. After examining message properties, an application can remove a message under the cursor or leave it and go on to the next message in the queue.

If you want to use a queue cursor in `MQReceiveMessage()`, you can create one by calling `MQCreateCursor()`. The cursor handle is passed as the seventh parameter in `MQReceiveMessage()`.

The third parameter in `MQReceiveMessage()` indicates how to read a message in the queue.

- When MQ_ACTION_RECEIVE is specified, the first message in the queue (when using no cursor) or the message under the cursor is removed.

- A value of MQ_ACTION_PEEK_CURRENT returns information about the first message in the queue when no cursor is specified or the message under the cursor. The cursor is not incremented after calling MQReceiveMessage().

- MQ_ACTION_PEEK_NEXT causes MSMQ to increment the cursor and to return information about the (next) message. A cursor is required when this constant is specified.

As described in ❸ , we created a structure indicating which message properties we want returned. The property structures we created are passed as the fourth parameter. If MQReceiveMessage() returns a message, properties values are returned in those structures.[3] The fifth and sixth parameters, used when receiving a message asynchronously, will be discussed later in the book. If we wanted to receive a message transactionally, we would pass an object representing a transaction context or a constant as the final parameter. In this example we are not within a transaction.

❺ We check for errors. If none are present, we print out the message body, the label, and the format name to which a response is to be sent.

❻ The response queue is opened. To do this we use the format name from the request message. We open the queue, with send access and queue sharing indicated. MSMQ returns a handle to the response queue as the last parameter.

❼ The response message body and the label properties are set, using the contents of the original message. The new message is then constructed.

❽ To send the message, we use the queue handle returned by MQOpenQueue() and pass the structure containing properties for our response message. If we were sending the message within a transaction context, we would pass as the third parameter an object representing the transaction context or a constant.

❾ When the message is sent, we no longer expect to use the response queue. To clean up, we close the queue, using the queue handle.

❿ The receiver procedure loops until it receives a request message body of "quit". When this occurs, the procedure breaks from the while loop and returns.

---

3. MQReceiveMessage() can return without a message after timing out. In this case the message property structure is not filled in.

5.7 The Hello World Sender

So far we have talked very little about how Hello World functions in sender mode. In fact, the sender procedures are nearly identical to the receiver procedures. A sender creates a response queue by calling `createQueue()` or finds a local one, using `locateQueueByType()`. A sender also uses `locateQueueByType()` to find a request queue. Similar code is also used to open queues for sending and receiving messages, closing and deleting queues, constructing messages, and sending and receiving them. Consequently we won't walk through the code here. You're encouraged to have a look at the Hello World application in detail, to experiment with it, and to improve it.

```
// sender() sets up the environment for the sending application
// then, it calls sendMessages() which appears below

void sender(int args, char ** argv) {
    HRESULT hResult;                           // Standard Windows result
                                               // indicator

    char qLabel[DESC_LENGTH +1];               // Optional queue descriptor
    WCHAR rspFormatName[NAME_LENGTH];          // Holds the formatted name
                                               // of a queue
    DWORD rspFormatLength = NAME_LENGTH;       // Format name length
    QUEUEHANDLE mQHandle, rQHandle;            // Queue handles
    WCHAR msgFormatName[NAME_LENGTH];          // Holds the formatted name
                                               // of a queue
    DWORD msqFormatLength = NAME_LENGTH;       // Format name length

    printf("sender >>\n");
    // Locate message queue
    printf("sender :: calling locateQueueByType\n");
    hResult = locateQueueByType(&msgQueueType, msgFormatName,
        &msqFormatLength);
    printf("sender :: Formatted Name :: %S\n", msgFormatName);

    // Create response queue pathname and queue label
    swprintf(qPathName, L"pswtech\\HelloWorldResponseQ");
    printf("Hello World Response Queue PathName :: %S\n", qPathName);
    sprintf(qLabel, "Response Queue created by %s", argv[0]);

// Create response queue or get formatName for existing queue
if (args > 1) {
    hResult = createQueue(qPathName, &rspQueueType, qLabel,
        rspFormatName);
```

```
        if (hResult == MQ_ERROR_QUEUE_EXISTS)
            PRINTERROR("sender :: queue already exists"", hResult, ABORT);
    } else {
        hResult = locateQueue(&rspQueueType, rspFormatName,
            &rspFormatLength);
        PRINTERROR("sender :: Cannot retrieve format name!",
            hResult, ABORT);
    }


    // Open response queue
    printf("Formatted Name :: %S\n", rspFormatName);
    printf("sender opening response queue :: calling MQOpenQueue\n");
    hResult = MQOpenQueue(
            rspFormatName,        // Queue format name
            MQ_RECEIVE_ACCESS,    // Will receive responses on this queue
            0,                    // Queue can be shared
            &rQHandle);           // Queue handle
    PRINTERROR("sender :: Cannot open response queue!",
        hResult, ABORT);

    printf("sender opening message queue :: calling MQOpenQueue\n");
    hResult = MQOpenQueue(     // Open message queue
            msgFormatName,        // Queue format name
            MQ_SEND_ACCESS,       // Will send message to this queue
            0,                    // Queue can be shared
            &mQHandle);           // Queue handle
    PRINTERROR("sender :: Cannot open message queue!", hResult, ABORT);

    // Send messages to receiver
    sendMessages(mQHandle, rQHandle, rspFormatName, rspFormatLength);
    MQCloseQueue(mQHandle); // Close message queue
    MQCloseQueue(rQHandle); // Close response queue

    if (args > 1) { // Delete message queue if one was created
        hResult = MQDeleteQueue(rspFormatName);
        PRINTERROR("sender :: Cannot delete queue", hResult, RESUME);
    }
    printf("sender <<\n");
}
```

```
void sendMessages(QUEUEHANDLE mQHandle, QUEUEHANDLE rQHandle,
                  WCHAR *rFormatName, DWORD rFormatLength) {
    MQMSGPROPS mProps;                   // Structure of message
                                         // property IDs and values
    MQPROPVARIANT propVar[PROPERTIES];   // Array of message property
                                         // values
    QUEUEPROPID propId[PROPERTIES];      // Array of message property
                                         // identifiers
    DWORD nProps = 0;                    // Property counter
    char mBuffer[BUFFER_LENGTH];         // Message buffer
    char rMBuffer[BUFFER_LENGTH];        // Response message buffer
    WCHAR msgLabel[BUFFER_LENGTH];       // Message label
    HRESULT hResult;                     // Standard Windows result
                                         // indicator
    printf("sendMessages >>\n");
    while (1) {
        // Get input string
        printf("Enter a message_body or \"quit\": ");
        if (gets(mBuffer) == NULL)
            break;

        // Prepare properties of message to send
        swprintf(msgLabel, L"HelloWorld"); // Assign a message label

        // Set the message body property
        nProps = 0;
        propId[nProps] = PROPID_M_BODY; // Set the message body
        propVar[nProps].vt = VT_UI1 | VT_VECTOR;
        propVar[nProps].caub.cElems = sizeof(mBuffer);
        propVar[nProps].caub.pElems = (unsigned char *)mBuffer;
        nProps++;

        propId[nProps] = PROPID_M_LABEL; // Set the message label
        propVar[nProps].vt = VT_LPWSTR;
        propVar[nProps].pwszVal = msgLabel;
        nProps++;

        propId[nProps] = PROPID_M_RESP_QUEUE; // Set the response queue
        propVar[nProps].vt = VT_LPWSTR;
        propVar[nProps].pwszVal = rFormatName;
        nProps++;
```

```
mProps.cProp     = nProps; // Create an MSGPROPS structure
mProps.aPropID   = propId;
mProps.aPropVar  = propVar;
mProps.aStatus   = NULL;

// Send the message to the message queue
hResult = MQSendMessage(          // Send the message
         mQHandle,                // Message queue handle
         &mProps,                 // Message properties
         MQ_NO_TRANSACTION);      // Sending is not transactional
PRINTERROR("sendMessages :: Cannot send message!", hResult, RESUME);

// Prepare properties of receiving a message
nProps = 0;
propId[nProps] = PROPID_M_BODY; // Set the message body
propVar[nProps].vt = VT_UI1 | VT_VECTOR;
propVar[nProps].caub.cElems = sizeof(rMBuffer);
propVar[nProps].caub.pElems = (unsigned char *) rMBuffer;
nProps++;

propId[nProps] = PROPID_M_LABEL; // Set the message label
propVar[nProps].vt = VT_LPWSTR;
propVar[nProps].pwszVal = msgLabel;
nProps++;

propId[nProps] = PROPID_M_LABEL_LEN; // Set message label length
propVar[nProps].vt = VT_UI4;
propVar[nProps].ulVal = BUFFER_LENGTH;
nProps++;

mProps.cProp     = nProps; // Create an MSGPROPS structure
mProps.aPropID   = propId;
mProps.aPropVar  = propVar;
mProps.aStatus   = NULL;

// Receive a message from the response queue
hResult = MQReceiveMessage(
      rQHandle,          // Message queue handle
      INFINITE,          // Wait a long time for a message
```

```
                MQ_ACTION_RECEIVE,   // Receive, don't peek at the
                                     // message
                &mProps,             // Message properties
                NULL, NULL, NULL,    // Synchronous receives
                MQ_NO_TRANSACTION); // Nontransactional

        if (FAILED(hResult)) {
            PRINTERROR("sendMessages :: Cannot receive response msg!",
                hResult, RESUME);
        } else {
            printf("sendMessages :: Received message body :: %s\n",
            rMBuffer);
            printf("sendMessages :: Received message label :: %S\n",
            msgLabel);
        }

        // Should sending and receiving terminate?
        if (strcmp(mBuffer, "quit") == 0)
            break;
    } /* while (1) */
    printf("sendMessages <<\n");
}
```

5.8 Sample Program Output

The design of our Hello World application intentionally has a couple of flaws. The example is used because of its simplicity, but the sender and receiver applications are too tightly coupled. For example, the sender and the receiver exchange messages in lockstep. You can see this in the sample run that appears next. Ordinarily you would never design two queued messaging applications' communication to be this synchronized.

In the sample that follows, all human inputs are shown in italics. Queue format names have been eliminated, and text has been indented to make it more readable. Finally, spacing has been introduced to illustrate when screen input and output take place. In the run that follows, both the sender and the receiver use the −c switch, which causes queues to be created.

Sender

Receiver

```
D:\PSWTech\hello>hello -r -c
receiver >>
Hello World Message Queue PathName ::
  .\HelloWorldMessageQ
calling createQueue
  createQueue >>
  createQueue :: setting up queue
   properties...
  createQueue :: calling
   MQCreateQueue...
  createQueue <<
  Formatted Name :: PUBLIC=...
 receiver opening message queue ::
  calling MQOpenQueue
  receiveMessages >>
```

```
D:\PSWTech\hello>hello -s -c
Sender >>
 sender :: calling locateQueue
 locateQueue >>
 locateQueue ::
  calling MQLocateBegin
 locateQueue ::
  calling MQLocateNext
 locateQueue ::
  Formatted Name ::
    PUBLIC=…
 locateQueue ::
  calling MQLocateEnd
 locateQueue <<
sender :: Formatted Name ::
 PUBLIC=…
Hello World Response Queue PathName ::
.\HelloWorldResponseQ
 createQueue >>
 createQueue ::
  setting up queue
    properties...
 createQueue ::
  calling MQCreateQueue...
 createQueue <<
```

Sender	**Receiver**

```
Formatted Name :: PUBLIC=…
sender opening response queue ::
 calling MQOpenQueue
sender opening message queue ::
 calling MQOpenQueue
 sendMessages >>
 Enter a message_body or "quit":
  MSMQ is so cool!
```

```
                              receiveMessages ::
                               Received message body  ::
                                MSMQ is so cool!
                              receiveMessages ::
                              Received message label ::
                               HelloWorld
                              receiveMessages ::
                               Response queue ::
                                    PUBLIC=...
```

```
sendMessages ::
 Received message body ::
  Response to message ::
   MSMQ is so cool!
sendMessages ::
 Received message label ::
  HelloWorld response label
Enter a message_body or "quit":
 MTS is neat!
```

```
                              receiveMessages ::
                               Received message body  ::
                                MTS is neat!
                              receiveMessages ::
                               Received message label ::
                                HelloWorld
                              receiveMessages ::
                               Response queue ::
                                    PUBLIC=...
```

```
sendMessages ::
 Received message body  ::
  Response to message ::
   MTS is neat!
```

Sender   **Receiver**

```
                                        receiveMessages ::
                                         Received message body ::
                                          MTS is neat!
                                        receiveMessages ::
                                         Received message label ::
                                          HelloWorld
                                        receiveMessages ::
                                         Response queue ::
                                          PUBLIC=...
sendMessages ::
 Received message body ::
  Response to message ::
   MTS is neat!
sendMessages ::
 Received message label ::
  HelloWorld response label
Enter a message_body or "quit":
 Microsoft rocks!
                                        receiveMessages ::
                                         Received message body  ::
                                          Microsoft rocks!
                                        ReceiveMessages ::
                                         Received message label ::
                                          HelloWorld
                                        receiveMessages ::
                                         Response queue ::
                                          PUBLIC=...
sendMessages ::
 Received message body ::
  Response to message ::
   Microsoft rocks!
sendMessages ::
 Received message label ::
  HelloWorld response label
Enter a message_body or "quit":
 quit
                                        receiveMessages ::
                                         Received message body ::
                                          quit
```

```
                                         receiveMessages ::
                                          Received message label ::
                                           HelloWorld
                                         receiveMessages ::
                                          Response queue ::
                                            PUBLIC=...

    sendMessages ::
     Received message body  ::
       Response to message :: quit
    sendMessages ::
     Received message label ::
       HelloWorld response label
      sendMessages <<                         receiveMessages <<
    sender <<                             receiver <<
    D:\PSWTech\hello>                         D:\PSWTech\hello>
```

5.9 Conclusion

In this chapter we have demonstrated how to use the MSMQ API to create queues, to look them up in the MQIS, to open and close queues, and to send and receive messages. Although the MSMQ API does not have the same object-oriented programming qualities of the COM components, it leverages the object-oriented design of MSMQ while providing a simple C language interface.

The design of our Hello World application intentionally has a couple of flaws. The sender and the receiver applications are too tightly coupled, and some anomalies exist under certain conditions. In Chapter 6 we review our design, identify the flaws, and show why it is important to develop a queue and message architecture that satisfies application assumptions and requirements.

5.10 Resources and References

Microsoft Message Queue Explorer Administrator's Online Help.

Microsoft Message Queue Server Online Help.

Rogerson, D. 1997. *Inside COM*. Redmond, WA: Microsoft Press.

6 Chapter

MSMQ Queue and Message Design Considerations

This chapter will be useful to all readers but is especially important to application architects and developers. Developing a good queue and messaging architecture up front will save you time later. In this chapter we briefly examine the Hello World program in the context of various assumptions. Then we discuss some MSMQ queue and message design options that meet particular application requirements. This discussion will focus on message format issues and how queues are used by one or more applications.

There are other design considerations for messages and queues. Message properties can be used to secure communications or to improve reliability and recovery from failures. Queue properties also facilitate these goals. We'll defer a discussion of these topics until later in the book. They are important issues, but they are also separable from this discussion.

6.1 Hello World Program Analysis

The simple Hello World applications created for Chapters 4 and 5 were designed to make the introduction of MSMQ tractable to readers. In those chapters we ignored some problems associated with those applications. In this section we'll examine the problems or limitations of those implementations. We'll also suggest ways in which the programs can be improved.

The Hello World application as developed with the MSMQ API exhibits two design flaws.

- The sender uses a synchronous processing model, sending a request message and waiting for a response. That user could wait a very long time if a receiver is not running or does not process a request and send a response immediately. A better sender design would use an event-driven processing model that allowed the user to perform other tasks until the response arrived.

- Processing in the sender and receiver applications is coupled too tightly. For example, the user running the sender program enters `"quit"` to terminate processing. Then the sender packages the text in the message body and sends it. The receiver receives it, prepares and sends a response, and then exits. The sender receives the response, and it exits. Thus any user can shut down a receiving process even if other senders are active. There should be an alternative way to stop a receiving application.

The COM sender has a less synchronous design. A request is sent when the user clicks the Send button: A response is received when the user clicks the Receive button. Processing is more event-driven.

Now let's look at how Hello World performs when there is more than one sender and one receiver:

- *Several senders are on separate machines.* Each sender can create a local response queue. The intended recipient (the sender of the original message) receives all responses. No sender receives a response intended for another process.

- *Several senders share an existing response queue.* The sender programs don't implement any algorithm or facility that helps to distinguish responses intended for user 1 from responses intended for user 2. There is a chance that one sender may receive another's response when two or more processes share the same response queue.

- *Several senders create response queues on the same machine.* When two or more senders attempt to create response queues, a name collision occurs. A better design would make the pathname for a queue configurable at start-up.

- *Several receivers create request queues on the same machine.* A name collision occurs. A better design would make the pathname for a queue configurable at start-up.

In summary, Hello World works fine with one sender and one receiver or when several receivers read messages from the same queue. However, the design starts to break down when a response queue is shared by two or more processes. In that case response messages do not always go to the intended recipient.

In designing distributed applications for MSMQ (or any message queuing technology), you should invest time up front to define a queue and messaging architecture that satisfies the assumptions and requirements of the application. MSMQ provides several queue and message properties—among them message and queue labels, queue names and types, message correlation IDs—that can be used in a design.

6.2 Queue Options

In MSMQ messages are always sent to a queue. A queue is a physical message store, but it can satisfy many logical purposes. For example, one or more queues can be associated with an individual user, a service, an event stream, and so on.

- *A queue can be associated with a user.* When a message needs to be sent to the queue, you can look the queue up no matter where it is located. If you'd like, you can name the queue after the user. The queue does not have to be located by a user; it can be anywhere in the MSMQ enterprise. Access controls can restrict access as needed.

- *A queue can be associated with a service.* One or more queues can be used to store service requests. If several related service requests are defined, a single queue can be implemented to store all requests, or separate queues can be used for each request type. For example, a catalog company may accept orders for apparel and accessories. Separate queues can be defined for each type of merchandise. If two queues are used, you could assign an identical service type for both queues and use the queue label to distinguish between apparel and accessory queues with identical service types. An alternative is to define different service types for apparel and accessory orders. Your applications that send messages to these queues will need to know the rules for looking up these queues so that accessory orders are not sent to the apparel queue or vice versa.

- *A queue can be associated with an event stream.* One or more applications may manage or monitor a particular resource. An event stream can be created from information that is relayed about the resource. When reporting or forwarding events related to the resource, applications would send a message to a queue used as a sink for the information. From there the information could be placed in a database, forwarded to other processes, and so on.

As part of a queue architecture design, several related issues need to be considered. The first issue is whether the queue is to be shared. By design a queue can have any number of processes placing messages on it. Access can be granted to one process, to many processes concurrently, or to many senders but to only one receiver at a time.

In queue architectures the number of sending applications that write to a queue is usually not critical. However, the number of processes that can remove messages is important.

A queue can usually be shared when several identical processes reading messages from a queue are interchangeable. In this situation you don't care whether a message goes to process A or to process B.

Problems arise when several processes read from a queue and a message needs to go to a particular process. When two applications read messages from the same queue, you automatically increase the complexity of your receiving applications. Consider the catalog order entry example. Assume that one application processes apparel orders and that another processes accessory orders. If both applications read messages from the same queue, both applications will need additional logic to differentiate between apparel and accessory orders.

The conclusion to draw is that it is a bad idea to use a queue for mixed purposes. Queues are cheap to create and manage. Applications can have several queues open at any time, and MSMQ makes it easy to respond to incoming messages by using asynchronous, or event-driven, processing. You don't need to conserve on the number of queues that are defined.

The second design issue relates to finding a queue. Briefly, an application can search for a queue by using a label or a type property. These properties ensure location independence. You should use a pathname only when you need to explicitly address a queue at a given location.

The third issue in designing a queue architecture relates to message ordering. Suppose that you are writing an application that sends several messages to a service and that each successive message modifies information contained in a previous message. Perhaps the first message creates an insurance policy, and follow-on messages add or delete policy options. In this case your application needs messages to be processed in order, without duplicate messages being delivered by the underlying messaging infrastructure.

Message ordering is difficult to guarantee if more than one process is removing messages from a queue. For example, process A could remove message 53 from a queue and then come to the end of its slice of CPU time. The operating system might then start process B, which removes message 54 from the queue, processes it, and obtains an error. You will find it much easier to ensure message ordering when a single process performs destructive reads.

To ensure that messages are delivered to a queue in order and without duplicates, they must be sent within a transaction. A transaction guarantees exactly-once delivery. If several messages are sent as part of the same transaction, they are guaranteed to arrive on the target queue in order. We'll go into more detail on this feature of MSMQ in Chapter 11.

6.3 Messages and Message Property Options

By now you've undoubtedly gleaned an important lesson from this discussion, namely, that your queue and messaging architectures cannot be defined in isolation. Your queue design must be reviewed with your message-processing design. Two related topics should be considered as you define a message architecture for your applications. The topics have to do with whether it is necessary to distinguish between messages in a queue and how to construct the body of a message.

6.3.1 Message Types

MSMQ gives you several properties for distinguishing messages from one another.

- *Labels.* A label is a natural way to identify a kind of service request, report, or event.
- *The application-specific property.* Applications can assign values to `PROPID_M_APPSPECIFIC` or to `MSMQ.AppSpecific` as a distinguishing message characteristic.
- *The message body.* Many applications embed codes into a message body to distinguish messages.

The correlation ID property is also available, although it has a very specific purpose: to help a sending application correlate a sent message and a response message.

A message label is probably the most semantically meaningful way to distinguish messages, since a label is a string of Unicode characters. However, be careful when using a label. Uppercase and lowercase letters, spaces, periods, and null characters introduce complexity into the message-selection process. For example, your application may have to handle customer order messages that have any of the following labels:

```
Customer order
customer   order
Customer Order.
```

The application-specific message property, an unsigned integer, is easier to use correctly than a message label is. It's very easy to determine whether the application-specific property of a message is equal to 3. Unfortunately an integer is also limiting.

A message body can contain any type of data and mixed kinds of data. A message body offers more flexibility than a message label and the application-specific property.

6.3.2 Message Body Structure

In most messaging environments two general message structures are used: fixed-length records and self-defining record structures. Users of MSMQ COM components have a third option: sending typed objects within a message. Let's examine the strengths and weaknesses of these types of record structures.

Perhaps the majority of messaging users pass fixed-length, variant records as a message body. A record usually contains a fixed-length record identifier as the first field. That identifier indicates to the receiving application how the rest of the record is structured. Two variant records appear in Figure 6-1.

Message bodies that use variant records are easy to construct and to read. However, at least two problems are possible when fixed records are used in a message body. First, variant-record definitions are very static. Suppose that you were using MSMQ to develop an application 20 years ago. You might have allocated a 5-character field to hold a customer's zip code. Since that time, 9-character zip codes have been introduced. Problems with the length of a message field will arise in your systems when you use variant records. Most companies handle changes by defining a new variant type. Unfortunately this strategy can lead to an increasing number of record types that need to be recognized. Eventually the logic for distinguishing between records can become more complex than the logic to service the request. A second problem with variant records can occur when very large records are passed in a message. In some applications most fields may be left blank. Unfortunately space— whether it is used or not—must be defined in the record. Fields that do not contain real information are simply left empty (or padded with blanks). Thus applications can pass very large records, but much of a record may contain no real information.

To address the problems associated with fixed-length record definitions, some companies use self-defining, or self-describing, syntaxes. In HTML, an example of a self-describing syntax, tags describe the string of text that follows the tag. Messages can be dynamically constructed by a sender and processed by a receiver.

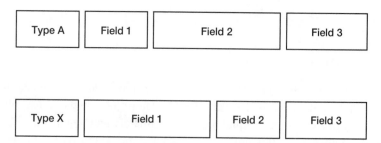

Figure 6-1   Two variant-record message bodies

In such tag/value/delimiter syntaxes the basic idea is to tag each field in the message and to place a delimiter between fields. It's worth noting that Microsoft decided to use a self-describing syntax for report messages. The message syntax is similar to HTML:

```
<MESSAGE ID>{message ID}</MESSAGE ID>
<TARGET QUEUE>{target queue format name}</TARGET QUEUE>
<NEXT HOP>{IP or IPX address of the next hop}</NEXT HOP>
<HOP COUNT>integer</HOP COUNT>
```

The MSMQ report message structure is rather flat. Additional structuring can be defined within the message, if necessary. Consider the following example:

```
<CUSTOMER ORDER>
    <CUSTOMER INFO>
        <FNAME>John</FNAME> <LNAME>Smith</LNAME>
        <Address>4 Main Street</Address>
        <CITY>Pleasantville</CITY> <STATE>CO</STATE>
        <ZIP>80002</ZIP> <TN>303-222-1212</TN>
    </CUSTOMER INFO>
    <ORDER ITEM>
        <COLOR>Blue</COLOR>
        <ID>X1234></ID> <SIZE>Medium</SIZE>
        <DESCRIPTION>Womens blouse</DESCRIPTION>
    </ORDER ITEM>
    <ORDER ITEM>
        <ID>Y98763</ID> <COLOR>Red Plaid</COLOR>
        <COLOR2>Purple</COLOR2> <SIZE>Small</SIZE>
    </ORDER ITEM>
</CUSTOMER ORDER>
```

In this example several variable-length subrecords are nested within another record. The subrecords begin with <CUSTOMER INFO> and <ORDER ITEM>.

The main strengths and weaknesses of a tag/value/delimiter syntax should be obvious. This kind of syntax offers substantial flexibility. All fields can have variable lengths. Optional fields are included in a message only if they contain information. Records can be nested within other records. Further, the message body can contain one or more ORDER ITEM records included within the CUSTOMER ORDER record. The first record includes an optional description field. The second includes an optional second-color preference. The ID and COLOR fields are reversed in the second ORDER ITEM record. Since all fields are delimited, they are of variable lengths.

A self-describing syntax has two weaknesses, however. First, the syntax is more difficult to process than are fixed-length records. Processing a record is much easier when fields have a known length and come in a predictable order.[1] Second, the tags and the delimiter characters help eliminate unnecessary fields from records, but they also add to the message's length. In a record in which few fields go unused, message length can increase substantially when a tag/value/delimiter syntax is used. On the other hand, the overall message length might be reduced if most fields are not used.

6.4 Summary

Since your queue and messaging architectures cannot be defined in isolation, it may be useful to define a checkpoint in your project schedule to carefully review assumptions, requirements, and designs. Examining the issues outlined in this chapter may catch design flaws and help your project team to understand the overall processing model for your distributed application. As you perform this review, you should also consider message reliability, as well as message security and queue security. These topics are discussed in Chapters 8 and 9, respectively.

6.5 Resources and References

Microsoft Message Queue Server Online Help.

---

1. Several products on the market use rules engines to process and to construct message syntaxes like the ones shown in this chapter. Do not let processing complexity dissuade you from using a self-describing syntax, unless your project is cash-starved.

7
Chapter

Solutions to Message
Problems

This chapter, intended primarily for developers, discusses programming solutions to typical application problems. It is expected that developers will refer to sections of this chapter as they seek solutions to particular messaging problems. The programming solutions in the chapter build on the Visual Basic example developed in Chapter 4 and the MSMQ API example of Chapter 5. Managers may want to read the introductory paragraphs of each major section to understand the messaging problems that are solved.

Messaging applications frequently need more than the simple ability to send a request and to receive a response. Usually a variety of messaging requirements need to be satisfied in production applications. In this chapter we'll address the following seven issues that are common in many MSMQ messaging applications:

- Converting a message identifier or a correlation identifier to a string
- Correlating two messages, for example, a request and a response
- Being notified when a message has arrived on a queue
- Receiving messages of an undetermined size
- Sending and receiving information that is broken into two or more related messages (another form of correlated messages)
- Shipping objects within a message
- Sending messages from an independent client while it is off line

7.1 Converting Message and Correlation IDs to Strings

When you open up MSMQ Explorer and look at messages, their message identifiers and correlation IDs are displayed as strings. The Explorer represents a message identifier (and correlation ID) as a machine GUID, followed by some numbers.

{8756B532-AC71-11D1-907C-00400521EF0C}\1885640

However, these identifier values are sent as blobs (binary large objects) guaranteed to be unique.

No direct translation from blob to string is available to us through MSMQ or Win32 APIs. However, when debugging your programs, you may sometimes want to obtain the Explorer representation of these values. The following code converts a Visual Basic message identifier from a blob to the Explorer representation:

```
Function GetMSMQMsgId(Msg As MSMQMessage) As String
    Dim Id(25) As String
    Dim MsgId As String
    Dim I As Long

    On Error GoTo GetMSMQMsgIdHandler
    For Counter = LBound(Msg.Id) To UBound(Msg.Id)
        Id(Counter) = ""
        If Len(Hex(Msg.Id(Counter))) = 1 Then
            Id(Counter) = "0"
        End If
        Id(Counter) = Id(Counter) & Hex(Msg.Id(Counter))
    Next Counter
    MsgId = "{" + Id(3) + Id(2) + Id(1) + Id(0) + "-" + Id(5) + Id(4) _
        + "-" + Id(7) + Id(6) + "-" + Id(8) + Id(9) + "-" + Id(10) + Id(11) _
        + Id(12) + Id(13) + Id(14) + Id(15) + "}\"
    I = Msg.Id(16) + 256 * Msg.Id(17) + 65536 * Msg.Id(18) _
        + 16777216 * Msg.Id(19)
    MsgId = MsgId + Str(I)
    GetMSMQMsgId = MsgId
Exit Function
```

```
GetMSMQMsgIdHandler:
    StatusText.Text = "GetMSMQMsgIdHandler :: Error: " _
        + Str$(Err.Number) + " :: " + "Reason: " + Err.Description
    GetMSMQMsgId = ""
End Function
```

Keep in mind that Microsoft does not guarantee to honor this format in the future.

7.2   Request and Response Correlation

Why would it be necessary to correlate two messages? An example readily comes to mind. In work flow environments a manager handles processing of requests on behalf of clients. To maximize throughput the manager may process several client requests simultaneously. When a client request arrives, the manager begins working on it. In order to satisfy a client's request, the manager may turn around and request processing by one or more downstream services. Perhaps the manager needs to merge data from two or more systems to satisfy the client request.

At any instant, two or more client requests may be in different stages of completion. When a response message arrives, the manager will need to correlate it with a client request and to figure out which task to initiate next as part of the client's work flow. A piece of information from the response is needed that relates the response message back to work in progress. The work flow manager typically uses information contained in the message envelope or embedded in the message for this purpose.

In this section we will develop a Visual Basic example that demonstrates message correlation. Requests and responses can be correlated in lots of ways. For example, you might examine the body of a message and correlate it with a previous message. Or you could use a message label: If message Y has a particular string of characters, it must be a response to message X. But these methods of correlating messages don't guarantee correct results, as nothing ensures that a message label or the message contents are unique. Applications need a foolproof way to correlate messages.

MSMQ provides two simple-to-use properties to help you uniquely identify an initial message and to correlate responses to it: the message identifier (PROPID_M_MSGID or MSMQMessage.Id) and the correlation identifier (PROPID_M_CORRELATIONID or MSMQMessage.CorrelationId). MSMQ assigns a unique message identifier to each message. When the correlation identifier from message B is identical to the message identifier for message A, we say that the two messages are correlated. This scenario is pictured in Figure 7-1.

How does the message correlation process work? Once message A is sent, sender X retrieves the message identifier and stores it for use when receiving messages.

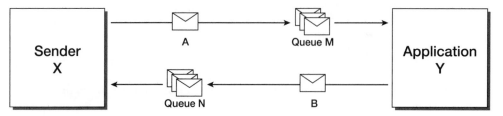

Message ID: {8756B532-AC71-11D1-907C-00400521EF0C}\1885640

Message ID: {8756B532-AC71-11D1-907C-00400521EF0C}\1885870
Correlation ID: {8756B532-AC71-11D1-907C-00400521EF0C}\1885640

Figure 7-1   Two correlated messages

Application Y receives message A and wants to send a correlated message in response. To do so application Y copies A's message identifier into the correlation identifier of message B. Thus the correlation identifier of message B will match the message identifier stored by sender X. Application Y sends message B to the response queue indicated by message A's response queue property. When retrieving messages that correlate with message A, sender X peeks at the correlation identifier of each message in the response queue. If a message's correlation identifier matches the stored message identifier, sender X performs a destructive read of the message.

7.2.1   Copying a Message Identifier into a Correlation Identifier

It is very easy for a responding application to facilitate correlation of messages. In COM, the procedure `Receive()` can be used. This procedure declares two message components, as well as a queue component for the response queue. A request queue is opened and a message is received. As the response is prepared, the message identifier is copied from the received message to the correlation identifier of the response message. Then the message is sent.

```
Private Sub Receive()
    Dim RecMsg As MSMQMessage
    Dim ResMsg As New MSMQMessage
    Dim openResponseQ As MSMQQueue

    On Error GoTo Receive_ErrorHandler
    ' Locate or create queue as demonstrated in Chapter 4
    ' Open queue for receiving messages if necessary -
    ' demonstrated in Chapter 4
    ' RecQueue represents an open queue
    Set RecMsg = RecQueue.Receive(ReceiveTimeout:=INFINITE)
```

```
                    ' Test whether a message was received or the Receive timed out
    ❶           If Not RecMsg Is Nothing Then
    ❷               MsgId = GetMSMQMsgId(RecMsg)
                    StatusText.Text = "Receive :: success :: message " _
                        + MsgId
                Else
                    StatusText.Text = _
                        "Receive :: No message was available to receive."
                    Exit Sub
                End If

                ' Prepare response
    ❸           ResMsg.Body = "Response Message to:: " + RecMsg.Body
                ResMsg.Label = "Response Label to:: " + RecMsg.Label
                ResMsg.CorrelationId = RecMsg.Id

                ' Open response queue
    ❹           Set openResponseQ = _
                    RecMsg.ResponseQueueInfo.Open(Access:=MQ_SEND_ACCESS, _
                        ShareMode:=MQ_DENY_NONE)
                ' Send response
                ResMsg.Send openResponseQ
                ' Close response queue
                openResponseQ.Close
                Exit Sub

        ReceiveEvent_ErrorHandler:
            StatusText.Text = "ReceiveEvent_Arrived :: " + Where _
                + " :: Error: " + Str$(Err.Number) + " :: " + "Reason: " _
                + Err.Description
        End Sub
```

❶ After each receive operation, we make sure that a valid message was received. It is possible that the MSMQQueue.Receive() method returned after timing out.

❷ We convert the message identifier into a string and print it out.

❸ A response message is prepared. The message body and the label are assigned. The third line is most critical. It copies the message identifier from the request message to the correlation ID of the response message. That enables the sender to correlate this response message with the request.

❹ We send the message, close the response queue, and exit the procedure.

7.2.2 Request and Response Message Correlation

Let's demonstrate how a program can send messages and then correlate responses. The program will send a message and store that message's identifier assigned to it by MSMQ. Later the program will examine the correlation identifier of messages in the response queue, attempting to correlate a response to the original message.

We'll develop a Visual Basic application for this purpose. Although our focus is on MSMQ, we delve into some VB mechanics so that a user can keep track of what is happening during execution, but we'll try to keep the VB handstands to a minimum.

The code this program uses is similar to the Hello World Sender application. However, after a message is sent, it is copied into a collection object, and the message identifier is placed into a list box.[1]

The collection is our primary repository for storing state—in this case a sent message. In production applications that need to recover state following a shutdown, the collection might be replaced by a database that is accessed through the COM data object `Recordset`.

The list box is incidental to our demonstration of message correlation. Each identifier in the list box represents a correlation identifier for a message the user expects to receive later on. When a user wants to receive the response message, he or she can double click on its identifier from the list box. The program retrieves the original message from the collection object. Next, messages in the response queue are examined one by one. If a correlated message is in the queue, it is removed, the message body and the label are displayed in text boxes, and the message identifier is deleted from the list box. If the correlated message is not sitting in the queue, the message identifier remains in the list box, and a status report is written in the status box. The form for this application appears in Figure 7-2.

The program adds one Visual Basic control, a list box, to those used by the Hello World Sender in Chapter 4. The property settings for the list box are as follows:

Control	Property	Setting
ListBox	Name	CorListId

To implement this program, we place the following declarations at the module level.

```
' Module-wide constants
Const RequestGUID = "{EFB01B40-49B3-11d1-902B-00400521EF0C}"
```

---

1. We could have placed the message body in the list box. A message body will have more meaning to users than a message identifier will. However, message bodies are not guaranteed to be unique, whereas a message identifier is. That is the rationale for using the message identifier; it is a better message property for demonstrating message correlation.

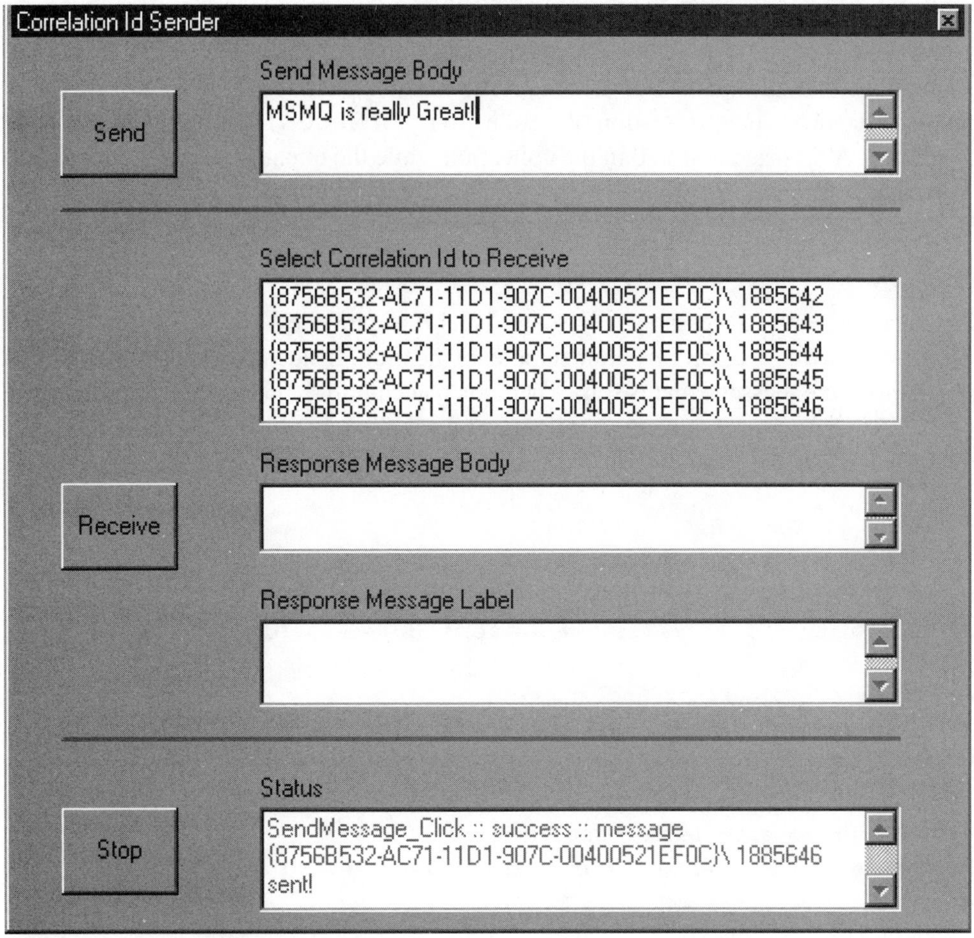

Figure 7-2 Screen used to send requests and to correlate responses

```
Const ResponseGUID = "{044F4C50-4A84-11d1-902D-00400521EF0C}"
Const ResponseQPath = "pswtech\CorrelationResponseQ"
Const ResponseQLabel = "Message Queue created by Correlation Sender"
Const RequestLabel = "Correlation Message"
Dim requestQ As MSMQQueueInfo
Dim responseQ As MSMQQueueInfo
Dim openRequestQ As MSMQQueue
Dim openResponseQ As MSMQQueue
Dim CorMsgCol As New Collection
```

There are few differences from the HelloWorld Sender program. Message labels, queue labels, queue type identifiers, and response queue pathnames have been changed so that this application and the HelloWorld application do not interact. The main difference is the declaration of a collection, `CorMsgCol`, of messages that have been sent. A message is stored in the collection while the client is waiting to receive a correlated response.

7.2.2.1 Sending a Message

When a user enters a message to be sent, Visual Basic invokes `SendMessage_Click()` in our sample application. Inside this procedure `ReqMsg` is the message that is sent. Then it is placed into `CorMsgCol`, a collection of `MSMQMessage` components. `SentMsgId` is a printable form of that message identifier. `Where` is used in status reports to indicate where a problem occurred.

```
Private Sub SendMessage_Click()
    Dim ReqMsg As New MSMQMessage
    Dim Where As String
    Dim SentMsgId    ' A printable form of ReqMsg.Id

    On Error GoTo ErrorHandler
    ' Locate or create a response queue as in Chapter 4
    ' Locate a request queue as demonstrated in Chapter 4
    ' Below, we open the queue where messages are sent
    If openRequestQ Is Nothing Then
        Set openRequestQ = requestQ.Open(Access:=MQ_SEND_ACCESS, _
            ShareMode:=MQ_DENY_NONE)
    End If

    Where = "Preparing request message body" ' Send message
    ReqMsg.Body = ReqBodyText.Text
    ReqMsg.Label = RequestLabel
    Set ReqMsg.ResponseQueueInfo = responseQ
    Where = "Sending request message"
    ReqMsg.Send openRequestQ

    SentMsgId = GetMSMQMsgId(ReqMsg)
    StatusText.Text = "SendMessage_Click :: success :: message " _
        + SentMsgId + " sent!"
    Where = "Adding Message identifier to List Box"
    CorIdList.AddItem (SentMsgId)
```

(4)
```
        Where = "Adding Message to Collection"
        CorMsgCol.Add ReqMsg, SentMsgId
    Exit Sub
    ErrorHandler:
        StatusText.Text = "SendMessage_Click :: " + Where _
            + " :: Error: " + Str$(Err.Number) + " :: " _
            + "Reason: " + Err.Description
    End Sub
```

(1) In your programs you will need to locate the queues to which a message is sent and its response is received. Code to do this is provided in Chapter 4. Then the queue to which a message will be sent is opened.

(2) The message body, the label, and the response queue are assigned. Then the message is sent.

(3) After the message is sent, we can retrieve the message identifier assigned to it by MSMQ. A printable version of the message ID is copied into `SentMsgId`, which is displayed as part of the final status message generated in this procedure and copied into the list box of request messages that have pending responses.

(4) A feature of Visual Basic collections is that elements can be added, accessed, and removed by using an index (integer) value or a key (string) value. `SentMsgId` is a representation of the message identifier, a value that is guaranteed to be unique, and is used as a key when accessing a message in `CorMsgCol`. Thus we are able to manage the association between message identifiers in the list box and elements in the collection of messages.

Suppose that you wanted to represent a message by its body in the list box. How would this procedure change? The code follows. The message body is placed into the list box and is used as the key into the collection of messages.

```
CorMsgCol.Add ReqMsg, ReqMsg.Body
CorIdList.AddItem (ReqMsg.Body)
```

7.2.2.2 Correlating a Response with a Request

`ReceiveMessage_Click()` demonstrates how to correlate messages in a response queue with a message selected by a user.

(1)
```
Private Sub ReceiveMessage_Click()
    Dim ResMsg As MSMQMessage
    Dim CorMsg As MSMQMessage
```

```
Dim Where As String
Dim ColKey
Dim LIndex As Integer
```

❷
```
LIndex = CorIdList.ListIndex ' Get the List index
' Retrieve a string version of the correlation ID
ColKey = CorIdList.List(LIndex)
' Retrieve the original msg using its message ID as a key
Set CorMsg = CorMsgCol.Item(ColKey)
```

❸
```
' Locate or create a response queue as in Chapter 4
' Open the response queue
If openResponseQ Is Nothing Then
    Set openResponseQ = _
        responseQ.Open(Access:=MQ_RECEIVE_ACCESS, _
        ShareMode:=MQ_DENY_NONE)
End If
```

❹
```
Where = "Receiving correlated response message"
openResponseQ.Reset
Set ResMsg = openResponseQ.PeekCurrent(ReceiveTimeout:=500)
Do While Not ResMsg Is Nothing
    If CorMsg.Id Like ResMsg.CorrelationId Then
        Set ResMsg = openResponseQ.ReceiveCurrent( _
```
❺
```
            ReceiveTimeout:=500)
        Exit Do
    End If
    Set ResMsg = openResponseQ.PeekNext(ReceiveTimeout:=500)
Loop
```

❻
```
If Not ResMsg Is Nothing Then
    ResBodyText.Text = ResMsg.Body
    ResLblText.Text = ResMsg.Label
    MsgId = GetMSMQMsgId(ResMsg)
    StatusText.Text = _
        "ReceiveMessage_Click :: success :: message " _
        + MsgId + " received :: correlates with " + ColKey + "!"
    CorMsgCol.Remove ColKey
    CorIdList.RemoveItem LIndex
Else
    StatusText.Text = "ReceiveMessage_Click :: " + Where _
```

```
              + " :: " + "No message was available to receive."
        End If
        Exit Sub

ErrorHandler:
        StatusText.Text = "ReceiveMessage_Click :: " + Where _
            + " :: Error: " + Str$(Err.Number) + " :: " + "Reason: " _
            + Err.Description
        CorIdList.ListIndex = -1  ' Reset list index
End Sub
```

1 Two `MSMQMessage` references are declared. `CorMsg` is used to reference a message in the `CorMsgCol` collection—the message associated with the message identifier selected by the user. There is an index value associated with each item in the list of pending messages. `LIndex` will be assigned the index value of the list item selected by the user. With that index value, we obtain `ColKey`, a message identifier used as the key to access a message in the `CorMsgCol` collection.

2 We retrieve an index for the list element selected. Then we obtain the list box entry corresponding to the selected list element. The list box entry is a string representation of a message identifier. The message identifier is used as a key in the `CorMsgCol` message collection. Thus we are able to reference a message corresponding to the message identifier selected by the user.

3 We locate and open the response queue for receiving messages if the queue has not been opened previously.

4 `CorMsg` references a message that was sent previously. In this block of code we examine one message at a time from the response queue and compare the correlation ID of the response message to `CorMsg.Id`, the message identifier assigned by MSMQ to the message we sent previously. If the correlation ID of a response matches `CorMsg.Id`, the response is removed from the queue, the message's body and label are displayed, and the message identifier is deleted from the list box. If the correlation ID of a response does not match `CorMsg.Id`, the message is left in the response queue, and we examine the next message. This process is repeated until a match occurs or we reach the end of the queue.

    `MSMQQueue` components maintain an internal cursor that holds a place in a queue. We reset the cursor to point to the first message in the queue. Then each message under the cursor is examined without moving the cursor. We don't move the cursor, because we want to remove the message if its correlation ID matches `CorMsg.Id`. To examine the message without moving the cursor, we call the

MSMQQueue.PeekCurrent method. If the message's correlation ID matches CorMsg.Id, we can remove the message by calling MSMQQueue.ReceiveCurrent() and we can exit the loop. Otherwise we move the cursor to the next message by calling MSMQQueue.PeekNext().

(5) Since this is a graphical program, we do not want a message peek or a receive to take an indefinite amount of time. Consequently each call is set to return in a half second or sooner.

(6) ResMsg is a reference to an MSMQMessage component. Once we exit the Do-loop in the previous code, ResMsg points at a correlated response or Nothing. If message correlation succeeded, we display the response contents and status information, remove the request message from CorMsgCol, and purge the message ID from the list box.

7.3 Asynchronous Message Processing

In a lot of computing contexts it is desirable to use an event-driven processing model. In this model the program processes events as they occur. A variety of events is possible. An event can be triggered by an external stimulus, as when a user clicks on a command button. Events can also result from internal occurrences. Perhaps an exception is raised or a timer goes off.

In many MSMQ applications it is desirable to treat a message arriving on a queue as an event. You may want a thread or a program to sleep when no messages are available to process. MSMQ allows the thread or process to sleep until a message arrives. This model also fits right in to the architecture of most desktop applications, in which application processing is caused by an external or internal event.

In this section we implement a simple program that automatically and asynchronously receives and responds to request messages. The program uses two COM components, MSMQQueue and MSMQEvent, to treat a message arriving on a queue as an event. Event notifications are enabled for a queue by using MSMQQueue, the component that represents a queue. The MSMQQueue component has a method, EnableNotification, which enables an event trigger. Once enabled, the trigger fires if a message has arrived on the queue or if a message did not arrive during a period specified by the application. In either case an MSMQEvent component method gets called. If a message has arrived, the Arrived method of the MSMQEvent component is called. Otherwise the ArrivedError method is called because the timer went off.

This example uses the following module-level declarations:

```
' Module-wide constants
Const MsgGUID = "{EFB01B40-49B3-11d1-902B-00400521EF0C}"
Const MsgQPath = "pswtech\CorrelationMsgQ"
Const MsgQLabel = "Msg Queue created by Asynchronous Receiver"
Dim msgQ As MSMQQueueInfo
Dim openMsgQ As MSMQQueue
Dim openResponseQ As MSMQQueue
Dim WithEvents ReceiveEvent As MSMQEvent
```

The GUIDs representing the queue type and the queue pathname are identical to those used by our correlation requester in the previous section. Indeed the two programs work well together.

An MSMQQueueInfo component, msgQ, is used to locate or to create the message queue. If the queue is created, we use MsgQLabel to assign a user-friendly label for it. Once the request queue has been opened, we represent it by openMsgQ throughout the program. We will enable event notification for the request queue represented by openMsgQ.

ReceiveEvent is an event handler component. The WithEvents keyword indicates to Visual Basic that ReceiveEvent will handle MSMQEvent events. All WithEvents variables must be declared as module-level variables. Later in this program we will relate the ReceiveEvent event handler to the request queue events by calling openMsgQ.EnableNotification().

A program that receives messages and sends a correlated response is available at http://www.psw.com/msmq/. The program uses the setup and asynchronous message receiving routines outlined next. Figure 7-3 shows a sample run of the program.

7.3.1   Setting Up to Receive Messages Asynchronously

When the user clicks on the SetUp For Requests button, Visual Basic starts a procedure called SetUpButton_Click(). This procedure begins by locating a request queue through the MQIS or creating one on the local machine. Next, the queue is opened with MQ_RECEIVE_ACCESS privileges. Once the request queue is open, we need to enable event notification.

```
Private Sub SetUpButton_Click()
    Dim Where As String

    On Error GoTo ErrorHandler
    ' Locate or create queue as demonstrated in Chapter 4
```

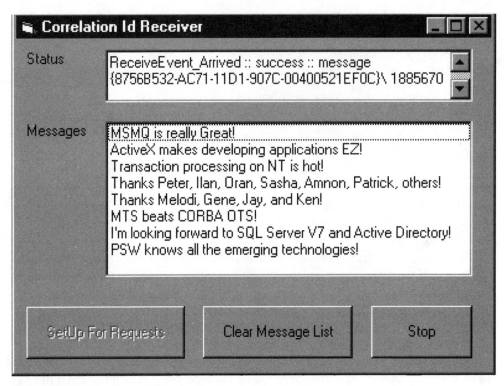

Figure 7-3 Asynchronously receiving messages with the correlation receiver program

```
      ' Open queue for receiving messages -
      ' openRequestQ represents the open queue

      ' Create ReceiveEvent for handling notifications
      Where = "Creating MSMQEvent"
      Set ReceiveEvent = New MSMQEvent

      ' Enable msg message notification
      Where = "Enabling msg message notification"
      openMsgQ.EnableNotification Event:=ReceiveEvent, _
          ReceiveTimeout:=1000
  Exit Sub

  ErrorHandler:
      StatusText.Text = "SetUpButton_Click :: " + Where _
          + " :: Error: " + Str$(Err.Number) + " :: " + "Reason: " _
          + Err.Description
  End Sub
```

① We create an `MSMQEvent` component and assign it to `ReceiveEvent`.

② In this code fragment event notification is started. `ReceiveEvent` is defined as the event handler. An event is triggered when a message exists in the queue represented by `openMsgQ` or after 1 second.

The `EnableNotification` method of an `MSMQQueue` component takes three parameters. The first parameter, a reference to an `MSMQEvent` component, is required. The second parameter, optional, controls the movement of the queue cursor. Three values are permitted.

- `MQMSG_FIRST`—By default MSMQ triggers an event notification when a message is in the queue.
- `MQMSG_CURRENT`—MSMQ triggers an event when a message is in the queue and at the current cursor position.
- `MQMSG_NEXT`—MSMQ increments the queue cursor and triggers an event when a message is in the queue and at the new cursor position.

A variety of scenarios for asynchronous message processing can be supported by using these cursor controls. In our example we are happy to process the first message in the queue. Consequently we implicitly specify `MQMSG_FIRST` by accepting the default.

The third parameter of `EnableNotification` is optional and allows us to specify a time to wait for a message to arrive. A wait period is expressed in milliseconds. The `Arrived` method will be called for `ReceiveEvent` if a message arrives before the timer goes off. Otherwise the `ArrivedError` method is called. The default behavior of `EnableNotification` is to wait an infinite length of time.

It's worth noting that registering for an event notification must be repeated after each event is triggered. When a message arrived or the wait timer goes off, it will be necessary to register `ReceiveEvent` again before this program can receive another event notification. You will see that `EnableNotification` is called again at the end of the `MSMQEvent_Arrived` and the `MSMQEvent_ArrivedError` functions to reregister for message arrival events.

We've seen how to register `ReceiveEvent` as an event handler. Now let's demonstrate how to asynchronously receive a message.

7.3.2 Receiving Messages Asynchronously

After `SetUpButton_Click()` executes, an `Arrived` event is triggered if a message sits in the queue represented by `openMsgQ` or arrives there in the next second. In this section we'll talk about how to process an `Arrived` event.

We want to read the message from the queue, copy its body to a list box, and respond to the message. `ReceiveEvent_Arrived` does this.

```
Private Sub ReceiveEvent_Arrived(ByVal msgQueue As Object, _
               ByVal Cursor As Long)
    Dim inMsg As MSMQMessage
    Dim ResMsg As New MSMQMessage
    Dim Where As String

    On Error GoTo ReceiveEvent_ErrorHandler
    Set inMsg = msgQueue.Receive(ReceiveTimeout:=0)
    If Not inMsg Is Nothing Then
        MsgList.AddItem inMsg.Body
        MsgId = GetMSMQMsgId(inMsg)
    StatusText.Text = _
            "ReceiveEvent_Arrived :: success :: message " + MsgId _
            + " received!"
    Else
        StatusText.Text = "ReceiveEvent_Arrived :: " + Where _
            + " :: " + "No message was available to receive."
        Exit Sub
    End If

    Where = "Preparing response"
    ResMsg.Body = "Response Message to:: " + inMsg.Body
    ResMsg.Label = "Response Label to:: " + inMsg.Label
    ResMsg.CorrelationId = inMsg.Id

    ' Open response queue
    Where = "Opening response queue"
    If inMsg.ResponseQueueInfo Is Nothing Then
        StatusText.Text = "Opening response queue — " _
            + "Response queue information not set"
        Exit Sub
    Else
        Set openResponseQ = _
            inMsg.ResponseQueueInfo.Open(Access:=MQ_SEND_ACCESS, _
                ShareMode:=MQ_DENY_NONE)
    End If

    ' Send response
    Where = "Sending message"
```

```
        ResMsg.Send openResponseQ
        ' Close response queue
        Where = "Closing response queue"
        openResponseQ.Close
(6)     msgQueue.EnableNotification Event:=ReceiveEvent, _
            ReceiveTimeout:=1000
        Exit Sub

    ReceiveEvent_ErrorHandler:
        StatusText.Text = "ReceiveEvent_Arrived :: " + Where _
            + " :: Error: " + Str$(Err.Number) + " :: " + "Reason: " _
            + Err.Description
(6)     msgQueue.EnableNotification Event:=ReceiveEvent, _
            ReceiveTimeout:=1000
    End Sub
```

(1) Two values are passed when an `MSMQEvent_Arrived` function is called: the queue component whose event is being handled and a cursor into the queue. In this function those variables are passed to `msgQueue` and `cursor`. The queue component is used to access messages in the queue. The cursor value indicates whether `EnableNotification` was called with `MQMSG_FIRST`, `MQMSG_CURRENT`, or `MQMSG_NEXT`.

(2) The following variables are declared. A received message will be referenced by `inMsg`. `ResMsg` is a message that will be generated in response. The queue to which the message is sent is represented by `openResponseQ`.

(3) The `Arrived` event indicates that a message arrived. Hence it is received with no wait-time.

(4) It is possible that no messages will be in the queue by the time this procedure executes. If several programs race to process a lone message just arriving on a previously empty queue, there can be only one winner. Therefore we checked for whether a valid message was received. If a valid message was received, the body is placed in the list box and its message identifier is converted to text and used as part of status text.

(5) A response message is prepared, the response queue is opened, the message is sent, and the response queue is closed.

(6) If this component is to continue receiving notifications, it must reregister to receive events. We use the `MSMQQueue` instance passed to us to reregister for notifications that follow and in the error-handling routine at the end of the procedure.

7.3.3 Processing Wait Timer Timeouts

After `SetUpButton_Click()` executes, an `ArrivedError` event is triggered if no message has arrived on the queue during the specified wait period. In some programs it might be very unusual for a message not to arrive during a wait period. In such a situation you might create a warning message to administrators, asking them to check the health of the underlying network or the status of other messaging applications.

In this program we simply write a status string in the status text box and reregister for message notifications. `ReceiveEvent_ArrivedError` does this.

```
Private Sub ReceiveEvent_ArrivedError( _
     ByVal msgQueue As Object, _
     ByVal ErrorCode As Long, ByVal Cursor As Long)

   StatusText.Text = _
     "ReceiveEvent_ArrivedError :: Error (N || C): " _
     + Str$(ErrorCode)
   msgQueue.EnableNotification Event:=ReceiveEvent, _
     ReceiveTimeout:=1000
End Sub
```

Three values are passed when an `MSMQEvent_ArrivedError` function is called: the queue component whose event is being handled, an error code indicating why no message arrived during the time period, and a cursor into the queue. The error code can be used to perform fine-grained error handling. For example, the error code might indicate that a queue manager is down or that program resources have been exhausted. A different processing strategy might be implemented for each kind of error.

7.3.4 Using the MSMQ API

In the MSMQ API you have three ways to asynchronously be notified that a message is available on a queue for processing.

- A *callback function* can be specified. The callback function is registered by using `MQReceiveMessage()`, the MSMQ API call for receiving messages. Then MSMQ calls the callback function if a message is available or if a timeout occurs.

   Here's a simple example to register `asyncReceive()` as a callback function.

```
// Receive a message
hResult = MQReceiveMessage(
    mQHandle,               // Message queue handle
    INFINITE,               // Wait a long time for a msg
    MQ_ACTION_RECEIVE,      // Receive the msg, not a peek
    &mProps,                // Message properties
    NULL,                   // Overlapped structure
    asyncReceive,           // Asynchronous callback
    NULL,                   // Not using a cursor
    MQ_NO_TRANSACTION);     // Nontransactional
```

The function signature for the callback function looks similar to
MQReceiveMessage(). Here's a simple implementation of the callback function.

```
void APIENTRY asyncReceive(HRESULT hResult, QUEUEHANDLE
            mQHandle, DWORD timeOut, DWORD action,
            MQMSGPROPS* mProps, LPOVERLAPPED lpO,
            HANDLE mCursor) {

    printf("asyncReceive: hResult = (0x%X)\n", hResult);
    if (FAILED(hResult)) {
            PRINTERROR(
            "asyncReceive :: Cannot receive response message!",
            hResult, RESUME);
    } else {
        printf(
            "asyncReceive :: Received message body :: %s\n",
            mProps->aPropVar[0].caub.pElems);
        printf(
            "asyncReceive :: Received message label :: %S\n",
            mProps->aPropVar[1].pwszVal);
    }
}
```

- MSMQ can signal the application by using the Windows event mechanism. In this case the hEvent member of an OVERLAPPED structure must contain a handle to a Windows event object.

- Processes within a Windows NT system can be notified through a completion port that a message has arrived.

7.4 Handling Variable-Length Messages

In many applications the size of messages can vary significantly. MSMQ supports messages of up to 4MB. You could define a single buffer that is large enough to hold your largest expected message. However, if most messages require 1K but one message requires 1MB, this strategy can be very wasteful. The alternative is to dynamically allocate a buffer just large enough to handle your message.

When COM components are used, dynamic buffer allocation is provided as part of the MSMQMessage component. If you need to copy a variable-length message to another data type, you can use the MSMQMessage.BodyLength property to ascertain how large the message is.

When using variable-length buffers with the MSMQ API, your program needs to handle dynamic buffer allocation. On the sender side things are pretty easy. Since you know what kind of message to send, you know how much buffer space to allocate for the message.

But how does the receiver know how much buffer space to allocate in order to receive a message sitting in a queue? The receiveMessage() procedure demonstrates how to do this. Since this procedure is similar to the receiveMessages() procedure described in Chapter 5, we'll focus primarily on the code to handle variable-length messages.

In this procedure we will first peek at a message in a queue to determine the length of the message body. That information is passed in the PROPID_M_BODY_SIZE property. We allocate a buffer big enough for the message body and then receive the message body, along with some other message properties.

We will adapt the Hello World program from Chapter 5 to demonstrate handling variable-length messages. In that program we created and sent a response message for each message received. As part of the code to build a response message, we will allocate a buffer big enough for the body of a response message. After the response is sent, we free the buffers used for receiving a message and sending a response.

Several declarations follow. Three merit some comment. Two pointers, pMBuffer and pRMBuffer, will point to two dynamically allocated message buffers. The value of the PROPID_M_BODY_SIZE property will be copied into bodySize, an unsigned integer.

```
#define BUFFER_LENGTH 100
#define PROPERTIES 10

void receiveMessages(QUEUEHANDLE mQHandle) {
    MQMSGPROPS mProps;                   // Structure of message property
                                         // IDs and values
    MQPROPVARIANT propVar[PROPERTIES]; // Array of message property values
```

```
        QUEUEPROPID propId[PROPERTIES];     // Array of message property
                                            // identifiers
        DWORD nProps = 0;                   // Property counter
        char mBuffer[BUFFER_LENGTH];        // Message buffer
        char *rMBuffer [BUFFER_LENGTH];     // Response message buffer
        WCHAR msgLabel[BUFFER_LENGTH];      // Message label
        WCHAR rMsgLabel[BUFFER_LENGTH];     // Response message label
        HRESULT hResult;                    // Standard Windows result
                                            // indicator
        WCHAR rFormatName[BUFFER_LENGTH];   // Response queue format name
        QUEUEHANDLE rQHandle;               // Response queue handle
        ULONG bodySize;                     // Message body Size

    Printf ("receiveMessages >>\n");
    while (1) {
        bodySize = 0; // Get the message body length
        nProps = 0;
        propId[nProps] = PROPID_M_BODY_SIZE;
        propVar[nProps].vt = VT_UI4;
        propVAR[nProps].ulVal = bodySize
        nProps++;

        mProps.cProp = nProps; // Create MSGPROPS structure
        mProps.aPropID = propId;
        mProps.aPropVar = propVar;
        mProps.aStatus = 0;

        //Receive a message
        hResult = MQReceiveMessage(
            mQHandle,               // Message queue handle
            INFINITE,               // Wait a long time
            MQ_ACTION_PEEK_CURRENT, // No peeking
            &mProps,                // Message properties
            NULL, NULL, NULL,       // Synchronous receives
            MQ_NO_TRANSACTION);     // Non-transactional

        if (FAILED(hResult)) {
            PRINTERROR(
                "receiveMessages :: Cannot receive response message!",
                hResult, RESUME);
        } else { // receive
```

(2)

```
printf("receiveMessages :: Peeked message :: %u\n",
    bodySize);

// Allocate a message buffer
pMBuffer = (char*) malloc(bodySize + 1);

// Prepare properties of message to receive
// Get the message body property
nProps = 0;
propId[nProps] = PROPID_M_BODY; // Get message body
propVar[nProps].vt = VT_UI1 | VT_VECTOR;
propVar[nProps].caub.cElems = sizeof(mBuffer);
propVar[nProps].caub.pElems = (unsigned char *) mBuffer;
nProps++;

propId[nProps] = PROPID_M_LABEL; // Get message label
propVar[nProps].vt = VT_LPWSTR;
propVar[nProps].pwszVal = msgLabel;
nProps++;

propId[nProps] = PROPID_M_LABEL_LEN; // Get label length
propVar[nProps].vt = VT_UI4;
propVar[nProps].ulVal = BUFFER_LENGTH;
nProps++;

propId[nProps] = PROPID_M_RESP_QUEUE; // Get resp queue
propVar[nProps].vt = VT_LPWSTR;
propVar[nProps].pwszVal = rFormatName;
nProps++;

propId[nProps] = PROPID_M_RESP_QUEUE_LEN; // Get length
propVar[nProps].vt = VT_UI4;
propVar[nProps].ulVal = BUFFER_LENGTH;
nProps++;

mProps.cProp = nProps; // Create MSGPROPS structure
mProps.aPropID = propId;
mProps.aPropVar = propVar;
mProps.aStatus = 0;
```

4
```
hResult = MQReceiveMessage( // Receive a message
    mQHandle,                  // Message queue handle
    INFINITE,                  // Wait a long time
    MQ_ACTION_RECEIVE,         // No peeking
    &mProps,                   // Message properties
    NULL, NULL, NULL,          // Synchronous receives
    MQ_NO_TRANSACTION);        // Non-transactional

if (FAILED(hResult)) {
    PRINTERROR(
        "receiveMessages :: Cannot receive message!",
        hResult, RESUME);
} else { //send
    printf(
        "receiveMessages :: message body :: %s\n", pMBuffer);
    printf(
        "receiveMessages :: message label :: %S\n", msgLabel);
    printf("receiveMessages :: Response queue :: %S\n",
        rFormatName);
```

5
```
hResult = MQOpenQueue( // Open response queue
    rFormatName,            // Queue format name
    MQ_SEND_ACCESS,         // Will receive responses on this
                            // queue
    0,                      // Queue can be shared
    &rQHandle);             // Queue handle
PRINTERROR("sender :: Cannot open response queue!",
    hResult, ABORT);
```

6
```
pRMBuffer = (char) malloc(bodySize + 50);
// Assign a message body
sprintf(rMBuffer, "Response to message :: %s",mBuffer);
// Assign a message label
swprintf(rMsgLabel, L"%s response label", msgLabel);

nProps = 0;
propId[nProps] = PROPID_M_BODY; // Set message body
propVar[nProps].vt = VT_UI1 | VT_VECTOR;
propVar[nProps].caub.cElems = sizeof(rMBuffer);
propVar[nProps].caub.pElems = (unsigned char *)rMBuffer;
nProps++;
```

```
        propId[nProps] = PROPID_M_LABEL; // Set message label
        propVar[nProps].vt = VT_LPWSTR;
        propVar[nProps].pwszVal = rMsgLabel;
        nProps++;

        mProps.cProp = nProps; // Create a MSGPROPS structure
        mProps.aPropID = propId;
        mProps.aPropVar = propVar;
        mProps.aStatus = NULL;
```

(7)
```
        hResult = MQSendMessage( // Send message
            rQHandle,          // Response queue handle
            &mProps,           // Response message properties
            NULL);             // Sending is not transactional
        PRINTERROR("receiveMessages :: Cannot send message!",
                hResult, RESUME);
```

(8)
```
        // clean up
        if ( bodySize == strlen("quit") )
            strcpy(mBuffer, pMBuffer);
        else
            strcpy(mBuffer, " ");
        MQCloseQueue(rQHandle);
```
(9)
```
        free(pMBuffer);
        free(pRMBuffer);
    }
        // Should sending and receiving terminate?
```
(8)
```
        if (strcmp(mBuffer, "quit") == 0)
            break;
        }
    } /* while (1) */
    printf("receiveMessages <<\n");
}
```

① We begin each loop by performing a nondestructive read, or peek, of a message to obtain its PROPID_M_BODY_SIZE property value. If no message is in the queue, we wait for one to arrive. The following code shows how the MQMSGPROPS structure is constructed and how the nondestructive read is performed.

② The PROPID_M_BODY_SIZE property value is copied to bodySize and printed out.

(3) A buffer is allocated to accommodate the message body, and an MQMSGPROPS structure is constructed to obtain the message body, the message label, and the response queue format name.

(4) We perform a destructive read of the message and print out three message properties.

(5) The response queue is opened.

(6) A second buffer for the response message is allocated. Then we construct an MQMSGPROPS structure for the response message.

(7) The response is sent.

(8) This is needed but uninteresting. Recall that in the Hello World message protocol, a receiving application exits this procedure and the program if a message body of "quit" is received. This procedure compares the contents of mBuffer with a "quit" literal to decide whether to exit the loop and program. Here we set up mBuffer.

(9) To clean up at the end of each loop, the request and response message buffers are freed, and the response queue is closed.

7.5 Multipart Message Sequences

A multipart message sequence is a stream of data that is passed in several MSMQ messages. There are always reasons why you may want to send a multipart message sequence:

- Your message size may exceed 4MB, the maximum message size supported by MSMQ.
- It may be efficient to pipeline the processing of data. You may want to divide a large amount of data into 5, 10, or 100 smaller blocks of data and to ship each block separately.

Whatever the reason, you may need to implement a multipart message sequence. Generally two requirements relate to any multipart messaging problem.

- The sender and the receiver must agree to a protocol for handling multipart messages. That is, the sender and the receiver must agree on how message properties are used when implementing a multipart message.[2]
- Messages that are part of multipart message sequence A must be distinguishable from messages that are part of multipart message sequence B.

The message identifier assigned to the first message in the sequence is guaranteed to be unique. Thus it can be used to correlate follow-on messages. Using the message identifier of the first message as the correlation identifier of other messages in the sequence satisfies the second requirement.

There are many ways to use MSMQ message properties to implement a multipart message. Agreement on property utilization is all that is really needed to satisfy the first requirement. Let's take a look at one approach.

In the following code we construct a multipart message sequence composed of four MSMQ messages. The message identifier assigned to the first message is copied into the correlation identifier of the other messages. In addition, a number is assigned to the application-specific message property of each message. We will also write a user-friendly label just in case a human user should need to manually investigate any problems.

```
' Module-wide constants
Const QGUID = "{4A0221A0-7F2C-11d1-9053-00400521EF0C}"
Const QPath = "pswtech\MultiPartMessageQ"
Const QLabel = "Multi-Part MessageQueue"
Const MLabel = "Multi-part Message :: "
Dim mpmQ As MSMQQueueInfo

Private Sub MPMButton_Click()
    Dim Msg1 As New MSMQMessage
    Dim Msg2 As New MSMQMessage
    Dim Msg3 As New MSMQMessage
    Dim Msg4 As New MSMQMessage
    Dim openMpmQ As MSMQQueue
    Dim I As Integer

    On Error GoTo ErrorHandler
    ' Locate or create a queue as described in Chapter 4
```

---

2. Senders and receivers also may need to agree on how the message content is processed. For example, are there semiautonomous parts that can be processed by themselves, or does the receiver need to reconstruct two or more message bodies into a single, contiguous whole? This problem is application-dependent and won't be discussed here.

```
' Open queue
If openMpmQ Is Nothing Then
    Set openMpmQ = mpmQ.Open(Access:=MQ_SEND_ACCESS, _
        ShareMode:=MQ_DENY_NONE)
End If
StatusText.Text = "Receive_Click :: Error: " _
    + Str$(Err.Number) + " :: " + "Reason: " + Err.Description
```

```
I = 1 ' Send message 1
Msg1.Body = "Some data - part " + Str(I)
Msg1.Label = MLabel + "Message " + Str(I)
Msg1.AppSpecific = 4 - I
Msg1.Send openMpmQ
StatusText.Text = "Send_Click :: success :: message " _
    + Str(I) + " sent!"
```

```
I = 2' Send message 2
Msg2.Body = "Some data - part " + Str(I)
Msg2.Label = MLabel + "Message " + Str(I)
Msg2.AppSpecific = 4 - I
Msg2.CorrelationId = Msg1.Id
Msg2.Send openMpmQ
StatusText.Text = "Send_Click :: success :: message " _
    + Str(I) + " sent!"
```

```
I = 3 ' Send message 3
Msg3.Body = "Some data - part " + Str(I)
Msg3.Label = MLabel + "Message " + Str(I)
Msg3.AppSpecific = 4 - I
Msg3.CorrelationId = Msg1.Id
Msg3.Send openMpmQ
StatusText.Text = "Send_Click :: success :: message " _
    + Str(I) + " sent!"
```

```
I = 4 ' Send message 4
Msg4.Body = "Some data - part " + Str(I) + " (final part) "
Msg4.Label = MLabel + "Message " + Str(I)
Msg4.AppSpecific = 4 - I
Msg4.CorrelationId = Msg1.Id
Msg4.Send openMpmQ
StatusText.Text = "Send_Click :: success :: message " _
    + Str(I) + " sent!"
openMpmQ.Close
Exit Sub
```

```
ErrorHandler:
    StatusText.Text = "Send_Click :: Error: " _
        + Str$(Err.Number) + " :: " + "Reason: " + Err.Description
    If Not openMpmQ Is Nothing Then
        openMpmQ.Close
    End If
End Sub
```

1 The application that receives this message will know that it is the first message in a sequence, because its correlation identifier property is empty and the application-specific property is not 0. The value of the application-specific property indicates how many additional messages are in the multipart message. Since four messages are in the sequence, the application-specific property is equal to 3.

2 As messages in the sequence arrive, the receiving application will use the correlation identifier of the first message to correlate other messages to it. The application-specific property is used to maintain message ordering. The application-specific message property is decremented every time a message is sent. The message with an application-specific property equal to 2 comes before the message with an application-specific property value of 1 in the sequence.

3 The application-specific property has a value of 0. This is the last message of the sequence.

Design Notes: There is a way to guarantee that message 1 arrives on the message queue ahead of message 2, that message 2 arrives ahead of message 3, and so on. If you send the four messages within a single transaction, MSMQ will guarantee that the messages arrive in order.

Note, however, that MSMQ doesn't guarantee that these messages are placed in the queue one immediately after another. An MSMQ queue manager accepts messages as they arrive. In a highly distributed world other messages can arrive at the destination queue between when message X and message X + 1 arrive. Given what we've learned in this chapter about peeking at messages and selecting correlated messages, it should be very easy for you to write a message-receiving application that selects pieces of a multipart message from a queue.

7.6 Object Shipping

One of the strengths of the MSMQMessage COM component is that it recognizes various types of objects that are placed into a message body. This facility includes relatively simple objects, such as character strings, and more complex objects are also supported. For example, you can place an Excel spreadsheet into a message body. MSMQ maintains the type information. In fact, MSMQ can ship several kinds of objects. You can even use MSMQ to send your own objects between applications.

Is Shipping Objects between Applications a Good Idea?

One segment of the industry frowns on designs in which an object's state is shipped between two applications. For example, the Common Object Request Broker Architecture (CORBA) defined by the Object Management Group provides no support for transferring an object between a client and a server. Rather clients create and interact with objects executing on a server. The ORB facilitates object creation and method invocation.

Why is shipping object state frowned on? There are philosophical, technical, and practical reasons for avoiding it.

- In any application it is desirable to be able to access an object in a location-transparent fashion. This rule can be broken when object state is shipped from one location to another.

- Problems can arise in a highly parallel and distributed system if object state is shipped without proper concurrency mechanisms. Suppose that two applications receive copies of the same object from a database application, change its state, and then ship the object back to the database application. How are the state changes merged back into the original object?

- Many objects evolve over time. To support a change in the definition of an object, you may need to upgrade all applications that use the object in lockstep, or the applications must be written to somehow support a changing object model. Either option can be costly.

Usually people ship object state across a network to optimize performance. It is more efficient to perform a large number of updates to an object locally, even when a large object is shipped across the network. The benefits erode when a small number of updates need to be made, even if the object is small.

Think carefully about the trade-offs before shipping objects in your applications. It may be advisable in some situations, but the decision should not be taken lightly.

In the examples that follow, you're shipping the object's state, not the binary object. The state of the object is copied into the body of a message and is sent across the network. When the message is received, the state is copied into a new object in the receiving application.

7.6.1 Sending and Receiving a Standard Microsoft Word Document

The following procedure, Send_Click(), demonstrates how an object is shipped to a receiving application. A Microsoft Word document will be inserted into the body of the message and a special label attached to it.

```
Private Sub Send_Click()
    Dim objQ As MSMQQueueInfo
    Dim openObjQ As MSMQQueue
    Dim Msg As New MSMQMessage
    Dim DocIn As Word.Document
    Const MLabel = "Shipped Object"

    On Error GoTo ErrorHandler
    ' Locate a queue for passing the object - A Word document
    ' Open queue as openObjQ, Access:=MQ_SEND_ACCESS

    Set DocIn = GetObject("c:\pswtech\obj\Infile.doc")
    Msg.Body = DocIn
    Msg.Label = MLabel
    Msg.Send openObjQ
    StatusText.Text = "Send_Click :: success :: message sent!"
    openObjQ.Close
    Exit Sub

ErrorHandler:
    StatusText.Text = "Send_Click :: Error: " _
        + Str$(Err.Number) + " :: " + "Reason: " + Err.Description
    openObjQ.Close
End Sub
```

① We prepare a message to be sent. A Microsoft Word document is loaded into DocIn, a Word.Document component. The document is inserted into the message body by using a simple assignment operator. (Programming can't be made simpler than this!)

② A message label is assigned, and the message is sent. To release resources, we close the queue before exiting.

You do not use SET to assign an object to the message body. If you use SET, you will receive an "Object Required" error. This is by design. A SET operation is used to assign a reference to an object. In this case we want to copy the object into the message body, not copy a reference into the message body.

Receive_Click() demonstrates how to use an object contained in a message. The Microsoft Word document will be removed from the body of the message and printed. The need for and use of MSMQ components should be obvious by now.

```
Private Sub Receive_Click()
    Dim objQ As MSMQQueueInfo
    Dim openObjQ As MSMQQueue
    Dim Msg As MSMQMessage
    Dim Obj As Object
    Dim DocOut As Word.Document

    On Error GoTo ErrorHandler
    ' Locate/create a queue for passing the Word document
    ' Opening queue as openObjQ, Access:=MQ_RECEIVE_ACCESS

    ' Receiving message
    Set Msg = openObjQ.Receive(ReceiveTimeout:=500)
    If Not Msg Is Nothing Then
        StatusText.Text = _
            "Receive_Click :: success :: message label :: " _
            + Msg.Label
        Set Obj = Msg.Body
        If TypeOf Obj Is Word.Document Then
            Set DocOut = Obj
            DocOut.PrintOut
        End If
    End If
    openObjQ.Close
    Exit Sub

ErrorHandler:
    StatusText.Text = "Receive_Click :: Error: " _
        + Str$(Err.Number) + " :: " + "Reason: " + Err.Description
    If Not openObjQ Is Nothing Then
        openObjQ.Close
    End If
End Sub
```

③ The message is received and its label placed in a status box.

④ The body is set into an object, and the object type is evaluated. If the object contains a Word document, it is printed out. The queue is closed before exiting, to release resources.

You don't need to explicitly test that the body contains a Word document. A run-time error is returned if COM fails to find the expected interfaces exported by a Word document.

7.6.2 Sending Data Records

ActiveX Data Objects `Recordsets`, a great way of representing data sent between applications, can be used to represent data returned from a query to a user or to replicate data. Technologies exist that make it relatively easy to send relational database records between two databases. For example, SQL Server provides data replication facilities for this purpose. However, many of these technologies are not especially well suited to replicating nonrelational data. Microsoft ActiveX Data Objects enable programmers to work with relational and nonrelational data, using a common set of components.

In the following example we derive several records of data from the *jobs* table that is part of the sample databases that come with SQL Server.

```
Private Sub SendButton_Click(Index As Integer)
    Dim RecSet As ADOR.Recordset
    Dim SQLStmt As String
    Dim DFact As Object
    Dim openAdoQ As MSMQQueue
    Dim adoMsg As New MSMQMessage

    On Error GoTo ErrorHandler
    ' Locate a queue for passing the object - An ADO Recordset
    ' Open queue as openAdoQ, Access:=MQ_SEND_ACCESS

    Where = "Making a query"
    Set DFact = CreateObject("AdvancedDataFactory")
    SQLStmt = "Select * from jobs"
    Set RecSet = DFact.query( _
        "driver={SQLServer};SERVER=.;database=pubs;uid=sa;pwd=",_
        SQLStmt)

    Where = "Preparing message"
    adoMsg.Body = RecSet
    adoMsg.Label = "Message containing an ADO RecordSet."
    Where = "Sending request message"
```

```
adoMsg.Send openAdoQ
StatusText.Text = StatusText.Text _
    + "SendMessage_Click :: success :: message sent!"
Exit Sub

ErrorHandler:
    StatusText.Text = "SendMessage_Click :: " + Where _
        + " :: Error: " + Str$(Err.Number) + " :: " + "Reason: " _
        + Err.Description
End Sub
```

① We use the COM `CreateObject()` function to create an `Advanced Data Factory` object. Then we formulate a SQL query. The results of the query are set into a `Recordset` object.

② The `Recordset` is placed into the body of the message and sent. Note that the Visual Basic `SET` command is not used.

Now let's receive the message and print out the contents of the `Recordset` in a text box.

```
Private Sub ReceiveButton_Click(Index As Integer)
    Dim adoRs As Object
    Dim RcrdSet As New ADOR.Recordset
    Dim openAdoQ As MSMQQueue
    Dim Msg As New MSMQMessage

    On Error GoTo ErrorHandler
    ' Locate a queue for passing the object - An ADO Recordset
    ' Open queue as openAdoQ, Access:= MQ_RECEIVE_ACCESS

    Where = "Receiving message"
    Set Msg = openAdoQ.Receive(ReceiveTimeout:=500)
    If Not Msg Is Nothing Then
        StatusText.Text = _
            "ReceiveButton_Click :: success :: message received!" _
            + vbCrLf
        StatusText.Text = StatusText.Text + "Message Label ::" _
            + Msg.Label + vbCrLf
        Set RcrdSet = Msg.Body
        RcrdSet.MoveFirst
        Do While Not RcrdSet.EOF
            StatusText = StatusText.Text + Str(RcrdSet(0)) + " | " _
```

③

```
                    + RcrdSet(1) + " | " + Str(RcrdSet(2)) + " | " _
                    + Str(RcrdSet(3)) + vbCrLf
            RcrdSet.MoveNext
        Loop
    Else
        StatusText.Text = "ReceiveButton_Click :: " + Where _
            + " :: No message was available to receive"
    End If
    Exit Sub

ErrorHandler:
    StatusText.Text = "ReceiveButton_Click :: " + Where _
        + " :: Error: " + Str$(Err.Number) + " :: " + "Reason: " _
        + Err.Description
End Sub
```

3 This block of code shows how to receive the message and then process the
Recordset, one record at a time. Each record is composed of a Fields collection.
Each Field collection contains zero or more Field objects. The *i*th Field in the
Fields collection from the *j*th record of data is found in the *i*th column of the *j*th row
returned by our query. You can write code to examine the Count property of the
Fields object and then iterate through each Field in the collection. I decided not
to do that, so that the code would look nice and simple.

7.6.3 Sending Your Own COM Objects

So far we have shown how to ship standard Microsoft objects. With a small amount of
code, you can ship your own objects, using MSMQ. To do this you must implement
the IPersistStream interface. Any object that implements this interface can send
its state.

IPersistStream is a standard COM interface definition that is used to copy
object state from an object into a buffer (or file) and from a buffer into an object.
Using this interface can make an object persistent; that is, the state survives failures
and can be released by a program when not in use.

How IPersistStream methods are implemented depends on the definition
of the object. In fact, you can store object state in a fixed-length record or use a tag/
value/delimiter syntax.

In Visual Basic the IPersistStream.Save method is called when your
object is assigned to a message body. When an object is copied from the message body
into an object, the IPersistStream.Load method is invoked.

It's almost as easy in Visual C++. You would instantiate your objects as usual. When you are ready to ship your object, you assign the IUnknown interface pointer to the MSMQMessage.Body property. MSMQ will locate the IPersistStream interface using the IUnknown interface and save the object's state into the MSMQMessage body. This is demonstrated as follows:

```
IMSMQMessagePtr Msg(__uuidof( MSMQMessage ));
ImyObjectPtr mine(__uuidof( myObject ));

Msg->Body = static_cast<IUnknown *> mine;
Msg->Send(someQueue);
```

We copied the state of a *myObject* object into the body of a message. MSMQ saves the class identifier (CLSID) of the object when it calls IPersistStream.Save. This makes it possible to determine what kind of object is in the body of a message.

A message body is in reality a variant. The variant contains a pointer to the IUnknown interface of the object. Consequently it is possible to test the object by asking for the *myObject* interface. The following code does this:

```
Msg = someQueue->Receive();
ImyObjectPtr mine((IUnknown *) Msg->Body );
if ( mine != NULL ) {
    // process the myObject
}
```

7.7   Working While Off Line

Applications can execute on independent clients to perform certain MSMQ operations while disconnected from the MSMQ environment, as long as no operation needs to use the MQIS. The application cannot locate queues, get or set queue properties or security descriptors, or attempt to create or delete public queues. While disconnected from the MSMQ environment, an application can create and delete private queues on the local machine and can send or receive messages.

In order to open a queue while an application is off line, you need the queue's format name. You can derive the format name while the application is connected to the MSMQ environment. As an alternative the format name can be stored in the executable, placed in a file, or read from an environment variable. A direct or a public format name is needed.

The following code demonstrates how to send a message while the independent client is disconnected from the MSMQ environment:

```
Private Sub Send_Click()
    Dim remQ As New MSMQQueueInfo
    Dim openRemQ As MSMQQueue
    Dim Msg As New MSMQMessage

    remQ.FormatName = _
        "PUBLIC=A00FEB2C-B95A-11D1-AB06-AE8CE9000000"
    Set openRemQ = remQ.Open(Access:=MQ_SEND_ACCESS, _
        ShareMode:=MQ_DENY_NONE)
    Msg.Body = "Message body sent while offline"
    Msg.Label = "Message label sent while offline"
    Msg.Send openRemQ
    openRemQ.Close
End Sub
```

In order for an application to receive messages from a queue while off line, the queue must reside on the independent client.

7.8   Conclusion

In this chapter we looked at the solution to seven requirements of MSMQ messaging applications. Certainly there are plenty of other messaging problems that you will encounter in your work with MSMQ. We probably addressed a couple of your most important issues in this chapter. One problem was left out: how to improve the reliability of communications between applications. We'll look at that problem in Chapter 8.

7.9   Resources and References

Gilman, L., and R. Schreiber. 1997. *Distributed Computing with IBM MQSeries.* New York: Wiley.

Lowe, A. 1997. *Porting Unix Applications to Windows NT.* Indianapolis, IN: Macmillan Technical Publishing.

Microsoft Message Queue Explorer Administrator's Online Help.

Microsoft Message Queue Server Online Help.

Richter, J. 1997. *Advanced Windows,* 3rd ed. Redmond, WA: Microsoft Press.

8 Chapter

Improving Message

Tracking and Recovery

This chapter, intended primarily for developers, discusses how to use MSMQ facilities to improve the tracking and recovery of messaging communications. The programming examples in the chapter build on the Visual Basic example developed in Chapter 4 and the MSMQ API example of Chapter 5. Managers may want to read the introductory paragraphs of each major section to gain a fuller awareness of MSMQ message tracking, acknowledgment, and journal features.

8.1 Overview of MSMQ Facilities

Many distributed computing technologies provide just one level of service: Requests are sent by using a nonrecoverable and unaudited communications protocol. Such protocols are nonrecoverable in that a request (or its response) is lost if the client, server, or network fails. They are also unaudited in that the technology doesn't record when operations succeed or fail. Unlike those technologies, MSMQ provides support for message recovery and tracks messages sent between applications.

The use of message recovery and tracking features has been left out of messaging examples up to this point in the book. Consequently the examples suffer from most of the problems that occur in distributed applications that communicate by using remote procedure calls (RPCs) or similar distributed computing technologies.[1]

Three kinds of recovery semantics are available from MSMQ.

- *Nonrecoverable, or express, messages* are never stored on disk and are lost if they reside in a queue whose queue manager stops.

- *Recoverable messages* are always stored on disk and are not lost. If they are in a queue and the queue manager stops or the system is halted suddenly, the messages will not be lost.[2]

- *Transactional messages* are stored to disk and are recoverable. In addition, since operations on these messages are transactional, once a message is sent and the transaction controlling the send operation commits, MSMQ guarantees delivery to the target queue. If an application fails after receiving a message and before committing a transaction in which the message was received, the message remains on the queue until another application chooses to process it. The distinguishing feature over express and recoverable messages is that messaging operations complete only if related work completes.

Using recoverable messages guards against losing messages if a queue manager or a host system fails or shuts down. Sending or receiving messages within transactions guarantees that message operations are coordinated with other related application processing.

MSMQ implements three facilities for keeping track of a message.

- *Writing messages to a journal.* As a message is sent from a source machine, MSMQ can write a copy of the message to the machine journal queue on the source machine. At the target machine the message can be copied to the journal queue of the destination queue as it is retrieved.

- *Tracing message routing.* As a message is routed from its source machine to its destination machine, MSMQ can generate messages that report routing progress.

- *Acknowledging message arrival.* A sender can request that MSMQ generate an acknowledgment indicating whether the message reached its target queue or was retrieved by a receiving application.

These facilities enable you to maintain a copy of the application message in a machine journal at the source machine, to monitor routing progress as the message traverses the network, to confirm that the message arrived at its target queue or was retrieved, and to copy the message to the target queue's journal as it is retrieved. These

---

1. This isn't to say that remote procedure calls or other technologies are unreliable or bad. However, RPCs fall short of recovery and audit requirements for many distributed applications.

2. This is true for messages in a target queue and those passing through the network en route to the target queue.

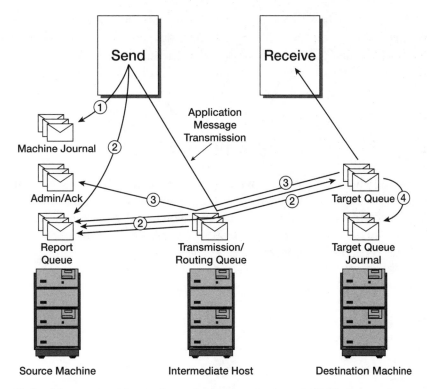

Figure 8-1 Message tracking by journal, report, and acknowledgment

interactions are pictured in Figure 8.1. The circled numbers correspond to the numbered steps that follow.

1. When the message is sent, it is copied into a machine journal on the source machine.

2. As the message is forwarded from the local machine, received and then forwarded by the intermediate host, and received by the destination machine, trace reports are sent to the report queue on the source machine.

3. An acknowledgment is returned to the administration queue when the message reaches its destination queue or is received. The kind of acknowledgment sent depends on the kind of acknowledgment selected by the application.

4. When the message is removed from the target queue on the destination machine, it is copied to a target queue journal.

Recovering and tracing message communications do come at a cost. Fewer recoverable or transactional messages can be sent or received per second than express messages. We'll look at the performance costs of recoverable and transactional messages in Appendix C.

Now let's look at how to make messages recoverable and how to configure MSMQ journal, trace, and acknowledgment facilities. We'll also consider how these facilities might be used so that you always know the state of an application message. The use of transactions and transactional messages is discussed in Chapters 10 and 11.

8.2 Making Messages Recoverable

By default MSMQ sends messages with express delivery. In many instances, however, you might want a message to survive a system shutdown. For example, messages should be made recoverable if you are sending them to or from a handheld device or a laptop that may roam from site to site or operate in disconnected mode.

The message delivery property must be set to MQMSG_DELIVERY_RECOVERABLE if messages need to be recoverable. The following code uses COM components to demonstrate this.

```
Dim Msg As New MSMQMessage
Dim openReqQ As MSMQQueue

Msg.Delivery = MQMSG_DELIVERY_RECOVERABLE
' Set other message properties
' Locate and open a queue referenced by openReqQ
```

The following code uses the MSMQ API to demonstrate the same example.

```
/* Data definitions */
MQPROPVARIANT propVar[PROPERTIES];  // Array of property variants
MSGPROPID propId[PROPERTIES];       // Array of property identifiers
HRESULT stats[PROPERTIES];          // Array of status indicators
MQMSGPROPS mProps;                  // Structure of properties &
                                    // values
DWORD nProps;                       // Property counter
QUEUEHANDLE mQHandle;               // Message queue handle

nProps = 0;
propId[nProps] = PROPID_M_DELIVERY; // Set the message delivery
                                    // property
propVar[nProps].vt = VT_UI1;
propVar[nProps].bVal = MQMSG_DELIVERY_RECOVERABLE;
nProps++;
// Set other message properties
```

```
mProps.cProp    =   nProps; // Construct the MSGPROPS structure
mProps.aPropID  =   propId;
mProps.aPropVar =   propVar;
mProps.aStatus  =   NULL;  // Status values are ignored

// Derive mQHandle - a handle to a message queue
// Send the message
hResult = MQSendMessage(
    mQHandle, // Message queue handle
    &mProps,  // Message properties
    NULL);    // Sending is not transactional
if (FAILED(hResult)) {
    return();
}
```

8.3 Setting Up Message and Queue Journals

In this section we'll briefly look at

- How to configure messages so that a copy is placed in the source machine queue journal as the message is sent
- How to configure queues so that messages are copied into a target queue's journal as they are retrieved by an application

Why would you want to journal messages? The primary reason is to provide a messaging environment that is resilient to failures.

On the sending side many applications log information when a message is sent. Rather than having an application log information or copy message content to a database, it is much easier to have MSMQ transparently save a copy of a message until it can be archived. On the receiving side there are several reasons for copying a message to a queue journal. You might do so to protect your business against repudiation of requests. Following the release of new versions of applications, it may be advisable to collect copies of messages in case the applications are found to have problems.

Note that all messages written to machine or target queue journals are treated as recoverable messages.

8.3.1 Message Journals

When you set up an MSMQ server or an independent client, MSMQ automatically creates a journal queue for the machine. To make MSMQ journal a message at the source machine is very simple. Just set the `MSMQMessage` journal property.

By default a message's journal property value is MQMSQ_JOURNAL_NONE; the message is not copied to the source machine journal queue. When the message's journal property is set to MQMSG_JOURNAL, the message is copied to the source machine's journal queue. You can also set the journal property of a message to MQMSG_DEADLETTER; the message is placed in the dead letter queue on the machine, residing there as it expires.

MSMQ allows you to set the message's journal to both MQMSG_JOURNAL and MQMSG_DEADLETTER. We use COM components to demonstrate this.

```
Dim Msg As New MSMQMessage
Dim openReqQ As MSMQQueue

Msg.Journal = MQMSG_JOURNAL + MQMSG_DEADLETTER
' Set other message properties
' Locate and open a queue referenced by openReqQ
Msg.Send openReqQ
```

Now we'll set a message journal property to MQMSG_JOURNAL and then use the MSMQ API to send the message.

```
/* Data definitions */
MQPROPVARIANT propVar[PROPERTIES];   // Array of property variants
MSGPROPID propId[PROPERTIES];        // Array of property identifiers
HRESULT stats[PROPERTIES];           // Array of status indicators
MQMSGPROPS mProps;                   // Structure of properties &
                                     // values
DWORD nProps;                        // Property counter
QUEUEHANDLE mQHandle;                // Message queue handle

nProps = 0;
propId[nProps] = PROPID_M_JOURNAL; // Set the message journal property
propVar[nProps].vt = VT_UI1;
propVar[nProps].bVal = MQMSG_JOURNAL;
// could use: propVar[nProps].bVal = MQMSG_JOURNAL & MQMSG_DEADLETTER;
nProps++;

// Set other message properties
mProps.cProp    =   nProps; // Construct the MSGPROPS structure
mProps.aPropID  =   propId;
mProps.aPropVar =   propVar;
mProps.aStatus  =   NULL; // Status values are ignored
```

```
// Derive mQHandle - a handle to a message queue
// Send the message
hResult = MQSendMessage(
    mQHandle, // Message queue handle
    &mProps,  // Message properties
    NULL);    // Sending is not transactional
if (FAILED(hResult)) {
    return();
}
```

8.3.2 Queue Journals

Whenever an application queue is created, MSMQ also creates a queue journal, which is used to track messages removed from a queue. By default a queue's journal property is set to MQ_JOURNAL_NONE; messages are not copied to a queue's journal as they are removed. To journal messages that are removed from a queue, the queue's journal property must be set to MQ_JOURNAL.

In the following code we use COM components to create a queue with its journal property set to MQ_JOURNAL.

```
Dim queue As New MSMQQueueInfo
' Pathname is required to create Q
queue.PathName = "pswtech\ackTraceQueue"
queue.Journal = MQ_JOURNAL
    ' Set other queue properties
queue.Create
```

Now we implement that same example with the MSMQ API.

```
/* Data definitions */
MQPROPVARIANT propVar[PROPERTIES]; // Array of queue property
                                   // variants

QUEUEPROPID propId[PROPERTIES];    // Array of queue property
                                   // identifiers

MQQUEUEPROPS qProps;               // Structure of queue property IDs
                                   // and values

DWORD nProps = 0;                  // Property counter
WCHAR PathName[NAME_LENGTH];       // Queue pathname
WCHAR FormatName[NAME_LENGTH];     // Queue format name
DWORD formatLength = NAME_LENGTH;  // Format name length
HRESULT hResult;                   // A status variable
```

```
nProps = 0;                          // Initialize the property counter
propId[nProps] = PROPID_Q_JOURNAL;   // Set the queue journal property
propVar[nProps].vt = VT_UI1;
propVar[nProps].bVal = MQ_JOURNAL;
nProps++;

propId[nProps] = PROPID_Q_PATHNAME; // Set PathName for queue creation
propVar[nProps].vt = VT_LPWSTR;
propVar[nProps].pwszVal = L"pswtech\\queueName";
nProps++;

// Set other queue properties

qProps.cProp = nProps; // Construct the MQQUEUEPROPS structure
qProps.aPropID = propId;
qProps.aPropVar = propVar;
qProps.aStatus = NULL;

// Create the queue
hResult = MQCreateQueue(
    NULL,               // Default security
    &qProps,            // Queue properties
    FormatName,         // Format name
    &formatLength);     // Format name length
if (IS_ERROR(hResult)) {
    return();
}
```

After a queue is created, you can also set a queue's journal property to
MQ_JOURNAL by using the MSMQ Explorer or by calling
MQSetQueueProperties(). In the MSMQ Explorer, right click on the queue's
icon within the Explorer window. This brings up a menu of options. Click on Properties. Then select the Advanced tab (shown in Figure 8-2) from the Queue Properties
window. Clicking on the Enabled check box and selecting OK initiates copying of
messages to the queue's journal.

The following example shows how to set a queue's journal property to
MQ_JOURNAL by calling MQSetQueueProperties(). First, we obtain the format name for the queue. Then we formulate an MQQUEUEPROPS structure. Finally,
we call MQSetQueueProperties() to modify the queue's properties.

```
// Variables, etc.
WCHAR qPathName[101];
```

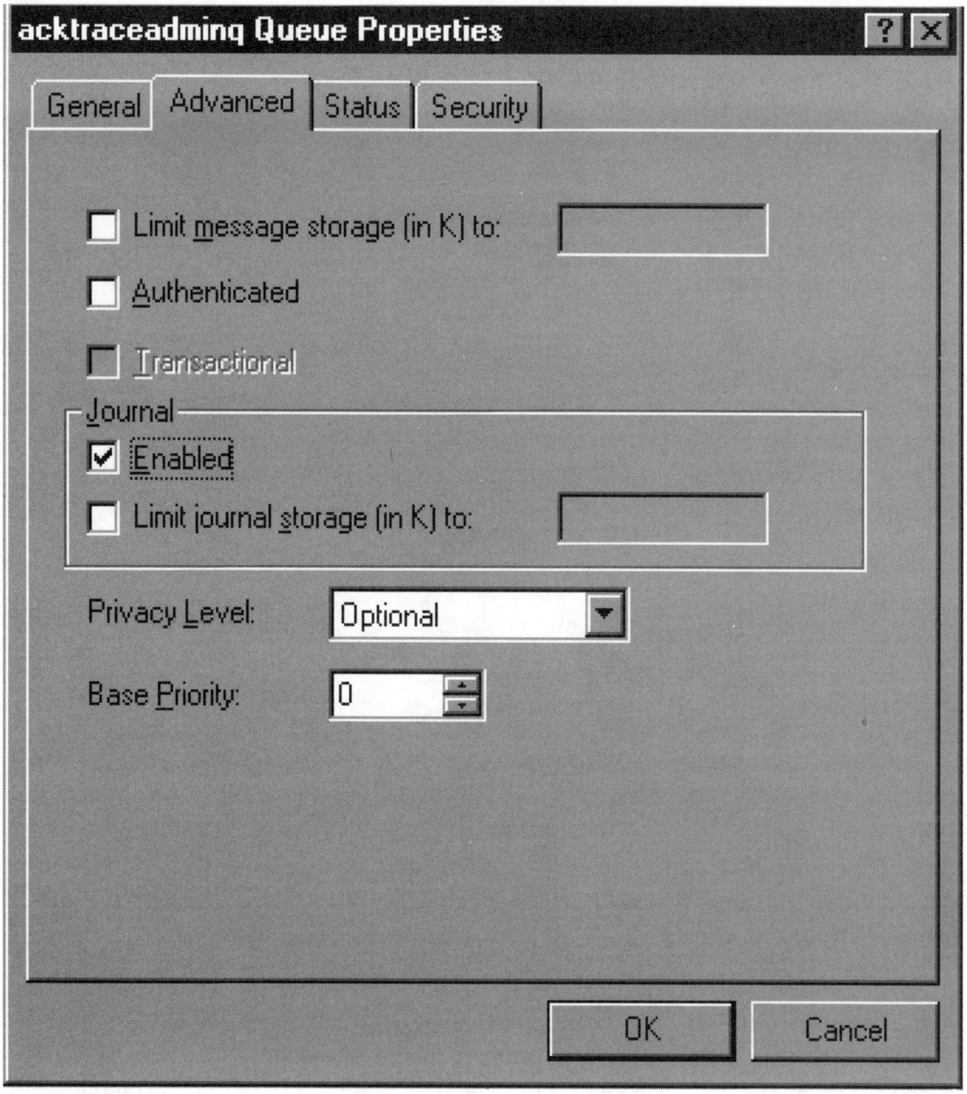

Figure 8-2 The Advanced tab of the Explorer Queue Properties window

```
MQQUEUEPROPS qProps;          // Structure of queue property IDs and
                              // values
MQPROPVARIANT propVar[5];     // Array of queue property values
QUEUEPROPID propId[5];        // Array of queue property identifiers
DWORD nProps = 0;             // Property counter
HRESULT hResult;              // Standard Windows result indicator
```

```
WCHAR formatName[100];     // Holds the formatted name of a queue
DWORD formatLength = 100;  // Format name length

// Set the queue pathname
swprintf(qPathName, L"pswtech\\someQueue");
hResult = MQPathNameToFormatName(
    (LPCWSTR) qPathName,    // Queue pathname
    formatName,            // Format name
    &formatLength);        // Format name length
PRINTERROR("Cannot get queue format name...", hResult, ABORT);

// Set queue journal property
propId[nProps]          = PROPID_Q_JOURNAL;
propVar[nProps].vt       = VT_UI1;
propVar[nProps].bVal     = MQ_JOURNAL;
nProps++;

// Construct the MQQUEUEPROPS structure
qProps.cProp     = nProps;
qProps.aPropID   = propId;
qProps.aPropVar  = propVar;
qProps.aStatus   = NULL;     // Will not inspect queue status values

// Set queue property in MQIS
hResult = MQSetQueueProperties( formatName, &qProps );
PRINTERROR("Cannot set queue properties...", hResult, RESUME);
```

8.4 Tracing Message Routing

In order to enable message tracing, a report queue must be configured on the source machine, and the trace property for your message must be set to MQMSG_SEND_ROUTE_TO_REPORT_QUEUE. To create a report queue on the source machine, you need to use MSMQ Explorer. Right click on the icon for the computer on which the report queue will be created. This brings up a list of options. Click on Properties and select the Tracking tab (see Figure 8-3). To create a new report queue, click the New button and enter a pathname for the queue to be created. Clicking on OK creates the queue. Then select Track all messages and click the OK button. This sets up the queue to receive report or message tracing messages.

Applications also need to enable tracing of messages by setting the trace property, which by default is set to MQMSG_TRACE_NONE; no report messages are generated. The application must explicitly set the message trace property to MQMSG_SEND_ROUTE_TO_REPORT_QUEUE. Then MSMQ will generate report

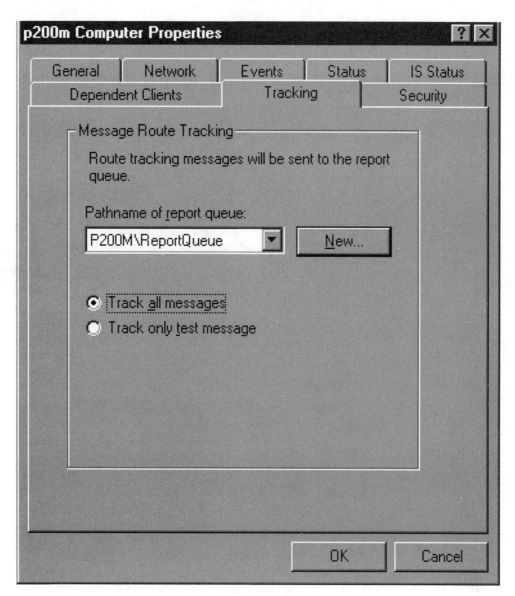

Figure 8-3 The Explorer Tracking tab of the Computer Properties window

messages and send them to the report queue. Note that MSMQ generates report messages only if a message leaves the source machine—in other words, if the message is routed.

The following code uses COM components to set the trace message property.

```
Dim Msg As New MSMQMessage
Dim openReqQ As MSMQQueue
```

```
Msg.Trace = MQMSG_SEND_ROUTE_TO_REPORT_QUEUE
' Set other message properties
' Open a queue referenced by openReqQ
Msg.Send openReqQ
```

Now we use the MSMQ API to set up message tracing.

```
/* Data definitions */
MQPROPVARIANT propVar[PROPERTIES]; // Array of property variants
MSGPROPID propId[PROPERTIES];      // Array of property identifiers
MQMSGPROPS mProps;                 // Structure of properties & values
DWORD nProps;                      // Property counter
HRESULT hResult;                   // A status variable
QUEUEHANDLE mQHandle;              // Message queue handle

nProps = 0;
propId[nProps] = PROPID_M_TRACE; // Set the message trace property
propVar[nProps].vt = VT_UI1;
propVar[nProps].bVal = MQMSG_SEND_ROUTE_TO_REPORT_QUEUE;
nProps++;

// Set other message properties
mProps.cProp     = nProps; // Construct the MSGPROPS structure
mProps.aPropID   = propId;
mProps.aPropVar  = propVar;
mProps.aStatus   = NULL; // Status values are ignored

// Derive mQHandle - a handle to a message queue
// Send the message
hResult = MQSendMessage(
    mQHandle,     // Message queue handle
    &mProps,      // Message properties
    NULL);        // Sending is not transactional
if (FAILED(hResult)) {
    return();
}
```

Following are the label and the body of two report messages generated when a message is routed from a source machine to a target queue on a destination queue in one network hop. The first report message was generated by machine psw200 and sent to its own report queue. The report indicates that an application message was sent to psw200m.

```
Label of report message 1:
20E6:22601 0 sent from psw200 to 1 111.111.111.124 at
01/01/98 , 20:33:42

Body of report message 1:
<MESSAGE ID>
20E66047-758B-11D1-904C-00400521EF0C\22601
</MESSAGE ID>
<TARGET QUEUE>
PUBLIC=79c57d0e-813b-11d1-83b3-006097c4cefc
</TARGET QUEUE>
<NEXT HOP>1 111.111.111.124</NEXT HOP>
```

The second message was generated by psw200m and sent to the report queue of psw200. The report indicates that an application message was received.

```
Label of report message 2:
20E6:22601 0 received by psw200m at 01/01/98 , 20:33:41

Body of report message 2:
<MESSAGE ID>
20E66047-758B-11D1-904C-00400521EF0C\22601
</MESSAGE ID>
<TARGET QUEUE>
PUBLIC=79c57d0e-813b-11d1-83b3-006097c4cefc
</TARGET QUEUE>
```

Each message label contains a simplified version of the report message body, as well as information on the time when the message was routed to machine psw200m. Each report message body contains the message identifier of the original message and the format name of the target queue. When a message is routed to the next machine, the report message label and the body include the IP address of the machine to which the message is being sent. When a message is received by the second machine, the report message label indicates the name of the machine on which the application message resides. The application message was on machine psw200m when the second report message was created.

8.5 Acknowledging Messages

A sender can request that MSMQ generate an acknowledgment message indicating whether the message reached its target queue or was retrieved by a receiving application. The acknowledgment message is sent to a queue designated by the sender.

To obtain an acknowledgment for a message, you must set its acknowledgment message property. The value you select specifies the kind of acknowledgment you want to receive. You also need to designate a queue to which acknowledgments should be sent. MSMQ creates the appropriate acknowledgment message and sends it to the intended queue.

A sending application can specify one of the following values for the acknowledgment message property:

- MQMSG_ACKNOWLEDGMENT_NONE, the default. No acknowledgment message is generated.

- MQMSG_ACKNOWLEDGMENT_FULL_REACH_QUEUE, a positive or negative acknowledgment generated depending on whether the message reached its target queue. A negative acknowledgment is generated if the TimeToReachQueue timer expires or the message cannot be authenticated.

- MQMSG_ACKNOWLEDGMENT_FULL_RECEIVE, a positive or negative acknowledgment generated based on whether the message was retrieved from the target queue. A negative acknowledgment is generated if the message is not retrieved from the target queue by an application before its TimeToBeReceived timer expires.[3]

- MQMSG_ACKNOWLEDGMENT_NACK_REACH_QUEUE, a negative acknowledgment generated if the message does not or cannot reach its target queue. For example, this acknowledgment would be sent if a transactional message is sent to a nontransactional queue or if an unauthenticated message is sent to a queue that accepts only authenticated messages.

- MQMSG_ACKNOWLEDGMENT_NACK_RECEIVE, a negative acknowledgment generated if an error occurs and the message is not retrieved by an application from the target queue before its TimeToBeReceived timer expires.

Using COM components, we demonstrate how to set the acknowledgment message property to MQMSG_ACKNOWLEDGMENT_FULL_RECEIVE and to send the following message.

```
Dim Msg As New MSMQMessage
Dim openReqQ As MSMQQueue
```

---

3. You would specify MQMSG_ACKNOWLEDGMENT_FULL_RECEIVE when the processing of information in a timely manner is critical or you need to know that a message was received. For example, this is one way to support nonrepudiation of requests by the receiving application.

```
Dim admQ As MSMQQueueInfo

' Locate or create administrative queue as demonstrated in Ch 4
' Then set admQ to reference it.
' Open target queue - openReqQ references the target queue when open

' Prepare and send request message
Msg.Ack = MQMSG_ACKNOWLEDGMENT_FULL_REACH_QUEUE
Set Msg.AdminQueueInfo = admQ
' Set up other message properties
Msg.Send openRegQ
```

We now use the **MSMQ API** for the same example.

```
/* Data definitions */
MQPROPVARIANT propVar[PROPERTIES];     // Array of property variants
MSGPROPID propId[PROPERTIES];          // Array of property identifiers
HRESULT stats[PROPERTIES];             // Array of status indicators
MQMSGPROPS mProps;                     // Structure of properties &
                                       // values

DWORD nProps;                          // Property counter
QUEUEHANDLE mQHandle;                   // Message queue handle
WCHAR *aFormatName;                    // Format name for the admin queue
HRESULT hResult;                       // A status variable

nProps = 0;
// Set the acknowledgment property
propId[nProps] = PROPID_M_ACKNOWLEDGE;
propVar[nProps].vt = VT_UI1;
propVar[nProps].bVal = MQMSG_ACKNOWLEDGMENT_FULL_REACH_QUEUE;
nProps++;

// Set the administration queue property -
// The format name for the administration queue was generated
// elsewhere
propId[nProps] = PROPID_M_ADMIN_QUEUE;
propVar[nProps].vt = VT_LPWSTR;
propVar[nProps].pwszVal = aFormatName;
nProps++;

// Set other message properties
mProps.cProp = nProps; // Construct the MSGPROPS structure
mProps.aPropID = propId;
```

```
mProps.aPropVar = propVar;
mProps.aStatus = NULL; // Status values are ignored

// Derive mQHandle - a handle to a message queue
// Send the message
hResult = MQSendMessage(
    mQHandle,                // Message queue handle
    &mProps,                 // Message properties
    NULL);                   // Sending is not transactional
if (FAILED(hResult)) {
    return();
}
```

8.6 Recovering and Tracing Messages

Now let's consider how the recovery and tracing facilities might be used so that you always know the status of an application message. First, we'll look at how nontransactional messages are recovered and traced. Then we'll consider the facilities for transactional messages.

8.6.1 Nontransactional Messages

As you might expect, a message's identifier plays a key role in enabling us to keep track of message activity.

- When a message is sent with the journal property set to MQ_JOURNAL, a copy is written into the journal queue of the source machine. The copy is given the same message identifier as the application message that is traversing the network toward its target queue.

- When MQMSG_SEND_ROUTE_TO_REPORT_QUEUE is assigned to a message's trace property, the message's identifier is assigned as the correlation identifier to all reports generated by MSMQ to trace the route of the message through the network.

- If a message is sent with the journal property set to MQMSG_DEADLETTER[4] and the message fails to reach its target queue before expiring, MSMQ places

---

4. Remember that the message journal property can be set to MQMSG_JOURNAL, to MQMSG_DEADLETTER, or to both. Setting the property to MQMSG_JOURNAL and MQMSG_ DEADLETTER may cause two copies of the message to be kept: one in the journal queue of the source machine and one in the dead letter queue on the machine on which the message expired.

the message in the dead letter queue of the computer on which it expired. The message in the dead letter queue retains the message identifier.

- A message's identifier is assigned as the correlation identifier when MSMQ generates a positive or negative acknowledgment message.

- If the target queue has its journal property set to MQ_JOURNAL, a copy of the message is written to the target queue's journal when it is retrieved. The copy is given the same message identifier as the message retrieved.

What's clear is that MSMQ gives you all the facilities necessary to never lose a message and to keep track of where copies reside if the message cannot be delivered.

A variety of strategies can be implemented to manage the copies of messages in journals or dead letter queues and the report and acknowledgment messages. For example, let's assume that important messages are sent with the following property configurations:

```
MSMQMessage.Delivery = MQMSG_DELIVERY_RECOVERABLE
MSMQMessage.Ack = MQMSG_ACKNOWLEDGMENT_FULL_REACH_QUEUE
MSMQMessage.AdminQueueInfo = ' local queue for receiving acknowledgments
MSMQMessage.Journal = MQMSG_JOURNAL + MQMSG_DEADLETTER
MSMQMessage.Report = MQMSG_SEND_ROUTE_TO_REPORT_QUEUE
```

You could create a message monitor to track the important outgoing messages, taking the following steps:

1. When a new message is written to the local machine's journal, the message identifier is recorded. We record the message identifier in scratch memory or in a database so that we have a way to correlate acknowledgments and reports with the original message. The journal copy of the message is left in the machine journal until the monitor receives confirmation that the message arrived at its target queue.

2. As messages arrive on the report queue, they are retrieved and correlated with application messages that have not yet reached their destinations. The correlation identifier of each report message is matched with the message IDs stored in scratch memory. The location of the message can be tracked by using information contained in the labels of each report message. The monitor might update scratch memory to track routing progress.

3. When an acknowledgment arrives, it is correlated with the message identifiers of messages that have not reached their target queues. The monitor program might inspect the class property of the acknowledgment message to determine whether the message successfully reached its target queue.

   a. *Success.* If the class property for an acknowledgment message is MQMSG_CLASS_ACK_REACH_QUEUE, the message arrived at its target queue. If the class property is `MQMSG_CLASS_ACK_RECEIVE`, the message arrived at its target queue and was received by an application. The message can be deleted from the machine journal, and scratch memory can be released.

b. *Failure.* If the class property is one of the several acknowledgments beginning with `MQMSG_CLASS_NACK`, the message did not arrive at its target queue and is sitting in a dead letter queue on a machine. The monitor could record the failure in the NT event log, write a failure message report in a file or database, and send a page to administrators, asking for manual assistance. Depending on how the monitor handles failures, it might also delete the message from the source machine journal and might free scratch memory.

These steps are illustrated in Figure 8-4.

Making messages recoverable guarantees that they will survive a machine or queue manager failure. If a message is important, you will want to take this precaution.

A monitor program like the one described will probably need to use `MSMQEvent` instances to process messages arriving on administrative, journal, and report queues. I suggest that you define an event handler for each queue to which messages are directed: one for the machine journal, one for the report queue, and one for each administration queue that MSMQ applications use.

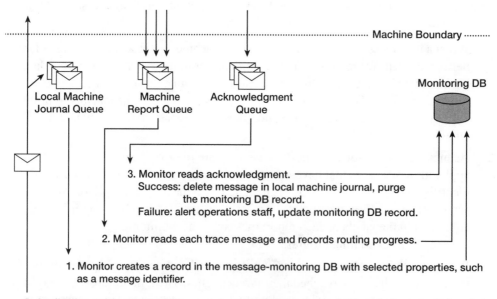

Figure 8-4 Processing of messages by a message monitor

Pipeline Application Group

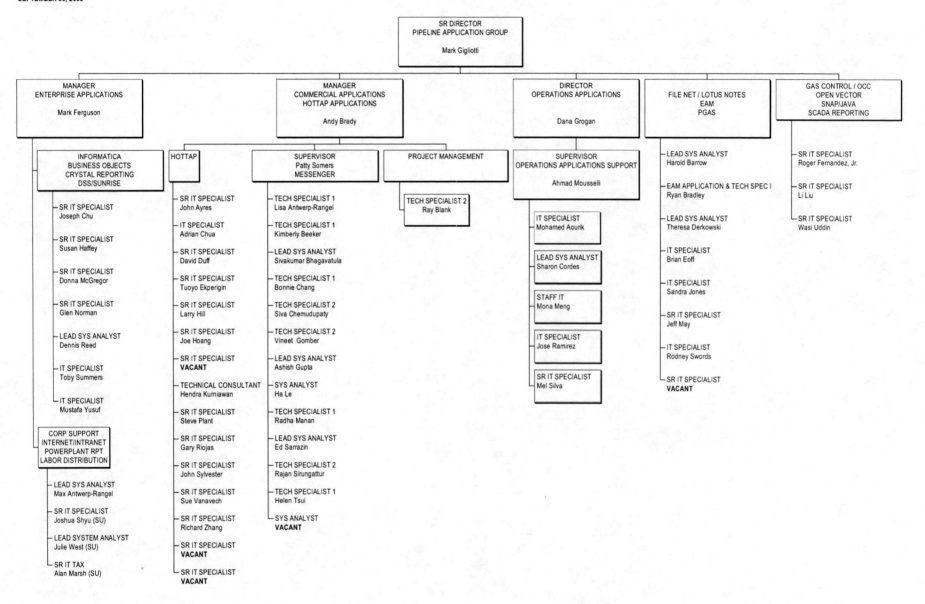

SR DIRECTOR
PIPELINE APPLICATION GROUP

Mark Gigliotti

MANAGER
ENTERPRISE APPLICATIONS

Mark Ferguson

MANAGER
COMMERCIAL APPLICATIONS
HOTTAP APPLICATIONS

Andy Brady

DIRECTOR
OPERATIONS APPLICATIONS

Dana Grogan

FILE NET / LOTUS NOTES
EAM
PGAS

GAS CONTROL / OCC
OPEN VECTOR
SNAP/JAVA
SCADA REPORTING

INFORMATICA
BUSINESS OBJECTS
CRYSTAL REPORTING
DSS/SUNRISE

HOTTAP

SUPERVISOR
Patty Somers
MESSENGER

PROJECT MANAGEMENT

SUPERVISOR
OPERATIONS APPLICATIONS SUPPORT

Ahmad Mousselli

Enterprise Applications — Informatica/Business Objects/Crystal Reporting/DSS/Sunrise

- SR IT SPECIALIST — Joseph Chu
- SR IT SPECIALIST — Susan Haffey
- SR IT SPECIALIST — Donna McGregor
- SR IT SPECIALIST — Glen Norman
- LEAD SYS ANALYST — Dennis Reed
- IT SPECIALIST — Toby Summers
- IT SPECIALIST — Mustafa Yusuf

**CORP SUPPORT
INTERNET/INTRANET
POWERPLANT RPT
LABOR DISTRIBUTION**

- LEAD SYS ANALYST — Max Antwerp-Rangel
- SR IT SPECIALIST — Joshua Shyu (SU)
- LEAD SYSTEM ANALYST — Julie West (SU)
- SR IT TAX — Alan Marsh (SU)

HOTTAP

- SR IT SPECIALIST — John Ayres
- IT SPECIALIST — Adrian Chua
- SR IT SPECIALIST — David Duff
- SR IT SPECIALIST — Tuoyo Ekperigin
- SR IT SPECIALIST — Larry Hill
- SR IT SPECIALIST — Joe Hoang
- SR IT SPECIALIST — **VACANT**
- TECHNICAL CONSULTANT — Hendra Kurniawan
- SR IT SPECIALIST — Steve Plant
- SR IT SPECIALIST — Gary Riojas
- SR IT SPECIALIST — John Sylvester
- SR IT SPECIALIST — Sue Vanavech
- SR IT SPECIALIST — Richard Zhang
- SR IT SPECIALIST — **VACANT**
- SR IT SPECIALIST — **VACANT**

Messenger (Supervisor Patty Somers)

- TECH SPECIALIST 1 — Lisa Antwerp-Rangel
- TECH SPECIALIST 1 — Kimberly Beeker
- LEAD SYS ANALYST — Sivakumar Bhagavatula
- TECH SPECIALIST 1 — Bonnie Chang
- TECH SPECIALIST 2 — Siva Chemudupaty
- TECH SPECIALIST 2 — Vineet Gomber
- LEAD SYS ANALYST — Ashish Gupta
- SYS ANALYST — Ha Le
- TECH SPECIALIST 1 — Radha Manan
- LEAD SYS ANALYST — Ed Sarrazin
- TECH SPECIALIST 2 — Rajan Sirungattur
- TECH SPECIALIST 1 — Helen Tsui
- SYS ANALYST — **VACANT**

Project Management

- TECH SPECIALIST 2 — Ray Blank

Operations Applications Support (Supervisor Ahmad Mousselli)

- IT SPECIALIST — Mohamed Aourik
- LEAD SYS ANALYST — Sharon Cordes
- STAFF IT — Mona Meng
- IT SPECIALIST — Jose Ramirez
- SR IT SPECIALIST — Mel Silva

File Net / Lotus Notes / EAM / PGAS

- LEAD SYS ANALYST — Harold Barrow
- EAM APPLICATION & TECH SPEC I — Ryan Bradley
- LEAD SYS ANALYST — Theresa Derkowski
- IT SPECIALIST — Brian Eoff
- IT SPECIALIST — Sandra Jones
- SR IT SPECIALIST — Jeff May
- IT SPECIALIST — Rodney Swords
- SR IT SPECIALIST — **VACANT**

Gas Control / OCC / Open Vector / SNAP/JAVA / SCADA Reporting

- SR IT SPECIALIST — Roger Fernandez, Jr.
- SR IT SPECIALIST — Li Liu
- SR IT SPECIALIST — Wasi Uddin

62

Now let's discuss some implementation details.

- *Administration queues are like any other application queue.* They have a pathname and a unique queue GUID. A type GUID can also be assigned to them. A message-monitoring program can use any of these properties to locate and open an administration queue.

- *Report queues are similar to application queues.* Every report queue has a pathname, a unique queue GUID, and a type GUID. MSMQ automatically assigns a special type GUID, {55EE8F32-CCE9-11CF-B108-0020AFD61CE9}, to report queues. A message-monitoring program can use the report queue's pathname, queue GUID, or type GUID to locate and to open the queue.

- *Machine journals are not like application queues.* Machine journals do not have a usable pathname, unique queue GUID, or type GUID. A message monitor can locate and open them only by using a format name. The general form of the format name for a machine journal queue is
  `MACHINE=machineGUID;JOURNAL`

- *Machine dead letter queues are similar to machine journals.* A message monitor can locate and open them only by using a format name. The general form of the format name for a machine journal queue is
  `MACHINE=machineGUID;DEADLETTER`

The machine GUID for these queues can be obtained by inspecting queue properties with Explorer or by deriving it programmatically. The MSMQ API provides a function, `MQGetMachineProperties()`, that can be used to return the machine GUID, as well as other properties. In COM, the `MachineIdOfMachineName()` method of the `MSMQApplication` component returns a string representation of a machine GUID. For example, the following code creates a format name for the pswtech machine journal:

```
Dim a As New MSMQApplication
b = "MACHINE=" + a.MachineIdOfMachineName("pswtech") + ";JOURNAL"
```

8.6.2 Transactional Messages

If you send messages within transactions, message monitoring becomes much simpler. When a transactional message fails to arrive successfully before its `TimeToReachQueue` expires or it is not received before its `TimeToBeReceived` timer expires, MSMQ automatically routes the message to the transactional dead letter queue, `XactDeadLetterQueue`, on the source machine. A program needing to know that a message was successfully sent need only examine the `XactDeadLetterQueue` queue after message timers have expired. If the message does not appear in that queue by the time its `TimeToReachQueue` and `TimeToBeReceived` timers expire, you are guaranteed that message communication has been successful. This makes it much easier to determine the status of a message.

How good is the guarantee that MSMQ gives? In the case of transactional messages MSMQ reserves space in the `XactDeadLetterQueue` before sending the message.

8.7 Conclusion

We have seen how MSMQ provides much wider support for handling failures than do most other on-line communication technologies. Messages can be made recoverable, written to journals on the source and destination machines, and tracked as they flow through the network. In addition, MSMQ will generate an acknowledgment message that describes the final disposition for a message.

Now it's time to look at message security. That topic is covered in Chapter 9.

8.8 Resources and References

Gilman, L., and R. Schreiber. 1997. *Distributed Computing with IBM MQSeries*. New York: Wiley.

Microsoft Message Queue Explorer Administrator's Online Help.

Microsoft Message Queue Server Online Help.

Chapter **9**

MSMQ Security

This chapter, intended for developers and managers, discusses how to use MSMQ security facilities. The programming solutions in the chapter build on the Visual Basic example developed in Chapter 4 and the MSMQ API example of Chapter 5.

MSMQ security services are quite attractive because they are fairly complete and easy to use. Security services make it possible to

- Authenticate and check message integrity, using X.509 certifications
- Encrypt messages sent from the source to the destination machine
- Grant or deny sender, receiver, and administrative access to queues and other MSMQ resources, based on Windows NT identity or group membership
- Audit the success and failure of MSMQ operations

These facilities will probably satisfy most users' security needs. Message authentication and encryption help to maintain the health of your applications. Access controls and auditing of operations help to maintain the health of the messaging environment, including your messaging applications.

Other aspects of security are equally important, including host system and network security. However, these topics are beyond the scope of this book. This chapter concentrates on authentication, message encryption, granting and denying access to MSMQ resources, and auditing MSMQ events.

Security services, along with transaction processing, leverage many features of the underlying Windows environment. MSMQ makes simple message authentication and encryption available to programmers without having to understand Windows security APIs. However, to use all of the MSMQ security features, you need to be able to program with security identifiers (SIDs), access control lists (ACLs), access control entries (ACEs), and security descriptors. These data types are defined as part of the base operating system. In this chapter we look at how to use these data types to secure MSMQ applications, but we do not work with them extensively.

9.1   Authentication

MSMQ message authentication allows the receiving application to verify the sender's identity and that message integrity has not been compromised. The queue manager on the source machine attaches a digital signature to the message. The queue manager of the target queue verifies the digital signature when the message arrives. The digital signature is also used to ascertain whether the message has been modified during transmission across the network.

Best of all, MSMQ hides most of the mechanics of message authentication from application developers. Authentication is as easy as setting one or two message properties. Before demonstrating how to use message authentication, let's understand exactly how the authentication process is implemented.

MSMQ uses an asymmetric key protocol based on *internal* or *external* certificates to sign each message. Certificates are issued by *certificate authorities* (CAs) and are used to certify the identity of a sender or a receiver. Internal certificates are generated by MSMQ; external certificates are issued by other certificate authorities, such as VeriSign Commercial Software Publishers.

Asymmetric key protocols use a key pair during authentication.[1] One key is made public, and the other is kept private.[2] When a sending application selects message authentication, the MSMQ runtime retrieves the sending application's internal certificate, external certificate, or the security context of the sender. The sender's private key is also obtained. Next, a hash value is computed for the message. Then the message is signed by encrypting the hash value with the sender's private key to make a digital signature, which is used to check the message's integrity once it reaches the destination queue manager. Finally, the sending application's internal or external certificate and the digital signature are attached to the message, and it is sent to the target queue.

---

1. The protocol is called asymmetric because one key is used to sign a digital signature or to encrypt some information. The other key is used to verify the signature or to decrypt the information. An asymmetric key cannot be used to both encrypt and decrypt. An alternative to asymmetric key protocols is a symmetric key protocol, such as Kerberos, which uses a single, private key and algorithms that enable the key to both encrypt and decrypt information.

2. This is also known as public key authentication, and the services that implement it are often called a public key infrastructure (PKI).

MSMQ supports several algorithms for creating the hash value used in the digital signature. A sender can use a hash algorithm message property to specify which algorithm to use in creating the signature.

The target queue manager computes the hash value for the message, using the hash algorithm indicated by the hash algorithm message property. Next, the sending application's public key is extracted from the certificate and is used to decrypt the digital signature. By comparing the two hash values, the queue manager can determine whether message integrity has been maintained during transmission across the network. Finally, the sender's identifier is retrieved from MQIS and compared with the message's sender ID property.

If the two hash values are the same and if the sender's identity is valid, MSMQ sets the message's authenticated property to TRUE, or 1. This is how MSMQ indicates to the receiving application that a message is safe to process. Unauthenticated messages are delivered to a receiving application with the authenticated property set to 0. If the hash values suggest that tampering has occurred, MSMQ discards the message. A negative acknowledgment will be returned, if the sending application requested one.

Infrastructure Designers

If you want to proactively monitor whether message tampering is occurring, you can adjust queue audit facilities to write an event record to the system event log any time a send fails. This subject is discussed later in this chapter.

MSMQ uses a hashing algorithm to create the digital signature for a message. MD5, a cryptographic checksum algorithm, is used by default. MD5 is a message digest algorithm that applies a one-way function to messages of arbitrary length to create a 128-bit message digest, or checksum. Modification of a message results in a different digest. Since MD5 is a one-way hash function, it is extremely difficult to recreate the signature. Programmers can select other hashing algorithms by specifying alternative values for the hash algorithm message property.

MD5 is generally preferred over other algorithms. For example, the algorithm computes a hash value with almost the same speed as MD4 and with fewer hash value collisions. By reducing the number of collisions, you increase the sensitivity to message tampering. MD2, another alternative, is optimized for 8-bit machines. MSMQ users should choose MD4 and MD5, since these algorithms were designed for 32-bit machines.

Internal and external certificates follow the X.509 certificate format, which is illustrated in Figure 9-1.

Version	The certificate's format
Serial Number	The unique serial number of the certificate authority
Algorithm	The algorithm and any necessary parameters used to sign the certificate
Issuer	The certificate issuer
Period of Validity	Two dates: *not valid before* and *not valid after*
Principal	User
Public Key	The public key algorithm, any parameters, and the public key
Signature	The certificate authority's digital signature

Figure 9-1   X.509 certificate format

Internal certificates can only be used with MSMQ. They contain a public key but have no additional sender information that can be used to authenticate a user. Thus internal certificates are recommended if you want to authenticate the sender but are not concerned that the certificate is backed by a well-known, trusted certificate authority.

External certificates can be used in MSMQ and non-MSMQ applications and usually contain information about the certificate authority, as well as information pertaining to the certified user. Why would an application want to use external certificates? They are becoming widely used on the Internet. An external certificate can be passed from a browser through a Web server to an application, where access control decisions are made using the user's credentials. In such an architecture the user delegates authority to the Web server to perform tasks on his or her behalf. In highly distributed applications delegation of authority makes it possible to develop finer-grained security models.

Internal and external certificates are managed from the MS Message Queue program under your system's control panel. From that program you can register, view, renew, and remove certificates, as well as cryptographic keys.

It's important to understand how queues treat authenticated and nonauthenticated messages and how applications use message authentication. We now turn to these topics.

9.1.1 Queue Authentication Options

It is possible to set a queue's authentication property to one of the following values:

- MQ_AUTHENTICATE—The queue accepts only authenticated messages.
- MQ_AUTHENTICATE_NONE—The queue accepts authenticated and nonauthenticated messages.

In the MSMQ API the PROPID_Q_AUTHENTICATE property for a queue can be set to MQ_AUTHENTICATE, using MQSetQueueProperties(). The format name for a queue is a required parameter in MQSetQueueProperties(). In the following code, we derive the format name for a queue, construct the necessary MSMQ API structures, and set the queue's properties to accept only authenticated messages.

```
// Variables, etc.
WCHAR qPathName[101];
MQQUEUEPROPS qProps;         // Structure of queue property IDs and
                             // values
MQPROPVARIANT propVar[5];    // Array of queue property values
QUEUEPROPID propId[5];       // Array of queue property identifiers
DWORD nProps = 0;            // Property counter
HRESULT hResult;             // Standard Windows result indicator
WCHAR formatName[100];       // Holds the formatted name of a queue
DWORD formatLength = 100;    // Format name length

// Set the queue pathname
swprintf(qPathName, L"pswtech\\secq");

hResult = MQPathNameToFormatName( // Derive queue's format name
    (LPCWSTR) qPathName,              // Queue pathname
    formatName,                      // Format name
    &formatLength);                  // Format name length
PRINTERROR("Cannot get queue format name...", hResult, ABORT);

// Set queue authentication property
propId[nProps]      = PROPID_Q_AUTHENTICATE;
propVar[nProps].vt  = VT_UI1;
propVar[nProps].bVal = MQ_AUTHENTICATE;
nProps++;
```

```
// Construct the MQQUEUEPROPS structure
qProps.cProp          = nProps;
qProps.aPropID        = propId;
qProps.aPropVar       = propVar;
qProps.aStatus        = NULL;

// Set queue property in MQIS
hResult = MQSetQueueProperties( formatName, &qProps );
PRINTERROR("Cannot set queue properties...", hResult, RESUME);
```

Using COM components makes the tasks even easier.

```
Dim targetQ As New MSMQQueueInfo
targetQ.PathName = "pswtech\secq"
targetQ.Authenticate = MQ_AUTHENTICATE
targetQ.Refresh
```

We set the pathname for the queue whose properties we want to change. Then the queue's authentication property is set to MQ_AUTHENTICATE. Finally, we call MSMQQueueInfo.Refresh to update the MQIS with queue property changes.[3] The MSMQQueueInfo component automatically finds the queue's format name when refresh is called.

It is also possible to set the authentication property by using MSMQ Explorer. Find the target queue and right click on its icon to bring up options. Select Properties. Choose the Advanced tab. The Advanced Properties tab is pictured in Figure 9-2. Now click on the Authenticated check box and then on OK.

If a target queue is configured with MQ_AUTHENTICATE, the queue rejects unauthenticated messages. When a message is rejected, MSMQ generates a negative acknowledgment, if requested by the sending application. When authentication is optional for your application, your target queue should be set up with MQ_AUTHENTICATE_NONE, since you want the queue to accept both authenticated and unauthenticated messages.

If you are developing an application and don't know whether a target queue is configured with MQ_AUTHENTICATE or with MQ_AUTHENTICATE_NONE, it's easy enough to check. Here's an example using COM components.

```
Dim targetQ As New MSMQQueueInfo
Dim openQ As MSMQQueue
Dim Msg As New MSMQMessage
```

---

3. This example assumes that the queue has already been created. MSMQQueueInfo.Refresh will fail if the queue has not already been created.

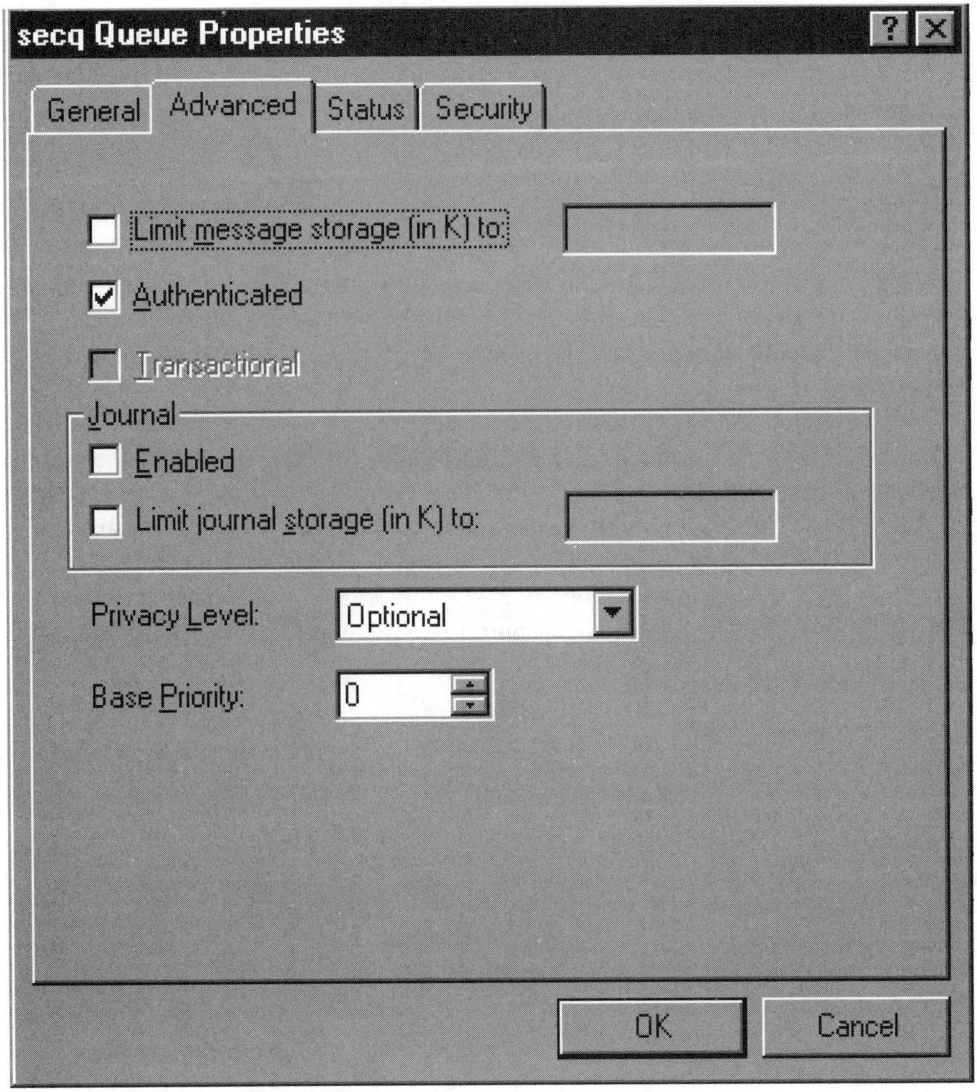

Figure 9-2 MSMQ Explorer Advanced Properties tab for a queue

```
targetQ.PathName = "pswtech\secq"
targetQ.Refresh
Msg.Body = "message body"
Msg.Label = "message label"
Set openQ = targetQ.Open(Access:=MQ_SEND_ACCESS, _
    ShareMode:=MQ_DENY_NONE)
```

```
If targetQ.Authenticate = MQ_AUTHENTICATE Then
    Msg.AuthLevel = MQMSQ_AUTH_LEVEL_ALWAYS
Else
    Msg.AuthLevel = MQMSQ_AUTH_LEVEL_NONE
End If
Msg.Send openQ
openQ.Close
```

This example shows how to send a message with authentication, using an internal certificate. We set the pathname for a queue, refresh (or load) its properties, and inspect the authentication property. If it equals MQ_AUTHENTICATE, we set the AuthLevel message property to MQMSQ_AUTH_LEVEL_ALWAYS, which tells MSMQ to authenticate the message. Otherwise the message is sent with the AuthLevel message property set to MQMSQ_AUTH_LEVEL_NONE, and the message is sent unauthenticated.

The following code, similar to the previous example, uses MSMQ API calls to test whether a queue requires authenticated messages—whether the queue's PROPID_Q_AUTHENTICATE property is MQ_AUTHENTICATE. Then the code sets PROPID_M_AUTH_LEVEL to an appropriate value.

```
// Variables, etc.
WCHAR qPathName[101];
MQQUEUEPROPS qProps;        // Structure of queue property IDs and
                           // values
MQPROPVARIANT propVar[5];   // Array of queue property values
QUEUEPROPID propId[5];      // Array of queue property identifiers
DWORD nProps = 0;           // Property counter
HRESULT hResult;            // Standard Windows result indicator
WCHAR formatName[100];      // Holds the formatted name of a queue
DWORD formatLength = 100;   // Format name length

// Set the queue pathname
swprintf(qPathName, L"pswtech\\secq");

hResult = MQPathNameToFormatName(   // Derive queue's format name
    (LPCWSTR) qPathName,            // Queue pathname
    formatName,                    // Format name
    &formatLength);                // Format name length
PRINTERROR("Cannot get queue format name...", hResult, ABORT);

// Get queue authentication property
propId[nProps]   =   PROPID_Q_AUTHENTICATE;
```

```
propVar[nProps].vt   =   VT_UI1;
nProps++;

// Construct the MQQUEUEPROPS structure
qProps.cProp           = nProps;
qProps.aPropID         = propId;
qProps.aPropVar        = propVar;
qProps.aStatus         = NULL;

// Get queue properties
hResult = MQGetQueueProperties( formatName, &qProps );
PRINTERROR("Cannot set queue properties...", hResult, RESUME);

if ( propVar[0].bVal == MQ_AUTHENTICATE ) { // if the queue requires it
    // Set PROPID_M_AUTH_LEVEL to MQMSG_AUTH_LEVEL_ALWAYS
}
// Send the message
```

9.1.2 Using Internal Certificates with Messages

Messages can be sent with or without authentication. The authentication-level property of a message can be set to one of two values:

- MQMSG_AUTH_LEVEL_ALWAYS to send an authenticated message
- MQMSG_AUTH_LEVEL_NONE to send an unauthenticated message

In the programming example in Section 9.1.1 we demonstrated how to set the MSMQMessage.AuthLevel property to MQMSQ_AUTH_LEVEL_ALWAYS or to MQMSQ_AUTH_LEVEL_NONE with COM components. On the receiving side you will want to check whether the queue manager could authenticate a message. To do this you receive the message and then check the IsAuthenticated property, as follows:

```
Dim targetQ As New MSMQQueueInfo
Dim openQ As MSMQQueue
Dim Msg As New MSMQMessage

targetQ.PathName = "pswtech\secq"
Set openQ = targetQ.Open(Access:=MQ_RECEIVE_ACCESS, _
    ShareMode:=MQ_DENY_NONE)
Set Msg = openQ.Receive(ReceiveTimeout:=1000)
```

```
If Msg.IsAuthenticated = TRUE then
    ' Process the message
    ' Perhaps evaluate access rights of the user - examine Msg.SenderId …
    ' and consider his/her group membership
Else
    ' Discard the message - possibly send an error as a response
End If
```

In Section 9.1.1 we used the MSMQ API to send an authenticated message. The following code shows how a receiver would check that a message was authenticated. We receive the message and check that PROPID_M_AUTHENTICATED has a value of 1.

```
MQQUEUEPROPS qProps;      // Structure of queue property IDs and values
MQPROPVARIANT propVar[5]; // Array of queue property values
QUEUEPROPID  propId[5];   // Array of queue property identifiers
DWORD        nProps = 0;  // Property counter
HRESULT hResult;          // Standard Windows result indicator

// Get PROPID_M_AUTHENTICATED with message
propId[nProps] = PROPID_M_AUTHENTICATED;
propVar[nProps].vt = VT_UI1;
nProps++;
// Prepare properties of message to send

// Create an MSGPROPS structure
mProps.cProp = nProps;
mProps.aPropID = propId;
mProps.aPropVar = propVar;
mProps.aStatus = NULL;
// Prepare other properties

// Open the queue - as demonstrated in Chapter 5.
// Now receive the message to the message queue

if ( propVar[0].bVal == 1) { // if 1, the message passed authentication
    // Process the message
    // Perhaps evaluate access rights of the user by examining the
    // PROPID_M_SENDERID property and consider his/her group membership
} else {
```

```
    // Discard the message - possibly send an error response.
}
```

9.1.3 Using External Certificates with Messages

An external certificate can be used once or repeatedly. We'll look at each case in turn.

9.1.3.1 Sending One Message

A certificate might be used once in an Internet solution, particularly if the Web server is multithreaded. The Web browser passes the user's certificate to the server as part of the HTTP. The server uses the certificate in an MSMQ call.

In the MSMQ API we work with a buffer containing the certificate. In the following code, we place an external certificate into PROPID_M_SENDER_CERT.

```
MQMSGPROPS mProps;                    // Structure of msg prop IDs and
                                      // values
MQPROPVARIANT propVar[PROPERTIES];    // Array of message property values
MSGPROPID propId[PROPERTIES];         // Array of message property
                                      // identifiers
unsigned char *certBuffer;            // Pointer to the external
                                      // certificate
DWORD certLength;                     // Byte length of the external
                                      // certificate
DWORD nProps = 0;                     // Property counter
char mBuffer[BUFFER_LENGTH];          // Message buffer
char rMBuffer[BUFFER_LENGTH];         // Response message buffer
WCHAR msgLabel[BUFFER_LENGTH];        // Message label
HRESULT hResult;                      // Standard Windows result
                                      // indicator
QUEUEHANDLE mQHandle;                 // Queue handle

// Load the external certificate into memory - to load a certificate
// from a certificate store, see the next example
// Set certBuffer to point to it.
// Set certLength to the length of buffer in bytes

// Set PROPID_M_SENDER_CERT
nProps = 0;
```

```
propId[nProps] = PROPID_M_SENDER_CERT;
propVar[nProps].vt = VT_UI1 | VT_VECTOR;
propVar[nProps].caub.cElems = certLength;
propVar[nProps].caub.pElems = certBuffer;
nProps++;
// Prepare properties of message to send

// Create an MSGPROPS structure
mProps.cProp    =   nProps;
mProps.aPropID  =   propId;
mProps.aPropVar =   propVar;
mProps.aStatus  =   NULL;
// Open the queue and send the message - as demonstrated in Chapter 5.
```

9.1.3.2   Setting a Security Context for Sending Multiple Messages

When an external certificate is going to be used repeatedly, it makes sense to set up a security context with the certificate. MQGetSecurityContext(), an MSMQ API function that does this, takes an external certificate as input and returns a handle to a security context. The handle is used with the PROPID_M_SECURITY_CONTEXT message property when messages are sent.

The sending program can use the *Certificate Helper* functions and the *Certificate Store* functions of Microsoft's CryptoAPI to derive a certificate that will be used as input to MQGetSecurityContext(). To obtain a certificate from a certificate store, one would acquire a handle for a cryptographic service provider (CSP), use it to open the certificate store and obtain a handle to it, step through each certificate, and select the one you want.

The following example briefly outlines how to obtain a certificate from a certificate store, derive a handle to a security context from the certificate by using MQGetSecurityContext(), and place the security context handle into PROPID_M_SECURITY_CONTEXT.

```
BOOL bRet;                      // Boolean return
HCRYPTPROV cryptProvider;       // Handle to a cryptographic provider
HCERTSTORE store;               // Handle to a certificate store
PCCERT_CONTEXT certContext;     // Pointer to a certificate context
PCCERT_CONTEXT prevContext;     // Pointer to the previous certificate
                                // context
HANDLE secContext;              // Security context created by
                                // MQGetSecurityContext
MQMSGPROPS mProps;              // Structure of msg prop IDs and values
```

```
MQPROPVARIANT propVar[PROPERTIES];   // Array of message property
                                     // values
MSGPROPID propId[PROPERTIES];        // Array of message property
                                     // identifiers
DWORD nProps = 0;                    // Property counter
HRESULT hResult;                     // Standard Windows result
                                     // indicator
QUEUEHANDLE mQHandle;                // Queue handle


// Acquire a CSP context
// bRet = CryptAcquireContext( &cryptProvider, NULL, NULL,
//                     PROV_RSA_FULL, NULL);
//
// Open the system certificate store
// store = CertOpenSystemStore( cryptProvider, "MY");
//
// certContext = prevContext = NULL;
// while (true) {
//     certContext = CertEnumCertificatesInStore( store, prevContext);
//     if (!certContext) {
//         when Null is returned, a certificate isn't found - BREAK and
//         clean up
//     } else {
//         test the certificate to see if it's the one to use
//         if it is {
//             MQGetSecurityContext( certContext->pbCertEncoded,
//                             certContext->cbCertEncoded,
//                             &secContext); // security context
//             BREAK;
//         }
//     prevContext = certContext;
// }
// clean up - close the store, free any prevContext, etc.


// Set PROPID_M_SECURITY_CONTEXT
nProps = 0;
propId[nProps] = PROPID_M_SECURITY_CONTEXT;
propVar[nProps].vt = VT_UI4$;
propVar[nProps].ulVal = secContext;
nProps++;
```

```
// Prepare properties of message to send

// Create an MSGPROPS structure
mProps.cProp = nProps;
mProps.aPropID = propId;
mProps.aPropVar = propVar;
mProps.aStatus = NULL;

// Open the queue - as demonstrated in Chapter 5.
// Now send the message to the queue
// When done with the security context, free it
MQFreeSecurityContext (secContext);
```

9.1.3.3 Receiving a Message

When a message is sent with an external certificate, MSMQ creates and validates the digital signature for the message. The target queue manager verifies the signature. In the MSMQ API `PROPID_M_AUTHENTICATED` is set to 1 if the message is authenticated. The `IsAuthenticated` property of an `MSMQMessage` component returns TRUE if the message is authenticated.

It is up to the receiving application to validate the certificate. The Certificate Helper functions of Microsoft's CryptoAPI will aid you in this purpose. How the certificate is validated is up to the application.

9.2 Message Encryption

All too often companies think nothing of sending unprotected data in clear text across networks. There are risks in doing this in a closed network environment. A contractor or a disgruntled employee can use a network sniffer to capture messages transmitted during the day to examine them off line for sensitive data or to figure out how to break into systems. The risks are magnified in large companies that share data over public networks or the Internet.

The MSMQ runtime makes it possible to send a private message across the network. Application programmers do not need to encrypt or to decrypt messages. The runtime does this on their behalf.

When a sending application chooses to send a private message, the source machine queue manager encrypts the message by using a symmetric key. Then the queue manager uses the destination machine queue manager's public key to encrypt the symmetric key. The encrypted symmetric key is sent with the encrypted message to the destination queue manager. The destination queue manager decrypts the symmetric key, using its private key. Next, the destination queue manager uses the symmetric key to decrypt the message and passes it along to the receiving application in clear text.

MSMQ uses RC2, a cipher encryption algorithm designed for RSA, as the default encryption algorithm. MSMQ also supports RC4. Message encryption is based on public key technology and uses the CryptoAPI with an underlying RSA provider. The CryptoAPI shields MSMQ from changes in the way keys are stored and how crypto-graphic algorithms are implemented. Thus your programs should not need to change when MSMQ is released on NT 5.0.

Dependent clients do not have any queue management functionality and rely on an MSMQ server to send or to receive messages. When an MSMQ dependent client application sends or receives a message, it is transmitted to or from its server across the network in clear text. This represents a security hole. If a company is highly concerned about security, applications should be deployed only on MSMQ servers or on independent clients.

It is important to understand how queues treat encrypted and nonencrypted messages and how applications use message encryption. These topics are discussed next.

9.2.1 Queue Privacy Options

Queues have a privacy property that can be set to one of three values:

- MQ_PRIV_LEVEL_NONE—The queue accepts only messages in clear text.
- MQ_PRIV_LEVEL_BODY—The queue accepts only private or encrypted messages.
- MQ_PRIV_LEVEL_OPTIONAL—The queue accepts both private and clear-text messages.

In the MSMQ API the PROPID_Q_PRIV_LEVEL property can be set to MQ_PRIV_LEVEL_BODY by using MQSetQueueProperties(). A format name for the queue must be passed in the call. In the following code we derive a format name for a queue, construct an MQQUEUEPROPS structure, and set the queue property.

```
// Variables, etc.
WCHAR qPathName[101];
MQQUEUEPROPS   qProps;            // Structure of queue property IDs and
                                  // values
MQPROPVARIANT propVar[5];         // Array of queue property values
QUEUEPROPID   propId[5];          // Array of queue property identifiers
DWORD         nProps = 0;         // Property counter
HRESULT hResult;                  // Standard Windows result indicator
WCHAR formatName[100];            // Holds the formatted name of a queue
```

```
DWORD formatLength = 100;      // Format name length

// Set the queue pathname
swprintf(qPathName, L"pswtech\\secureq");

hResult = MQPathNameToFormatName(// Derive queue format name
    (LPCWSTR) qPathName,           // Queue pathname
    formatName,                    // Format name
    &formatLength);                // Format name length
PRINTERROR("Cannot get queue format name...", hResult, ABORT);

// Set queue privacy property PROPID_Q_PRIV_LEVEL to MQ_PRIV_LEVEL_BODY
propId[nProps]       = PROPID_Q_PRIV_LEVEL;
propVar[nProps].vt   = VT_UI4;
propVar[nProps].ulVal = MQ_PRIV_LEVEL_BODY;
nProps++;

// Construct the MQQUEUEPROPS structure
qProps.cProp         = nProps;
qProps.aPropID       = propId;
qProps.aPropVar      = propVar;
qProps.aStatus       = NULL;

// Set queue properties
hResult = MQSetQueueProperties( formatName, &qProps );
PRINTERROR("Cannot set queue properties...", hResult, RESUME);
```

Using COM components makes this task even easier.

```
Dim targetQ As New MSMQQueueInfo

targetQ.PathName = "pswtech\secureq"
targetQ.PrivLevel = MQ_PRIV_LEVEL_BODY
targetQ.Refresh
```

It's also possible to set the privacy property by using MSMQ Explorer. Find the target queue and right click on its icon to bring up options. Select Properties. Choose the Advanced tab (shown in Figure 9-2), select a Privacy Level, and click OK.

When a target queue is configured with MQ_PRIV_LEVEL_BODY, the queue rejects unencrypted messages. If the target queue is configured with MQ_PRIV_LEVEL_NONE, the queue rejects encrypted messages. In these situations MSMQ generates a negative acknowledgment, if requested by the sending application.

If you don't know how a target queue is configured, it's easy enough to check. At the end of Section 9.1.1 we showed how to examine a queue's authentication property and to customize a message accordingly. With minor changes the MSMQ and COM examples can be modified to handle a queue's encryption property.

9.2.2 Sending and Receiving Private Messages

Messages can be sent with or without privacy. The privacy-level property of a message can be set to one of two values:

- `MQMSG_PRIV_LEVEL_BODY` to send a private message
- `MQMSG_PRIV_LEVEL_NONE` to send a clear-text message

Sending a private message couldn't be much simpler. Here's how to send an RC2 encrypted private message by using COM components.

```
Dim targetQ As New MSMQQueueInfo
Dim openQ As MSMQQueue
Dim Msg As New MSMQMessage

targetQ.PathName = "pswtech\secureq"
Set openQ = targetQ.Open(Access:=MQ_SEND_ACCESS, _
    ShareMode:=MQ_DENY_NONE)
Msg.PrivLevel = MQMSG_PRIV_LEVEL_BODY
Msg.Body = "message body"
Msg.Label = "message label"
Msg.Send openQ
OpenQ.Close
```

By default MSMQ implicitly uses RC2. To specify RC4, you would insert the following line of code:

```
Msg.EncryptAlgorithm = MQMSG_CALG_RC4 ' Not using MQMSG_CALG_RC2
```

On the receiving side it's possible to check whether the message was encrypted and what the encryption algorithm is by inspecting the `PrivLevel` and `EncryptAlgorithm` properties.

```
Dim Msg As New MSMQMessage

' Check Privacy
If Msg.PrivLevel = MQMSG_PRIV_LEVEL_BODY Then
    StatusText.Text = "Message was encrypted "
```

```
' Check algorithm
    If Msg.EncryptAlgorithm = MQMSG_RC2 Then
        StatusText.Text = StatusText.Text + "using RC2."
    Else
        StatusText.Text = StatusText.Text + "using RC4."
    End If
Else
    StatusText.Text = Message was not encrypted."
End If
```

The following code shows how to send a private message when using the MSMQ API.

```
MQMSGPROPS mProps;                      // Structure of msg prop IDs and
                                        // values
MQPROPVARIANT propVar[PROPERTIES];      // Array of message property
                                        // values
MSGPROPID propId[PROPERTIES];           // Array of message property
                                        // identifiers
DWORD nProps = 0;                       // Property counter
char mBuffer[BUFFER_LENGTH];            // Message buffer
char rMBuffer[BUFFER_LENGTH];           // Response message buffer
WCHAR msgLabel[BUFFER_LENGTH];          // Message label
HRESULT hResult;                        // Standard Windows result
                                        // indicator
QUEUEHANDLE mQHandle;                   // Queue handle

// Set PROPID_M_PRIV_LEVEL to MQMSG_PRIV_LEVEL_BODY
propId[nProps] = PROPID_M_PRIV_LEVEL;
propVar[nProps].vt = VT_UI4;
propVar[nProps].ulVal = MQMSG_PRIV_LEVEL_BODY;
nProps++;

// Prepare other message properties

// Create an MSGPROPS structure
mProps.cProp    = nProps;
mProps.aPropID  = propId;
mProps.aPropVar = propVar;
mProps.aStatus  = NULL;

// Open the queue - as demonstrated in Chapter 5.
// Then send the message
```

The receiving application can check the `PROPID_M_PRIV_LEVEL` message property to determine whether the message was sent encrypted. The encryption algorithm can be determined by using the `PROPID_M_ENCRYPTION_ALG` message property.

9.3 MSMQ Access Controls

MSMQ makes it possible to assign Special Access Permissions to users or groups. These permissions control elementary operations on an enterprise, sites, connected networks, computers, and queues.[4] MSMQ also provides a set of standard Type of Access profiles for these MSMQ objects. Each Type of Access profile is composed of a set of Special Access Permissions for an MSMQ object. Type of Access profiles are used when the enterprise is installed and as new sites, connected networks, computers, and queues are created. Consequently you have tremendous ability to customize access controls as necessary, but MSMQ leaves nothing to chance; it automatically secures your messaging environment as sites, connected networks, computers, and queues are created and modified.

Permissions are stored in an *access control list* (ACL). Every MSMQ object has an ACL associated with it. The ACL is composed of *access control entries* (ACE). Each ACE contains two pieces of information: a user or group that is granted access to the object and the permissions granted. The user or group is identified by its *security identifier* (SID).

Permissions for each MSMQ object can be examined or modified by using MSMQ Explorer. To examine or modify the access control list for an MSMQ object, use MSMQ Explorer to find its icon. Right click on the icon and select Properties. In the Properties window choose the Security tab and press the Permissions button. This brings up a Permissions window for the object you selected.

Figure 9-3 shows a Queue Permissions window, a visual representation of the ACL for the queue with a pathname of `pp200\objectq`. To add a user or a group to the ACL, click on the Add button. To remove an entry, click on Remove. To change Type of Access permission for a user or a group already in the list, select one of the entries from the Type of Access combo box. You can also specify Special Access Permissions from the Type of Access combo box.

Table 9-1 shows the Special Access Permissions for an enterprise, sites, connected networks, computers, and queues.

---

4. In a sense a message is an object defined by MSMQ. However, no specific access controls are associated with a message; only the queues that store messages have access controls.

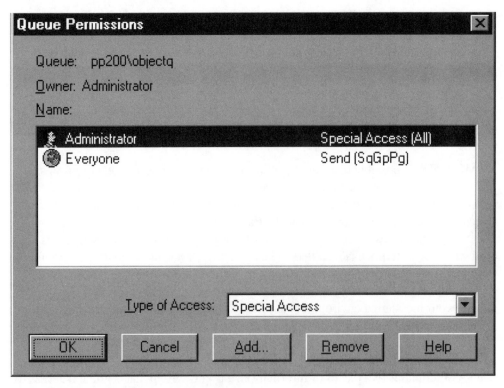

Figure 9-3 Queue Permissions window

Table 9-1 Special Access Permissions by MSMQ Object

MSMQ Object	Access Controls
Enterprise	Create a Site (Cs)
	Create a CN (Cc)
	Create a User (Cu)
	Set Enterprise Properties (Sp)
	Delete the Enterprise (D)
	Get Enterprise Permissions (Pg)
	Set Enterprise Permissions (Ps)
	Take Ownership of the Enterprise (O)

continued

Table 9-1 *continued*

MSMQ Object	Access Controls
Site	Create a Routing Server (Cr)
	Create a BSC (Cb)
	Create a Computer (C)
	Set Site Properties (Sp)
	Delete the Site (D)
	Get Site Permissions (Pg)
	Set Site Permissions (Ps)
	Take Ownership of the Site (O)
Connected Network	Open a Connector Application or Service on the local host
	Set CN Properties (Sp)
	Delete the CN (D)
	Get CN Permissions (Pg)
	Set CN Permissions (Ps)
	Take Ownership of the CN (O)
Computer	Receive Messages from the Computer's Dead Letter (Rd)
	Peek Messages in the Computer's Dead Letter (Pd)
	Receive Messages from the Computer's Journal (Rj)
	Peek Messages in the Computer's Journal (Pj)
	Create a Queue (C)
	Set Computer Properties (Sp)
	Delete the Computer (D)
	Get Computer Permissions (Pg)
	Set Computer Permissions (Ps)
	Take Ownership of the Computer (O)
Queue	Receive Messages from the Queue's Journal (Rj)
	Receive Message from the Queue (Rq)
	Peek Message from the Queue (Pq)
	Send Message to the Queue (Sq)
	Set Queue Properties (Sp)
	Get Queue Properties (Gp)
	Delete the Queue (D)
	Get Queue Permissions (Pg)
	Set Queue Permissions (Ps)
	Take Ownership of the Queue (O)

MSMQ also provides the programmatic means to examine and assign permissions for a queue. This feature is discussed in Section 9-4.

When using MSMQ Explorer to grant Receive Dead Letter (Rd), Receive Journal (Rj), or Receive Message (Rq) permissions, MSMQ automatically assigns Peek Dead Letter (Pd), Peek Journal (Pj), or Peek Message (Pq) permissions, respectively, to the user or the group. It is necessary to programmatically assign permissions if you wish to assign the Receive permission to a queue without the Peek permission.

Each Type of Access profile is composed of a set of Special Access Permissions for an enterprise, site, connected network, computer, and queue. Table 9-2 lists the permissions in each Type of Access profile and indicates to whom the profile is automatically assigned.

9.4   Managing Queue Access Programmatically

The MSMQ API provides a way to inspect and to modify queue access permissions. `MQGetQueueSecurity()` provides a shorthand way to derive a standard Windows NT security descriptor for queue access controls. To set a queue access control, you use `MQSetQueueSecurity()`.

A security descriptor contains the security information associated with a secured object and can include the following security information:

- Security identifiers (SIDs) for the owner and the primary group of an object
- A discretionary ACL (DACL) indicating what kinds of access are granted to users or groups
- A system ACL (SACL) specifying the kinds of access attempts that are audited
- Control bits

`SECURITY_DESCRIPTOR` is the data type, a structure, for obtaining a SID, DACL, SACL, and control bits. To derive a queue's security descriptor, you must pass the queue's format name to `MQGetQueueSecurity()` and identify the kinds of security information to be returned in the descriptor. Just as four kinds of information are in a security descriptor, four constants define security information that can be passed in a call to `MQGetQueueSecurity()`.

- `OWNER_SECURITY_INFORMATION`
- `GROUP_SECURITY_INFORMATION`
- `DACL_SECURITY_INFORMATION`
- `SACL_SECURITY_INFORMATION`

Table 9-2   Type of Access Profiles by MSMQ Object

MSMQ Object	Profile	Permissions
Enterprise	Full	The administrator who installs an enterprise is granted Full control permission. (Cs, Cc, Cu, Sp, D, Pg, Ps, O)
	Read	Everyone is granted Read permission to retrieve permissions (Pg) and to register certificates (Cu).
	Write	A user or a group can create sites (Cs), create connected networks (Cc), retrieve permissions (Pg), and register certificates (Cu). MSMQ doesn't automatically grant these privileges.
Site	Full	The administrator who installs a site is granted Full control permission. (Cr, Cb, C, Sp, D, Pg, Ps, O)
	Read	A user or a group can retrieve permissions for that site (Pg). MSMQ doesn't automatically grant these privileges.
	Write	Everyone has Write permission to retrieve permissions for that site (Pg) and to create a computer in the site (C).
Connected Network	Full	The administrator who installs a connected network is granted Full control permission. (Open Connector, Sp, D, Pg, Ps, O)
	Read	Everyone is granted Read permission to retrieve permissions for the connected network (Pg).
	Write	Identical to Read permissions.
Computer	Full	The administrator who installs a computer is granted Full control permission. (Rd, Pd, Rj, Pj, C, Sp, D, Pg, Ps, O)
	Read	A user or a group can receive messages from a computer's journal (Rj, Pj) and dead letter queues (Rd, Pd) and can retrieve permissions for the computer (Pg). MSMQ doesn't automatically grant these privileges.
	Write	Everyone has Write permission to retrieve permissions for the computer (Pg) and to create queues (C).
Queue	Full	The queue administrator on a given computer is granted Full control permission. (Rj, Rq, Pq, Sq, Sp, Gp, D, Pg, Ps, O)
	Send	Everyone is granted Send permission to retrieve queue properties (Gp) and permissions (Pg) and to send messages to the queue (Sq).
	Receive	A user or a group can retrieve the queue's properties (Gp) and permissions (Pg) and can peek (Pq) and receive messages from the queue (Rq).

SECURITY_INFORMATION is the data type that describes this information. To indicate more than one type in a call, any of the preceding constants can be added together.

Once you have obtained a security descriptor, you can examine and modify it, using access control functions provided as part of Windows 32-bit Platform Software Development Kit (SDK). You set the security descriptor for a queue by calling MQSetQueueSecurity().

The subject of working with Windows access control structures and functions to programmatically examine and modify security descriptors is worthy of a book and will not be covered here. However, some options are outlined as part of the following example. It shows how to derive a security descriptor by using MQGetQueueSecurity() and to reset it with MQSetQueueSecurity().

```
HRESULT hResult; // Standard Windows result indicator
WCHAR formatName[100]; // Holds the formatted name of a queue
DWORD formatLength = 100;      // Format name length
SECURITY_INFORMATION secInfo;  // Security Information structure
PSECURITY_DESCRIPTOR secDesc;  // Security descriptor
DWORD more = 0;                // Additional length needed for the
                               // descriptor

// Create message queue pathname and derive its format name
swprintf(qPathName, L"pswtech\\objectq");
hResult = MQPathNameToFormatName(
    (LPCWSTR) qPathName,       // Queue pathname
    formatName,                // Format name
    &formatLength);            // Format name length
PRINTERROR("Cannot get queue format name...", hResult, RESUME);

// Obtain the queue's security descriptor
secInfo = OWNER_SECURITY_INFORMATION + GROUP_SECURITY_INFORMATION;
secInfo += DACL_SECURITY_INFORMATION + SACL_SECURITY_INFORMATION ;
hResult = MQGetQueueSecurity(
    (LPCWSTR) formatName,
    secInfo,
    &secDesc,
    GetSecurityDescriptorLength(secDesc),
    &more);
PRINTERROR("Getting queue permissions...", hResult, ABORT);

// To examine the queue's security descriptor
// GetSecurityDescriptorOwner - obtain the queue owner's SID
```

```
// GetSecurityDescriptorGroup - obtain queue owner's primary group SID
// GetSecurityDescriptorDacl - obtain queue DACL
// GetSecurityDescriptorSacl - obtain queue SACL
// GetAclInformation - get information about an ACL
// GetSecurityDescriptorLength - obtain byte length of the security
// descriptor
// IsSecurityDescriptorValid - tests components of the security
// descriptor

// To modify the queue's security descriptor
// InitializeSecurityDescriptor - initialize a new security descriptor
// GetUserName - get user name of the current thread
// LookupAccountName - get SID for an account
// InitializeAcl - initialize a new ACL
// SetAclInformation - set information about an ACL
// SetSecurityDescriptorOwner - modify queue owner's SID
// SetSecurityDescriptorGroup - modify queue owner's primary group SID
// SetSecurityDescriptorDacl - modify queue DACL field
// SetSecurityDescriptorSacl - modify queue SACL field

// Reset the queue's security descriptor
hResult = MQSetQueueSecurity(
    (LPCWSTR) formatName,
    secInfo,
    &secDesc);
PRINTERROR("Setting queue permissions...", hResult, RESUME);
```

9.5 Access Event Auditing

Administrators can set up MSMQ to audit access operations on an enterprise, sites, connected networks, machines, and queues. MSMQ writes audit records to the event log on the system where an operation is performed. However, where records are written is not always obvious. If you are working on system A and create queue XYZ on system B, an event record is written on system B, where the queue was created. Now suppose that you change one or two properties for XYZ. Even though the queue resides on system B, the change to the queue's property was initiated on system A. In this case an audit record is written into system A's event log.

To configure auditing for an enterprise, site, connected network, machine, or queue, use MSMQ Explorer to find the object's icon. Right click on the icon and

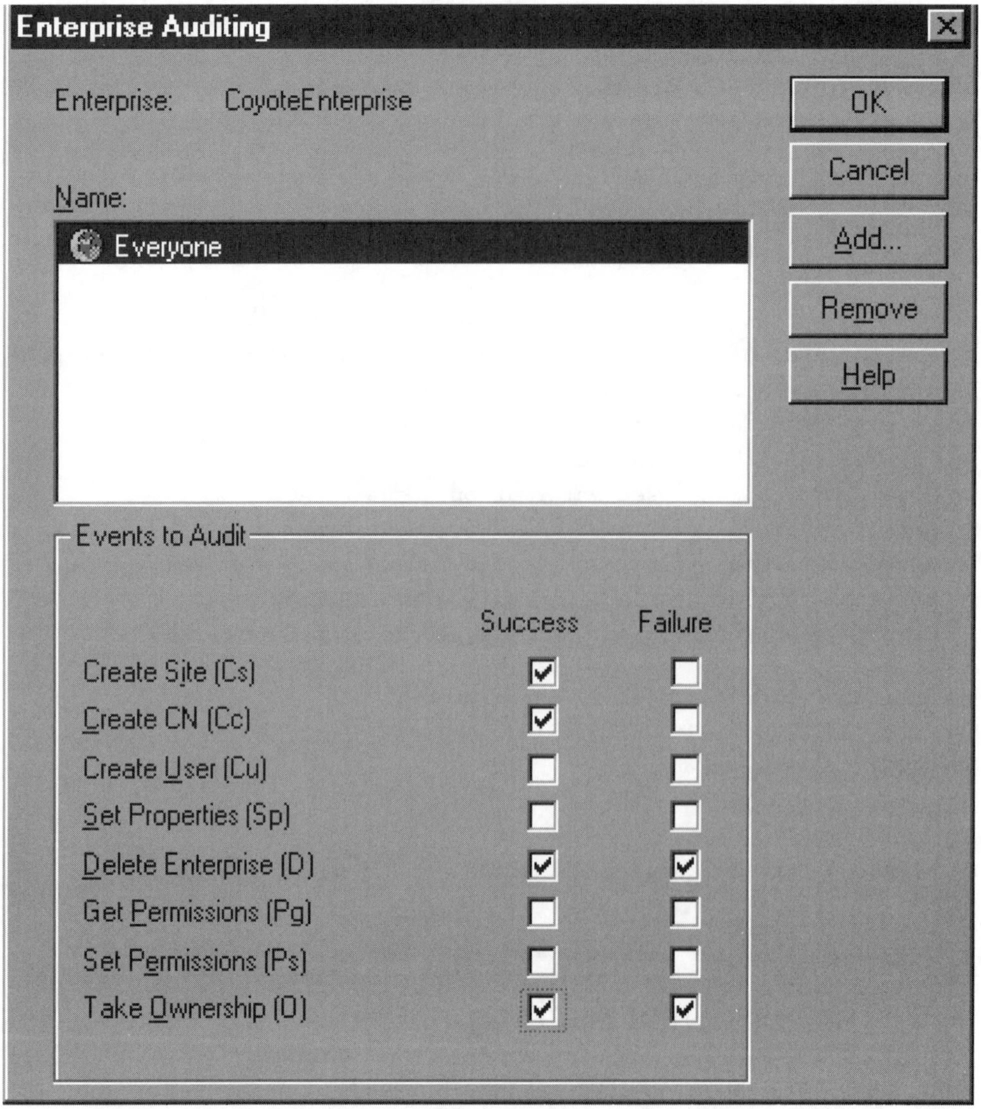

Figure 9-4 Configuring auditing in an MSMQ enterprise

select Properties. In the Properties window choose the Security tab and press the Auditing button.

Figure 9-4 shows an Auditing window for an MSMQ enterprise. We have set up enterprise auditing to audit all accesses that successfully create sites or connected networks and any attempts to delete the enterprise or take ownership of the enterprise.

You can add audit profiles for an MSMQ resource by clicking the Add button.

This brings up an Add Users and Groups window. Select the users and groups to be added and click the OK button. Back in the Auditing window, select the user or group and choose the kind of events and outcomes that should be audited. Then click the OK button. As you can see, auditing access is extremely easy to configure.

Each type of MSMQ object has its own set of events that can be audited. We commonly think of queues as the primary objects that need to be secured, but that is because few distributed computing services have as elegant an architecture as MSMQ. It's important to review the audit configuration of all MSMQ objects in your enterprise.

9.6 Conclusion and Recommendations

The facilities discussed in this chapter should satisfy the security needs of most users. Following are some brief thoughts on how to approach authentication, message encryption, access control, and auditing of activities.

As an application architect, I use authentication to understand who is accessing data or processing resources, what their role is, and so on. An application request can be satisfied or denied based on a user's authenticated identity or group membership. The sensitivity of data determines whether it should be encrypted for network communications. Encryption is rather expensive, so only the most sensitive data should be encrypted.[5]

When defining a security architecture for a company, I spend a lot of time looking at how its IT functions are structured. In particular I focus on what groups are responsible for the various pieces of operational support and how administration of security is organized. It is important to understand the responsibilities of each group and the tasks they need to perform, where they are located, and so on. This information enables me to outline what permissions each group needs in order to perform its IT function. This information can be used to configure the access rights to MSMQ and application resources, based on the *Principle of Least Privilege:* Assign each group only the privileges it needs to perform its job.

Another critical consideration is whether configuration of the computing environment is tightly or loosely controlled. If a company maintains strong configuration controls, it makes sense to develop a detailed ACL definition for all objects in the environment. On the other hand, detailed planning is a poor investment of one's time if there are no change controls or when they are ignored.

---

5. The cost of encryption is not borne by the application, since the queue managers encrypt and decrypt messages. However, the cost does subtract from the CPU cycles available to your applications. Encryption using private key technologies, such as Kerberos, has been demonstrated to add 16% to 17% to ordinary communications costs. Encryption based on public keys is significantly greater.

Another factor to take into consideration is the kinds of threats against the environment. As a rule, the more threats that can be enumerated, the better you are able to react to them. You need to consider the likelihood of human error, as well as the possibility of malicious actions. Auditing events helps you to detect human errors and malicious actions. If you collect information about these events, you are better able to tune access controls so that threats are minimized.

Remember that MSMQ is one part of a larger computing infrastructure. In defining a security architecture, I like to organize my thinking into four layers: the network, the operating system and attached devices, infrastructure services, and applications. Technologies or techniques are available that enable you to secure each layer, to audit events, and to take active or reactive steps to counter attacks against resources.

Since this chapter is about security, it may be useful to identify features that are not implemented in MSMQ and to discuss any risk associated with them. The computing world is full of security risks, so we'll restrict the discussion to risks associated with application-to-application communication.

Two security features not provided by MSMQ are mutual authentication and nonrepudiation. In *mutual,* or two-way, *authentication,* the sending application is authenticated to the receiving application, and the receiving application is authenticated to the sender.

The nature of asynchronous messaging makes it difficult to implement mutual authentication; the receiver may not be known or on line when a message is sent. Even in on-line applications mutual authentication is rarely required, because the protocol support for mutual authentication adds significant overhead to communications. It's also not clear that mutual authentication is necessary; in any queued messaging environment the queue manager acts as a trusted third-party service provider, authenticating senders and receivers and granting or denying access to queues, based on their identities. In most situations it's more important (or at least sufficient) that queues be set up properly and that the host environment be secured and periodically audited.

Nonrepudiation ensures that senders or receivers cannot repudiate their actions. With nonrepudiation an investor can always be held accountable for a request to buy stocks, and a stock broker cannot refute that he or she received a sell order. In order to implement nonrepudiation, one or more irrefutable pieces of evidence must be provided by the sender or the receiver and stored in order to resolve disputes later.

Nonrepudiation is a relatively new requirement in distributed computing systems. It is not needed when two systems within the same company exchange information and is rarely implemented, under any circumstances.

If needed, nonrepudiation can be implemented by sending and receiving applications; evidence can be sent within the body of messages. However, the evidence or information used to ensure nonrepudiation must be selected carefully. Bad guys can always electronically sniff a network for digitized evidence, such as fingerprints, and reuse it. All sort of attacks are possible if the returns are sufficiently attractive. And if the returns aren't very attractive, implementing nonrepudiation may be more trouble than it is worth.

9.7 Resources and References

Brain, M. 1998. *Win32 System Services,* 2d ed. Upper Saddle River, NJ: Prentice Hall.

Microsoft Corp. 1998. Microsoft Developer Network Platform SDK, Windows Base Services, Security.

Microsoft Message Queue Explorer Administrator's Online Help.

Microsoft Message Queue Server Online Help.

Sutton, S. 1997. *Windows NT Security Guides.* Reading, MA: Addison-Wesley.

Tuvell, W. 1996. Challenges Concerning Public-Key In DCE, Open Software Foundation DCE Request For Comments: 98.0.

10 Chapter

Introduction to Transaction Processing

This chapter is intended for IT managers, application designers, and developers. First, transaction processing is introduced for readers who are unfamiliar with the topic. Then the chapter compares and contrasts on-line distributed transaction processing with transactional queued messaging. Recommendations for when to use each are included at the end of the chapter.

Transaction processing, concerned with such attributes as reliability, performance, and availability, also simplifies application development. When one or more operations are executed under the control of a transaction, the operations either all succeed or all fail together; partial results cannot occur.

Two forms of distributed transaction processing (DTP) are used today. *Transactional queued messaging* is the form that MSMQ supports. A transaction context can be wrapped around one or more messages that are placed in a queue and removed from a queue. The context ensures that message operations either all succeed or all fail. *On-line distributed transaction processing* makes it possible to modify resources distributed throughout the network environment with transactional guarantees. Microsoft Transaction Server supports this form of transaction processing.

Transactional queued messaging and on-line distributed transaction processing offer very different benefits but are also complementary technologies. A transaction can be used to control several messaging operations and updates to data spanning a network environment. When each technology is used properly, it is possible to develop extremely scalable, high-performance distributed applications. However, you have to understand the strengths and weaknesses of each technology.

10.1 Basics of Transaction Processing

A transaction is a unit of work. Each unit of work may be composed of one or more operations, but the transaction as a whole can be treated as a single event. For example, a unit of work called "take an order" could involve these four operations:

- Create an order in an order database.
- Add one or more items to the order.
- Prepare a shipping record within the shipping database.
- Write a billing record in the billing database.

A transaction enables the tasks to be handled as a single unit of work.

A transaction has four important properties, as follows:

- *Atomicity*—All operations that make up a transaction execute completely or not at all.
- *Consistency*—Data moves from one well-defined state to another well-defined state.
- *Isolation*—Changes made within the context of a transaction are not visible to others until the transaction commits.
- *Durability*—Once the transaction completes, results will survive a failure of the TP system.

In the TP world these are known as the *ACID* properties.

10.1.1 Transaction Processing Systems

Today nearly all application developers create transaction processing systems by using services made available by transaction managers and databases.[1] Details differ across TP environments. For example, some TP systems provide presentation services, and others do not. Still, most transaction processing systems function in similar ways.

---

1. In many, or perhaps most, TP applications an "open," or generalized, transaction manager may not have been used. Rather those applications used the transaction manager embedded in the database. Embedded transaction managers are limited by their ability to control transactions across heterogeneous database systems. However, this discussion also applies to those transaction managers.

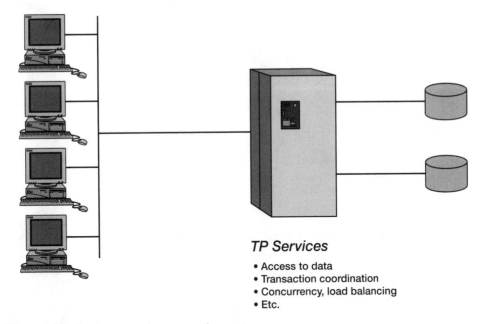

TP Services
- Access to data
- Transaction coordination
- Concurrency, load balancing
- Etc.

Figure 10-1   A transaction processing system

Users and application programs access transactional resources, such as data, through services provided by a TP environment (see Figure 10-1). Some TP services, including access to data and control of the transaction, are visible to application developers. Other services, including load balancing, request prioritization, and transaction coordination, are transparent.

The following pseudocode illustrates how transaction services are accessed in a Microsoft environment.

```
/* Initializations: log onto TP system, open databases */
Result = DtcGetTransactionManager( &TxMgr );

CheckResult( Result ); // Check that connect is successful
Result = TxMgr.BeginTransaction( &Tx ); // Create a transaction
CheckResult( Result ); // Check that the transaction was created

/* Do what is necessary to create an order */
While ( more_items_to_order ) {
    /* Add an item to the order */
    if ( done )
        break;
}
```

```
/* Prepare items for shipping */
/* Bill the customer */


/* Now commit the transaction if all tasks were successful */
if ( Ok ) {
        Result = Tx.Commit( ); // Commit all work
        CheckResult( Result ); // Check results
} else {
        Result = Tx.Abort( ); // Abort all work
        CheckResult( Result ); // Check results
}
```

The application initializes the transaction environment and tells the transaction manager to create a transaction. Next, the application performs one or more operations. Numerous database records may be created, updated, or deleted. Services of other transactional application programs may be invoked. Messages may be sent or received from a queue. Each new database, transactional application program, and queue becomes a participant in the transaction as it is accessed.

When an application is ready to complete its work, it tells the transaction manager to *commit* the transaction. The transaction manager ends the transaction and makes all changes permanent. If the application did not complete its work successfully, it tells the transaction manager to *abort* the transaction. The transaction manager ends the transaction and nullifies all changes. That is, the transaction is *rolled back*. Should the application fail before its work is completed, the transaction manager automatically aborts the transaction, and changes are rolled back.

The transaction manager coordinates transaction completion across all resources and manages recovery activities when failures occur. How databases and other resource managers handle transaction completion and recovery is discussed later in the chapter. The term resource manager is frequently used to describe a facility that manages a specific set of computing resources. In addition to databases, resource managers could include transactional file systems, print queue managers, and communications protocol engines, such as MSMQ.

The engineering of any software system is based on a set of assumptions. The same is true for TP environments. Two common assumptions in transaction processing systems are that most transactions succeed and that transaction system failures are rare. A corollary to these assumptions is that vendors optimize TP environments to commit transactions quickly. Application design should also optimize for successful transaction completion.

10.1.2 Goals of Transaction Processing

Consider what transaction processing could mean to your systems. Bernstein and Newcomer provide the following succinct description of TP system goals: "In summary, transaction processing (TP) systems have to efficiently handle high volumes, avoid errors due to concurrent operation, avoid producing partial results, grow incrementally, avoid downtime, and never lose results" (page 3). Let's dissect this description clause by clause.

- To *"efficiently handle high volume."* Concurrency enables TP systems to handle high volumes. One or more "threads of execution" may execute within a single process. Several identical processes may offer the same TP services on a single host. TP services can also be offered on multiple hosts. Today's transaction processing products implement infrastructure services that enable your company to develop and to deploy applications scalable to thousands or tens of thousands of users and a billion transactions a day.

- To *"avoid errors due to concurrent operation."* TP managers and databases work cooperatively to avoid errors due to concurrent operation. Through their communications protocol and database locking, they enforce the property of isolation between transactions.

- To *"avoid producing partial results."* Transaction processing allows you to group one or more tasks into a single, logical unit of work. All operations that comprise the unit of work succeed or fail together; partial results cannot occur. Applications and databases that are distributed throughout the enterprise and that run on a variety of platforms, ranging from Windows-based desktops to mainframe servers, can share the property of atomicity.

- To *"grow incrementally."* TP systems provide a framework in which new applications and host systems can be added incrementally. New applications can offer new services, and existing applications can be upgraded to take advantage of these services. As the demand for host system resources reaches a saturation point, application services can be moved to more powerful hosts, redeployed to less utilized hosts, or both. Many TP systems are designed to scale to hundreds or thousands of hosts.

- To *"avoid downtime."* Airline reservation systems deliver approximately 99 percent availability—about one and one-half hours a week of scheduled and unscheduled down time. Such levels of availability are possible for a couple of reasons. TP systems provide failure resilience and failover capabilities to application clients. TP systems also support monitoring of applications servers and automatically attempt to restart failed services. When TP systems fail, they are expected to recover quickly. The transaction abstraction aids fast recovery by enabling systems to recover to a clean state.

- To *"never lose results."* Data is always written to the database when a transaction completes. This enables the data to survive a TP system failure. Other technologies can be used to enhance the durability of data. Software disk mirroring, or RAID solutions, eliminates the risk that a system will lose data from a single disk failure.

10.1.3 Complementary TP Technologies—Clustering

For years system vendors have been able to grow systems incrementally and to reduce down time by using machine *clusters*. A cluster is two or more hosts that can share selected resources, primarily disks and network addresses.

When a TP system needs to grow incrementally, a new host is added to the cluster, and resources are redeployed across the hosts that make up the cluster. When a host goes down because of scheduled down time or as a result of a failure, another machine in the cluster can take over the network address, and applications can be restarted. TP services remain available while the failed machine is brought back into service. Applications that use a stateless protocol may experience no impact from the failure or only a brief period of inactivity similar to what occurs when a network gets momentarily saturated.

Microsoft has introduced Cluster Server (MSCS), code named Wolfpack, a host clustering facility for Windows NT. Through MSCS a system administrator can define and implement failover strategies for Microsoft Message Queue, Transaction Server, SQL Server, and the application programs that use them. Companies that deploy their mission-critical applications on Windows NT should consider using MSCS to implement a clustered computing environment.

10.2 The ACID Properties

Now let us examine the ACID properties more closely. As we discuss each property, we'll also consider the developer's role in ensuring the property.

10.2.1 Atomicity

The property of atomicity implies that a set of operations can be structured to all succeed or all fail. Partial results can be highly detrimental in many programs, causing data to become inconsistent. Fixing such problems can be very costly to companies. Atomicity ensures that partial results do not occur.

Atomicity enables application behavior to mimic business events and makes developing complex applications much simpler to program. Analogies to atomic events abound in real life. An automobile retailer and a buyer cannot do business unless both agree to a fair price for a car. Banks will not issue funds from an account unless a customer identifies himself or herself and the exchange is properly documented. In other words, success is achieved only at the end of a series of steps.

Let's consider a simple example to see how atomicity simplifies application programming. We'll refine the order entry example from earlier in the chapter. Suppose that you need to develop a program so that a bookstore can order books for its customers. The design includes several steps.

1. An order record is created in the order database.

2. A record from the customer database is accessed (and perhaps updated), or a new record is created.[2]

3. Author, title, publisher, and pricing information is recorded for one or more books in the order database.

4. The total cost of the order is calculated and recorded in the order database.

5. An up-front deposit is collected by the bookstore personnel and recorded in the accounting and the order databases.

6. An order number is assigned, and the order process completes.

With a transaction, if an error or a problem is encountered that would prevent full completion of the order entry process, the application can simply call the transaction manager to abort the routine and to perform incidental processing to clean up. Thus it might free data structures and return to the initial order entry screen. The transaction manager and the databases handle the rollback of data to its original state. Records created as part of the order are purged automatically.

A programmer who did not have transactional guarantees would need to develop logic to reverse, or roll back, each operation. Programming the rollback of several complex operations can involve substantial costs. A transaction reduces costs by simplifying programming.

Designers and developers also need to understand the limitations of atomicity. Databases and some file systems can participate in a transaction, but many other computing resources do not, including graphical user interface technologies, printers, fax machines, standard file systems, and humans!

How should these nontransactional resources be handled? Some designers have taken the approach of updating nontransactional computing resources first. If an error occurs while updating the nontransactional computing resources, the transaction is aborted. Like a lot of designs, this works fine until a failure occurs. Consider the

---

2. A separate transaction might be used to update the customer's record.

example of ordering books at a bookstore. Before committing the transaction, the order entry system might display the order number to a clerk. The clerk will give the order number to the customer and will collect a deposit for the books.

If the program fails after the customer's money is accepted and before transactional updates are committed, no record of the order will appear in any database. This is the situation pictured in Figure 10-2. If our assumption holds that transaction system failures are rare, the bookstore is unlikely to have many irate customers. However, a few customers will have paid their money and will expect their books to be ordered. Those customers won't be happy.

An alternative is to commit the transaction first and to then update nontransactional computing resources. Suppose that the transaction commits but that a network failure occurs before nontransactional resources (including the clerk's screen, in this case) are updated. Books will be ordered, and an accounting record for the deposit is entered in the accounting database. However, the clerk may not collect the deposit, because the program appears to have failed. Or the clerk may reenter the order. Re-entering the order causes books to be ordered twice and inserts duplicate collection records in the accounting database. For most bookstores it may not be a problem if a book is ordered twice. However, the accounting database will contain invalid records. Manual intervention will be needed to clear invalid records from the database.

Nontransactional computing resources can be accommodated if the TP programs log transaction information during processing. At a minimum the application should log information that is needed to fix problems manually. In sophisticated programs you would log the order number, issue the number to the screen, commit the transaction, and validate that the order made it into the system.

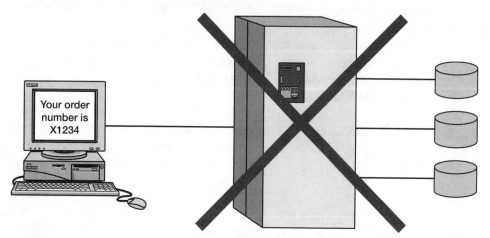

Problem: The order results are printed before the transaction completes. A failure wipes out any record of the order.

Your order number is X1234

Figure 10-2   A failure occurring after the order number is printed

Altering the system design slightly can also help eliminate problems. The system could allow a clerk to query for order numbers in the order database and to fix problems as they occur.

Programmer Responsibilities

During application processing, the programmer needs to implement the processing logic that addresses a business problem. This logic includes informing the transaction manager to create a transaction, detect errors, and signal transaction completion by calling a commit or an abort function.

10.2.2 Consistency

Perhaps no ACID property is more important than consistency, because data, whether it is kept on note cards or as records in a database, is so vital to the functioning of a successful enterprise. Manufacturing and financial companies make huge investment decisions on the basis of data represented as snapshots or trends. Regulatory agencies levy heavy fines on utilities and telecommunications companies that do not maintain accurate data. In the extreme licenses may be revoked and companies may be shut down if their record keeping is found to be unsatisfactory. Enormous sums of money are spent yearly by companies seeking to keep data accurate and consistent.

For databases, consistency is satisfied when it applies integrity constraints. These mechanisms offer a limited form of consistency that applies only to records within the database. The transaction manager extends this notion of consistency across one or more cooperating databases. However, the old adage "garbage in, garbage out" applies here. Primary responsibility for ensuring data consistency rests with data modelers and programmers.

Programmer Responsibilities

A data-oriented definition of consistency is required before one can achieve consistency through transaction processing. Many organizations employ data modelers who are responsible for defining and maintaining a logically consistent data model across a set of systems. Their job is to define the set of database tables, keys, integrity constraints, and predicates that apply to data processing within the organization. In addition, database administrators are responsible for creating databases, configuring integrity constraints, and applying predicates during processing.

10.2.3 Isolation

There are two ways of looking at the property of isolation. First, changes made within the scope of a transaction are not visible outside the transaction until they are committed. Suppose that you are a bookstore manager who wishes to monitor daily cash receipts, using the accounting database. As you calculate current cash receipts, I initiate a large book order and offer a deposit of $100. If your program returns before my book order transaction commits, your daily cash receipts total will not reflect the $100 I tendered toward the purchase of books. My order record has been allocated in the database, but it has not been placed in the index of records that your program is reading.

A second way to look at the property of isolation is in terms of serialization. A set of transactions is considered isolated if the effect of running them is as if they were running one at a time.

Isolation is important to data consistency. If changes were visible outside a transaction, most TP systems would achieve data consistency only when transaction processing has stopped, if at all.

Programmer Responsibilities

No additional programming is required by programmers to satisfy the property of isolation. They need only to inform the transaction manager when to create a transaction, detect errors, and signal transaction completion by calling a commit or an abort function.

10.2.4 Durability

This last property is straightforward. Durability means that updates, once committed, will survive a TP system failure. To satisfy this property, the TP system almost always records changes to data on disk storage.

Programmer Responsibilities

No additional programming is required by programmers to satisfy the property of durability. They need only to inform the transaction manager when to create a transaction, detect errors, and signal transaction completion by calling a commit or an abort function.

Some readers may find this property uninteresting, but it is vital to many companies. For insurance companies and airlines, for example, contractual arrangements may be associated with some transactions. Utilities and telecommunications companies can suffer financial penalties for loss of data.

10.3 Distributed Transaction Processing

So far we've been talking about transactions very generally and have assumed that there is an application, a transaction manager, and a database. But this simplistic model won't scale for larger corporations. Most companies have multiple databases.

How can two or more databases be updated within a transaction? What if these databases are distributed across a network? What complications are thereby introduced?

Several complications are introduced with multiple databases. First, one database may be able to commit updates but another cannot. Second, a database manager can fail during the transaction. Additional points of failure are introduced when data is distributed across a network. A host may fail, the network may go down or introduce unacceptable latencies, and communications processes can fail.

Most corporations don't have the ability to place all data in a single database. First, this strategy doesn't scale. Every computer has a maximum number of disk drives that can be connected to it, systems can process a finite amount of file accesses in an interval of time, and databases have upper limits on the amount of data they can manage. Second, most corporations need to live with legacy decisions. If a company did not place all data in a single database when it began using information technology, it's unlikely to consolidate data into a single database later. Consequently distributed databases are a reality.

The same arguments apply to applications. Frequently companies strive to reuse existing applications distributed across a network. Thus distribution of data and applications is a reality to almost all users of information technologies.

Generally speaking, two complementary forms of distributed transaction processing can be used to manage resources distributed across an enterprise: on-line distributed transaction processing and transactional queued messaging. Microsoft Transaction Server (MTS) supports on-line distributed transaction processing. MSMQ provides transactional (and nontransactional) queued messaging. The rest of this chapter covers a range of DTP issues, some beyond the scope of MSMQ, to help application designers determine how and when to use MSMQ with MTS.[3]

---

3. Keep in mind that not all high-performance applications require full transactional properties. MSMQ also supports recoverable messages, a powerful but weaker form of messaging than transactional messaging. See Chapter 8 for more on this topic.

10.3.1 On-Line Distributed Transactions

On-line distributed transaction processing lessens the complications associated with program failures, network latency, and resource exhaustion. In this model applications, transaction managers, and databases can be distributed across a network. Transaction managers ensure that applications and databases cooperatively deliver information-processing services with the same transactional guarantees of a single-system TP environment. A distributed transaction processing system is pictured in Figure 10-3.

The on-line model makes a key assumption, namely, that all participants are ready and able to work on behalf of the transaction. If one application or database is inaccessible due to failure or network latency, no work can be performed. No progress can be made.

A client application asks the transaction manager to start a transaction. Then the client can update resources locally or remotely. As each new database is accessed, it

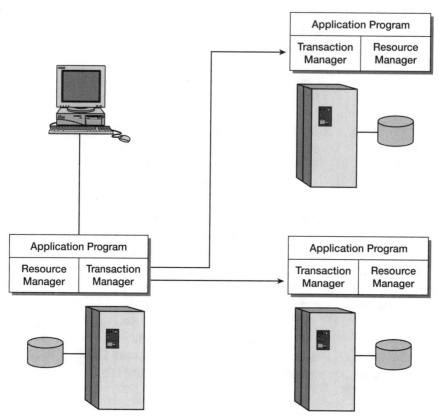

Figure 10-3 An on-line distributed transaction processing system

becomes a participant in the transaction. If the client application requests the services of remote transactional application programs, those services are invoked, using communications facilities provided by or registered with the transaction manager. Transaction managers on the remote systems join the transaction and coordinate the activities of resource managers accessed by its transactional applications. The local and remote transaction managers cooperate to ensure that ACID properties span all systems. When the client application completes its work, it asks the local transaction manager to commit or to abort the transaction. The transaction manager interacts with local resource managers to commit or to abort updates to local resources. An indication to commit or to abort work is also communicated to remote transaction managers that act as proxies for the local transaction manager on remote systems.

Transactional guarantees are extended to a distributed environment by using a two-phase commit (2PC) protocol. In the next section we'll look at how the 2PC protocol works.

10.3.2 Two-Phase Commit

So far we've talked about transactions as if they happen "automagically." How is it that TP environments implement transactions?

Most TP managers, working in cooperation with databases, implement transactions by using a two-phase commit protocol. It's useful to understand how the protocol works. As you will see, it is a little complex, but do not despair. When an application is ready to complete work, all it needs to do is tell its local transaction manager to commit or to abort the transaction. The transaction managers and the resource managers hide the 2PC complexity from developers.

10.3.2.1 Aborting a Transaction

Let's begin with the simple case. If the application doesn't want to commit a transaction, it calls a transaction abort function supplied by the transaction manager. The local transaction manager will send a message to all resource managers, informing them to abort the transaction. The resource managers discard updates, release locks, and acknowledge the abort.

10.3.2.2 Committing a Transaction

If the application wishes to commit its changes, the transaction manager initiates a two-phase commit process with resource managers that are transaction participants. The initial phase of the two-phase commit protocol is pictured in Figure 10-4. In this phase the transaction manager at the top of the illustration initiates the two-phase commit protocol. Responsible for coordinating the *global transaction,* the transaction

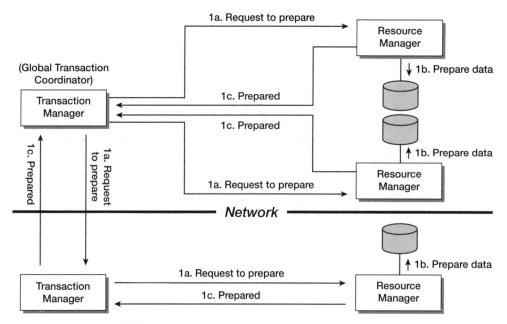

Figure 10-4 Phase 1 of the two-phase commit protocol

manager requests that each local resource manager and remote transaction manager involved in the transaction prepare to commit the transaction.

Each resource manager prepares to commit the transaction. In order to support durability, a resource manager writes to disk the old and new versions of data it manages so that it can recover even if the system fails. If a resource manager can prepare successfully, it sends the transaction manager a message indicating that it is prepared. If a resource manager cannot prepare successfully for any reason, it returns a transaction abort indication. When a remote transaction manager is involved in the transaction, it forwards the prepare-to-commit request to its local resource managers involved in the transaction and returns a consolidated response indicating whether resources were prepared.

If any participants in the transaction are unable to prepare updates to be committed, the transaction manager marks the transaction as aborted and sends an abort indication to local resource managers and remote transaction managers. Each resource manager purges changes and deallocates resources. If all participants are able to prepare updates to be committed, the transaction is marked as committed, and the second phase of the 2PC protocol is executed.

In the second phase of the 2PC protocol (Figure 10-5) the transaction manager tells each resource manager and remote transaction manager to commit changes. Each resource manager updates its data in the database and returns a positive

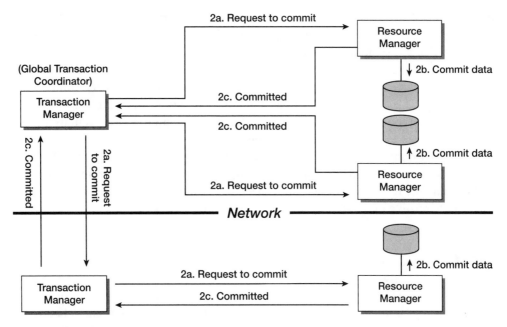

Figure 10-5 Phase 2 of the two-phase commit protocol

acknowledgment. Remote transaction managers forward the commit indication on to resource managers under their direct control. Acknowledgments flow from the remote resource managers to the remote transaction manager and then on to the global transaction manager.

10.3.2.3 Handling Failures

Between the first and second phases of the 2PC protocol, a resource manager waits until it gets an indication from a transaction manager to commit or to abort. The resource manager does not know whether the transaction committed or aborted until it receives an indication. The resource manager is said to be *in doubt* about the outcome of the transaction between these phases. To sustain the property of isolation, the resource manager continues to hold locks on the data modified by the transaction.

What if a resource manager fails while the transaction is in doubt? Before the resource manager can begin processing transactions again, its state must reflect all of the effects of committed transactions and none of the effects of aborted transactions. After the resource manager restarts, it must resolve all transactions in doubt. All transactions that were not prepared prior to the failure are aborted. If a transaction was committed but resources were not updated prior to the failure, resources are updated during the restart. The resource manager will ask its local transaction manager about the outcome of any in-doubt transactions. The transaction manager indicates the outcome of each in-doubt transaction to the resource manager, and the resource manager processes that information accordingly.

Suppose that a computer fails and then restarts. This type of failure impacts the host's resource managers and transaction manager. What happens when a resource manager asks the transaction manager about in-doubt transactions? The transaction manager on that computer must determine the outcome of all in-doubt transactions. To do this it reviews its log file to determine the outcome of transactions it coordinated.

Transactions initiated from other systems can't be resolved without help. Associated with each *incoming transaction* is a transaction manager that coordinates the transaction. The restarted transaction manager will query a coordinating transaction manager to resolve the status of each incoming in-doubt transaction.

10.3.3 Nested Transactions

We've seen that a transactional application, program A, can begin a transaction and can call another transactional application, program B. Can program B call other transactional applications, programs C and D, within the scope of program A's transaction? Yes, at least in most transaction processing environments. A *nested* transaction (Figure 10-6) is one begun within the scope of another transaction. In the case of programs A, B, C, and D the transaction initiated by program A is a *parent* transaction to the *child* (nested) transaction started by program B.

Nested transactions fit perfectly into structured and object-oriented methodologies, encouraging the design and development of smaller, well-defined units of computation that can be invoked from other transactional programs as needed. Nested transactions are critical to the development of distributed, transactional, component-based systems.

Two kinds of nested transactions exist: *subtransactions* and *nested top-level transactions*. Most TP environments support subtransactions, whereby the parent and the child share the same transaction context. Program B may have some code that is bracketed by transaction begin, commit, and abort calls. As a subtransaction, program B will still execute within the scope of the parent transaction begun by program A. This means that if program B commits but the parent transaction aborts, the effects of both transactions are rolled back. On the other hand, the parent transaction can commit or abort its transaction even if the subtransaction in program B aborted.

If the transaction started by program B is a nested top-level transaction, it executes outside the scope of its parent transaction and can commit or abort independently. Nested top-level transactions are not widely supported in TP environments. Microsoft's Distributed Transaction Coordinator supports both kinds of nested transactions.

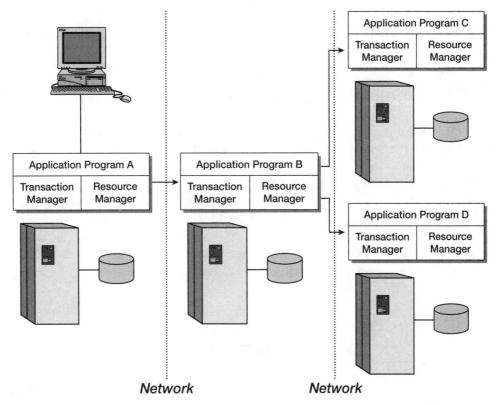

Figure 10-6 Nested transactions

10.3.4 Overhead

On-line distributed transaction processing adds overhead to processing in two ways. The two-phase commit protocol is a heavyweight. Two sets of messages need to be sent in order to commit a transaction. The transaction managers and the resource managers must log both resource changes and state changes, for example, whether the transaction was prepared. Also, locks cannot be immediately released when the application is finished working; they need to be held through the second phase of the commit protocol. Although the overhead of a two-phase commit is occasionally necessary, it's important to look for ways to minimize its impact in high-performance, distributed applications.

On-line distributed transaction processing also adds wait states to application processing. When it sends a request to program B, program A usually waits for a reply before proceeding with other work. While waiting for a reply from program B, program A consumes memory or swap space, and database records remain locked.

One way to minimize the dollar cost of transactions is to eliminate as much re-source contention as possible. How can a developer do this? We look at that topic next.

10.4 Transactional Queued Messaging

The semantics of queued messaging change slightly when a message is sent or received within a transaction. Suppose that an application, a sender, wants to get some information from another application and that transactional queued messaging is used. The interactions among a sender, a receiver, and a queue manager are illustrated in Figure 10-7(a). The three transactions that send a request, process the request and create a response, and retrieve the response are illustrated.

The sender will locate and open Queue A if it is not open already. Then the sender creates a transaction to ensure that the message is delivered without duplication. Next, the sender places a message on the queue and commits the transaction.

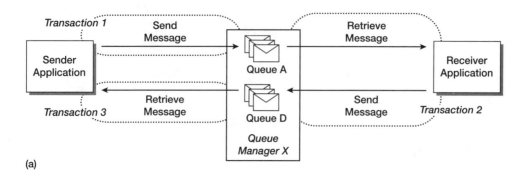

(a)

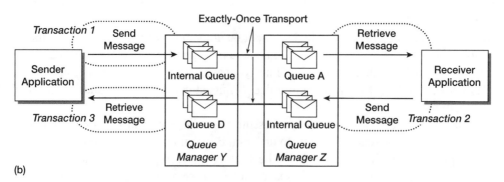

(b)

Figure 10-7 (a) Transactional queued messaging; (b) with remote queues

When it is ready to receive the message, the receiver locates and opens Queue A if it is not open already. Then the receiver may create a transaction and remove messages off the queue and process the transaction. Since the message is a request for information, the receiver must prepare a response. Then the receiver locates and opens the response queue, Queue D, if it is not open already. The transaction is committed to guarantee that the request was removed from Queue A, and the response is sent to Queue D.

When it is ready to receive the response, the sender opens Queue D if it is not open already. Then the sender removes the message as part of another transaction.

With MSMQ all transactional operations are to local queues. But how, then, can an application send a message to a remote queue?

The answer is that MSMQ also implements an *exactly-once transport* protocol. When a transactional message is sent to Queue A, the transaction controls whether the message is placed on an internal queue on the local system. Once the transaction commits, MSMQ is free to forward the message to Queue A, using its exactly-once transport protocol. At the destination machine another local transaction is executed to read the message and to send a response. Then the response is forwarded to Queue D by the exactly-once transport protocol. When the response is read from Queue D, a third local transaction is executed. These interactions are illustrated in Figure 10-7(b).

Two comments relating to performance should be mentioned. Since a transaction does not span the network, an application is blocked for a very short period as a transactional send or receive is committed. Second, writing a message to a queue or removing a message from a queue is far less complicated than inserting or removing several records from tables in a relational database. Thus MSMQ transactions are fairly lightweight.

The request-response scenario described here is but one of many interactions that are possible by using transactional queued messaging. For example, it is possible to use transactions and messages to emit transactional asynchronous events between applications. The transaction guarantees message delivery without duplicates. Your applications retain all the benefits of ordinary queued messaging, including loose coupling, asynchronous processing, message reliability, and security.

Transactional queued messaging also makes it possible to coordinate a set of MSMQ operations. Indeed one or more MSMQ operations can be coordinated with updates to a database and interactions with transactional applications.

10.4.1 Error Handling

A variety of failures can occur in the queued messaging model. Queue managers can exit while a sender is placing a message on a queue, and receivers can fail while retrieving a message from a queue. Communications failures can occur during the sender or receiver operations. These scenarios add error-handling complexity.

Error handling is even more difficult if, for example, a sender needs to place two messages on two separate queues or if a receiver needs to remove two messages from two separate queues. If the sender places the first message on queue 1 and then queue 2 fails, what should the sender do? Ideally it would remove message 1 from its queue, but a receiver might have removed the message from the queue first!

The atomic property of transactions is useful in queued messaging. In this model a transaction spans one or more queue operations. An application will ask a transaction manager to begin a transaction, place one or more messages on one or more queues, remove one or more messages from one or more queues, and tell the transaction manager to commit or to abort the transaction. If the transaction is committed, all messages placed on queues remain there, and all messages read from queues are permanently removed. If the transaction is aborted, no new messages are placed on queues, and all received messages remain on their queues.

Under a transaction a queue manager behaves much like a resource manager in on-line transaction processing. The queue manager commits or aborts changes at the direction of a transaction manager. Also, multiple senders and receivers can be performing operations on the same queue or on separate queues concurrently.

10.4.2 Compensating Transactions

Committed transactions cannot be aborted. Yet many times in information systems, as in life, it may be necessary to reverse previous work. This is the purpose of a *compensating transaction*. Well-designed TP systems implement compensating transactions so that simple or common tasks can be undone.

It may appear simple to develop a transaction that reverses some previous work. If a record is created in a database as part of transaction A, its compensating transaction needs only to delete the record. In this case developing a compensating transaction is simple. Unfortunately things get complicated quickly.

What if transaction A is just the first step in a series of transactions that will occur? Consider the order entry system implemented using transactional queued messaging. Perhaps the order entry system converts an order into several request messages that are sent to downstream systems, indicating to remove items from inventory and to prepare them for shipping. Then the system determines that it cannot complete the order process. It may be possible to design and to develop compensating transactions that cancel requests that are pending. But how would you handle items that are on their way to shipping?

The direct effect of a transaction is usually simple and predictable. The secondary effects of a transaction are usually more difficult to predict and to reverse. When an item is removed from inventory, that event may trigger an inventory control transaction to replenish the current stock of items. Or a manager may observe a run on this item and adjust marketing plans for the item. How does the transaction programmer reverse these actions?

In the real world not all effects of a transaction can be reversed through automation. It's impractical or impossible to design a perfect or comprehensive compensating transaction. Some transactions will need to be reversed manually (repopulating inventory with recently ordered items), whereas others may be ignored (the inventory was going to need replenishing sooner or later).

10.4.3 Overhead

The flexibility and the power of queued messaging don't come for free. Figure 10-8 illustrates some of the overhead costs of on-line distributed transaction processing and transactional queued messaging. In many, though not all, on-line transaction processing environments a client and a server component communicate directly with each other when making a request and returning a response. This operation involves two sends and two receives, although the TP environment may hide some or all send and receive operations.

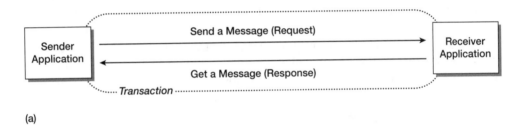

(a)

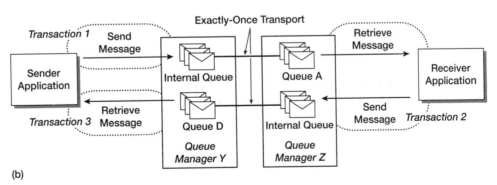

(b)

Figure 10-8 Communications and transaction overhead for (a) on-line DTP and (b) transaction queued messaging

When a message is sent and a response is returned using queued messaging, both the sender and the receiver do a send and a receive from a queue. Each send and receive operation involves an interaction with the queue manager on the local machine. Since communication with the queue manager uses shared memory, this element of queued messaging overhead is not substantial.

Transactions add additional overhead to on-line and queued messaging applications. A distributed on-line transaction spans the network, and several machines may participate in the transaction. As we saw previously, two additional round-trips to each machine are needed when committing an on-line distributed transaction. In addition, system resources are consumed throughout the transaction. In other words, a distributed transaction between one client and one server involves substantial overhead. That overhead grows as more participants are added to the transaction, especially if the participants are part of nested transactions.

In transactional queued messaging three lightweight transactions are executed if a message is sent and a response is returned. When an MSMQ internal transaction is executed, the transactional overhead is optimized and is much less expensive than an external transaction. However, neither form of transaction spans the network; the transaction includes only local participants. In addition, system overhead is incurred because MSMQ uses an exactly-once transport to send messages across the network.

Does an on-line distributed transaction incur more overhead than transactional queued messages? In general transactional queued messages incur less overhead, but this depends in part on how frequently compensating transactions need to be executed. What is clear is that on-line distributed transactions are more costly to applications. Applications incur most costs of an on-line distributed transaction. In addition to being blocked from the time a request is sent across the network until a response is received, applications may be blocked while the transaction is committed.

The overhead of transactional queued messaging is distributed between the application and the system. The two share the cost of three lightweight transactions. Applications don't block after sending a message and may not block when receiving a message. The system incurs the cost of all communications across a network.

10.5   When to Use On-Line or Queued Transactions

On-line distributed transaction processing and transactional queued messaging are complementary ways of constructing transaction processing systems. A catalog business might construct an order entry system that records orders in a database, queues messages to one or more order processing systems, and queues a message to the billing system. The database update and queuing of messages to separate systems can be controlled through a transaction.

Downstream systems can use the same processing approach. They may remove a message from a queue, update resources distributed across the network, place a response message on a queue, and send one or more new messages within a single transaction.

Many companies use queued messaging as the communications backbone that integrates transaction processing systems. Each system may implement a set of tasks that are tied together into a *work flow,* using messaging. When designing a transaction processing system, it is very important to understand the respective strengths and weaknesses of on-line transaction processing and queued messaging so that you can use each effectively. See Figure 10-9.

10.5.1 Strengths and Weaknesses of On-Line Distributed Transactions

On-line distributed TP is required when resources spanning several systems must be updated within a single transaction. Under a single transaction your applications incur no threat that data will be left in an inconsistent state. Thus error handling is

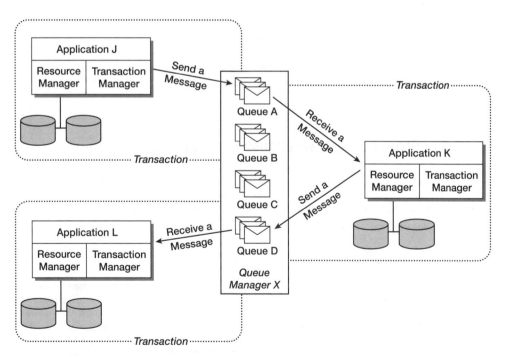

Figure 10-9 Transactional queued messaging with on-line distributed TP

simplified: When the transaction fails, the whole transaction fails. The programmer must handle the failure, but that effort is small in comparison with the effort to handle partial failures spanning multiple systems.

But on-line distributed transactions also have several weaknesses.

- Clients and servers must be on line in order for transaction processing to be performed. System availability is determined by the server. As more and more servers are integrated into a distributed transaction processing system, system availability can only degrade.

- Two-phase commit is a heavyweight protocol, and its weight increases with distribution and nesting of subtransactions.

- Most on-line transaction processing systems do not support prioritization of requests. Client requests are usually processed on a first-come, first-served basis.

- Load balancing is difficult to achieve. Some TP environments provide load balancing across a set of server processes on a host. Others provide only the raw mechanisms for selecting one server from a set of random servers. The raw mechanisms can exacerbate system performance. A set of clients can and probably will randomly select the same server at the same time during processing. In order to consistently balance requests across a set of servers, you cannot rely on randomness; requests need to be forwarded to servers based on information about their current loads.

In general, the lack of prioritization and load balancing in many on-line distributed transaction processing environments means that few engineers know how to tune these systems.

10.5.2 Strengths and Weaknesses of Queued Messaging

The use of queued messaging has several advantages.

- Senders and receivers need not be on line at the same time under queued messaging, because they interact through a queue manager.[4]

---

4. One might be tempted to argue that using queued messaging merely transfers availability requirements from the application to a queue manager: The queue manager must be available when a sender wants to queue a message or a receiver wants to process a message. Like a lot of things, it depends on several factors, such as whether the queue manager is remote and how it is used. For example, if a queue manager is on a remote host and is unavailable when a message needs to be sent, it can be queued on a server or independent client system for transmission to the destination queue once the queue manager becomes available. The fact that the remote queue manager is down has no impact on the sending program.

- Message processing is highly flexible. It is possible to assign priorities to messages as a way of determining the order in which they are processed. Other strategies are also possible, such as processing messages based on their time-to-live.

- Load balancing is trivial when queued messaging is used. When it is ready to process a message, a receiver removes one from the queue. In other words, the load is automatically balanced across all receivers.

With the ability to prioritize messages and to balance loads across receivers and queue managers, the tuning of queued messaging environments is better understood by engineers. A queue manager can be tuned much like a database. Additional disk storage, memory, or processors can be added to a host to reduce resource contention and boost performance.

Queued messaging is not without weaknesses, however.

- It is impossible to update resources spanning several systems in a single transaction without incorporating on-line distributed TP into the basic design.

- Transactional queued messaging incurs three transactions; on-line distributed TP incurs one transaction.

10.6   Conclusions and Recommendations

Our introduction to transaction processing can be summarized with the following statements.

- Transactions simplify error handling but add overhead to application processing.

- Use on-line distributed transactions *only* when two or more operations must succeed or fail together. Designers will opt to use distributed transactions to achieve atomicity and consistency. Your business-processing and data models should define the need for atomicity and consistency, but designers can often reformulate problems so that they do not require distributed transactions. For example, it may be possible to eliminate or to minimize the need for distributed transactions by designing processing models that take advantage of *pending states*.

- Minimize the nesting and frequency of distributed transactions as throughput requirements increase. Use queued messaging when processing needs to scale to high volumes of requests. Administrators will find it much easier to scale systems through the combined use of message priorities and load balancing across receivers and queue managers.

- Use queued messaging when asynchronous or event-driven processing is possible. Servers have historically used an event-driven computing model. An incoming request is an event to servers. With the advent of graphical front-end technologies, client applications are frequently structured for processing events. As a result queued messaging technologies fit nicely into their processing models.

    On-line distributed transactions do not fit an event-driven model as well. Distributed transactions can introduce potentially long wait states while a server is performing a request. Developers may be required to perform extra programming, using threads to minimize the impact of long wait states on graphical front ends.

- When evaluating transaction processing system designs, consider the complexity of developing compensating transactions as criteria to be weighed along with simplicity of implementation, performance, availability, and "manageability."

10.7   Resources and References

Bernstein, P. A., and E. Newcomer. 1997. *Principles of Transaction Processing.* San Francisco: Morgan Kaufmann.

Gray, J. N., and A. Reuter. 1992. *Transaction Processing: Concepts and Techniques.* San Francisco: Morgan Kaufmann.

Jennings, R., S. Gray, and R. Lievano, 1997. *Microsoft Transaction Server 2.0.* Indianapolis, IN: SAMS Publishing.

Sessions, R. 1998. *COM and DCOM: Microsoft's Vision for Distributed Objects.* New York: Wiley.

Umar, A. 1997. *Object-Oriented Client/Server Internet Environments.* Upper Saddle River, NJ: Prentice Hall.

X/Open. 1991. *X/Open CAE Specification: Distributed Transaction Processing: The XA Specification.* Cambridge, MA: X/Open.

———. 1996. *X/Open Guide: Distributed Transaction Processing: Reference Model, Version 3.* Cambridge, MA: X/Open.

11
Chapter

Implementing Transactions and Assessing Performance

This chapter, intended primarily for developers, discusses how to use MSMQ and other Microsoft transaction processing facilities. The programming solutions in the chapter build on the Visual Basic example developed in Chapter 4 and the MSMQ API example of Chapter 5. Managers may want to read the introductory paragraphs of each major section and the last section, on performance.

In Chapter 10 we reviewed several design topics in transaction processing. Now let's look at implementing applications that use the transactional support that MSMQ provides. For all the power that a transaction gives you, MSMQ makes transaction processing very easy!

Aside from enabling MSMQ operations to be coordinated with updates to other resource managers, using transactions delivers the following three benefits or features:

- *Exactly-once semantics.* If a message is sent within a transaction, you are guaranteed that no duplicates are received. Without a transaction, there is a risk that a message will be duplicated during transmission. MSMQ checks only for duplication of transactional messages.

- *Guaranteed delivery.* Transactions ensure that a message is delivered unless it expires. Nontransactional messages can be lost during transmission.

- *Ordered delivery.* When several messages are sent within a single transaction, they are guaranteed to arrive at the target queue in order. In fact, transactions within a host system are also ordered.

MSMQ provides the following ways to send or to receive messages within transactions:

- *DTC transactions.* Microsoft's Distributed Transaction Coordinator is a general-purpose distributed transaction manager. DTC transactions enable you to commit changes to resources managed by MSMQ, SQL Server, and other resource managers.

- *MTS transactions.* Microsoft Transaction Server is an object-oriented, distributed transaction process environment; DTC provides the transaction management. MTS facilitates remote creation and invocation of objects distributed across a network. MTS also implements an implicit transaction model: The application does not have to explicitly commit or abort a transaction.

- *XA transactions.* Through DTC, MSMQ can participate in transactions initiated from a foreign transaction processing environment. XA is a system-level interface that will be discussed later in this chapter.

DTC, MTS, and XA transactions are also called *external transactions;* they are coordinated outside MSMQ.

MSMQ itself can coordinate transactions; these *internal transactions* can occur in two types of situations.

- *When MSMQ is the only resource manager.* Internal transactions can be used to send and receive one or more messages. These transactions are optimized specifically for MSMQ.

- *For sending a single message.* A program can send a single transactional message without having to explicitly create a transaction or call a commit or an abort function.

For all five ways of sending or receiving messages, keep these constraints in mind.

- A transactional message does not reside in a queue until the transaction commits. You cannot be sent a message and then try to receive it within the same transaction.

- When using a transaction, a message must be sent to a transactional queue; messages cannot be delivered otherwise. However, it is possible to retrieve a message from a transactional queue without a transaction.

- Transactional messages can be sent to local or to remote queues.

- If a message is received within a transaction, the queue must be on the local machine. Applications cannot receive messages from remote queues within a transaction.

- Applications can receive messages from a remote transactional queue if the receive operation is not part of a transaction.

- Queues are designated as either transactional or nontransactional at creation time, and this property cannot be changed later.

11.1 Basics of Transactional Messaging

MSMQ applications can supply an optional transactional parameter when sending or receiving messages. The parameter describes the transactional property that applies to the operation. A transaction object or one of four constants may be passed as the parameter.

The four constants are as follows:

- `MQ_MTS_TRANSACTION`. The call is part of the current MTS transaction.
- `MQ_NO_TRANSACTION`. The call is not part of a transaction.
- `MQ_SINGLE_MESSAGE`. A single transactional message is to be sent.
- `MQ_XA_TRANSACTION`. The call is part of an externally coordinated, XA-compliant transaction.

As an alternative to these constants, a transaction object can be passed with the send or the receive call.

In the following sections we'll show how to create transaction objects. We'll also explain how to use the transaction objects and constants when sending and receiving messages.

11.2 External Transactions

An external transaction is coordinated by Microsoft's DTC, a general-purpose transaction manager that enables MSMQ, MTS, and SQL Server operations to share an "all-or-nothing" quality. The operations all succeed, or all changes are rolled back. The relationship among DTC, MSMQ, SQL Server, and MTS is illustrated in Figure 2-2 and described in detail in Section 2.4.2.1.

External transactions are not optimized for a particular kind of resource manager. As a result, they are slower than internal transactions, which are highly optimized for MSMQ.

11.2.1 DTC Transactions

The DTC interface follows an explicit transaction model: The application explicitly creates a transaction and either commits or aborts it. DTC transactions can be used with COM components and the MSMQ API.

11.2.1.1 Using COM Components

An MSMQCoordinatedTransactionDispenser component is used to create an external transaction. As a transaction dispenser, this component will dispense transactions to an MSMQ application, much as a PEZ dispenser supplies candy to children of all ages. You do not need to consume the first transaction before getting another. It is possible to hold several transactions at once.

An MSMQTransaction component is returned by the BeginTransaction method of an MSMQCoordinatedTransactionDispenser component. An MSMQTransaction component represents a transaction and can be used when sending or receiving transactional messages. Each instance of an MSMQTransaction component in a program represents a separate external transaction.

The following code shows how to create an external DTC transaction and receive a message.

```
Private Sub Receive()
    Dim Msg As MSMQMessage
    Dim openETQ As MSMQQueue
    Dim cTxnDisp As New MSMQCoordinatedTransactionDispenser
    Dim extTxn As MSMQTransaction

    ' Locate the desired transactional queue - as demonstrated in Ch 4.
    ' Open the queue - openETQ represents the open queue

    ' Create internal transaction
    Set extTxn = ctxnDisp.BeginTransaction

    ' Receiving a message
    Set Msg = openETQ.Receive(ReceiveTimeout:=500, Transaction:= extTxn)
    If Not Msg Is Nothing Then
        ' Process the message contents::
        ' Since we are using an external transaction, there could be other
        ' resource managers participating in the transactions, e.g., SQL
        ' Server
```

```
      ' If a processing error occurs, call extTxn.Abort - otherwise…
      extTxn.Commit
      StatusText.Text = "Receive_Click :: success :: transaction committed"
   Else
      extTxn.Abort
      StatusText.Text = "Receive_Click :: failure :: transaction aborted"
   End If
   openETQ.Close
Exit Sub
```

Two design notes are worth mentioning.

- In the preceding example the message is processed before the transaction is committed. What if we had reversed the order? Suppose that we retrieve the message, commit the transaction, and then process the message. If we update a database as part of message processing, those transactional resource managers do not share the same transaction as MSMQ. If a failure occurred after committing the MSMQ receive and before processing the message, the message would be lost, and other transactional operations might not be committed. In other words, you have lost all the benefits of an external transaction!

- Let's look at this problem from another angle. If you are going to process the message within an external transaction, the time to process the message shouldn't be extremely long, such as hours or days. You would prefer processing to be shorter. If message processing is a protracted task, consider copying the message to a local database in one external transaction. Then process the message as part of a separate database transaction.

Suppose that you are in a transaction but want to receive a message from a transactional queue outside that transaction. You could call the `MSMQMessage.Receive` method, using the `MQ_NO_TRANSACTION` constant.

```
Set Msg = openETQ.Receive(Transaction:= MQ_NO_TRANSACTION)
```

If you want to receive the message as part of another transaction, you will need to create a second `MSMQTransaction` component and receive the message with it.

To send a message using a transaction created by an `MSMQTransactionDispenser` component, you need to open the queue with `MQ_SEND_ACCESS` access and to send the message as follows:

```
Msg.Send( Transaction := extTxn )
```

Although these examples don't show it, it is possible to send and receive messages within the same transaction. In your application you may want to create a transaction, retrieve a message, process it, and send another message—no problem!

11.2.1.2 Using the MSMQ API

Now let's implement an external transaction with the MSMQ API. We need to use a DTC object, `ITransactionDispenser`, to create a transaction. `ITransaction` is the DTC object that represents a transaction.

`DtcGetTransactionManager()` is used to create an `ITransactionDispenser` object. This function returns a reference to the `ITransactionDispenser` object. You can reuse the `ITransactionDispenser` component to create new `ITransaction` components.

Not surprisingly `ITransactionDispenser` behaves like other transaction dispensers, such as `MSMQCoordinatedTransactionDispenser`. A programmer calls the `BeginTransaction` method of `ITransactionDispenser` to create an `ITransaction` object. We won't describe these functions and components in detail; they are documented in the *Guide to Microsoft Distributed Transaction Coordinator* shipped with SQL Server Books Online.

The following example demonstrates how to create an external DTC transaction and to send a message, using the MSMQ API.

```
void Sender(){
    ITransactionDispenser *txnDisp;   // Transaction Dispenser
    ITransaction *txnObj;             // Transaction object
    HRESULT hResult;                  // Status variable
    HRESULT txResult;                 // Transaction status variable
    // MSMQ and other declarations

    // Get a DTC transaction dispenser
    hResult = DtcGetTransactionManager(
            NULL,                       // Host name - assume local
            NULL,                       // Txn Mgr name - use local
            IID_ITransactionDispenser,  // We want a txn dispenser
            0, 0, 0,                    // Reserved words
            (void **) &txnDisp);        // Returned a pointer to the dispenser
    PRINTERROR("Sender :: Could not create transaction dispenser",
        hResult, ABORT);

    // Create a transaction
    hResult = txnDisp->BeginTransaction(
```

```
        NULL,           // punkOuter
        0,              // Isolation level
        0,              // Isolation flags
        NULL,           // Transaction options
        & txnObj);      // Returns a pointer to the transaction
PRINTERROR("Sender :: Could not create transaction",
        hResult, ABORT);


// Perform updates to SQL Server if necessary
// Create a message

// Send the message
hResult = MQSendMessage(
    mQHandle,           // Message queue handle
    &mProps,            // The message
    txnObj);            // Use the DTC transaction object

if (FAILED(hResult)) {
    // Abort the transaction and call an error routine
    txResult = txnObj->Abort(
        0,              // Not used by DTC
        FALSE,          // Not used by DTC
        FALSE);         // Perform an asynchronous abort
        PRINTERROR("Sender :: Could not abort transaction!",
        txResult, RESUME);
        PRINTERROR("Sender :: Could not send message!", hResult, ABORT);
}


// Commit the transaction
txResult = txnObj->Commit(
        FALSE,          // Not used by DTC
        0,              // No XACTTC enumeration values
        FALSE);
PRINTERROR("Sender :: Could not commit transaction!",
    txResult, ABORT);


// Now clean up - release methods are inherited from IUnknown
// Release the transaction
hResult = txnObj->Release();
PRINTERROR("Sender :: Could not release transaction",
    hResult, RESUME);
```

```
// release transaction dispenser
hResult = txnDisp->Release();
PRINTERROR("Sender :: Could not release transaction dispenser",
    hResult, RESUME);
}
```

11.2.2 MTS Transactions

In this section we will look at performing MSMQ operation within MTS transactions. We won't go into all the details of using MTS, the scope of which is another book. Rather we'll introduce the major MTS programmatic concepts. Then we'll show how to use MTS transactions with COM components and with the MSMQ API.

In a sense it's too bad that Microsoft chose the name Transaction Server for its on-line distributed transaction processing environment, because it's also a great environment for deploying nontransactional COM objects. Many compelling features, including distributed transactions, make MTS interesting.

- *Object brokering.* MTS handles the creation and destruction of COM objects on behalf of clients. All interactions take place with the benefits of location independence; that is, the client need not know whether a component is executing in the same process space as the client, in a separate process on the same host, or across the network.

- *Object pooling.* A small number of component instances can be shared by a large number of clients. MTS will create a pool of objects at start-up and will recycle them as clients come and go.

- *Resource pooling.* MTS manages threads and database connections on behalf of the programmer. A component can be developed as if it were single threaded. MTS creates a pool of threads and assigns components to them in response to client requests. Database connections are also pooled. MTS coordinates the communications between components and databases and puts the connections back into the pool as work is completed.

- *Security.* Declarative and programmatic security are provided. Declarative security enables an administrator to grant or to deny access to components executing under the control of MTS. Programmatic security allows the component to query MTS for information about the client, such as the client's role, and to modify its behavior accordingly.

- *Administrative controls.* MTS gives administrators considerable control over the properties of components in the runtime environment. Their location, transactional properties, and declarative security attributes are controlled through MTS Explorer.

As you can see, many of these features make developing and deploying components easier, and almost none of these features have anything to do with transactions!

MTS supports implicit transactions, or in MTS parlance *automatic transactions.* A component does not need to create a transaction. Rather it uses a transaction context created by MTS or inherits the context created by a client program. In fact, a component need not call a commit or an abort method.

The MTS Explorer allows an administrator to set a transaction property for every component. The property is used to indicate whether a component requires a transaction, requires a new transaction, or should not run in a transaction or whether transactions are optional.

- *Requires a transaction.* The component must execute within the scope of an MTS transaction. MTS will automatically create a transaction for the component if the client doesn't have a transaction.

- *Requires a new transaction.* The component must execute within its own transaction. MTS automatically creates a new transaction for the component.

- *Supports transactions.* The component can execute within the scope of a client transactions, but a transaction isn't required.

- *Does not support transactions.* The component should not execute within the scope of a transaction.

MTS uses the transaction property to determine whether the object should be created to execute within a transaction and whether the transaction is required or optional.

An MTS component, `ObjectContext`, enables application components to declare whether work is complete and whether it can be committed or should be aborted. When an update leaves a component in a consistent state, it calls the `EnableCommit` method of an `ObjectContext` instance. This indicates that transactional updates can be committed in their current form although the component's work isn't necessarily done. MTS doesn't deactivate the component. If the component's state isn't consistent, it calls `DisableCommit`. This method indicates that the transactional updates should not be committed but allows further processing to put the component into a consistent state. By default transactions are enabled.

MTS also allows transactional components to explicitly indicate when and how a transaction should be terminated. Two methods, `SetComplete` and `SetAbort`, are provided. `SetComplete` indicates that the component is in a consistent state, that the transaction can be committed, and that MTS can deactivate the component. A program uses `SetAbort` to indicate that the transaction cannot be successfully committed and that the component should be deactivated. For example, one of these methods might be called after a record has been deleted from a database.

MTS also supports explicit transactions, but it is not recommended by Microsoft (or by me). The implicit transaction model is more elegant, for several reasons. For one thing, it introduces a clear division between transaction demarcation and state consistency. The component focuses on what it understands best—whether its state is consistent or not. MTS determines when a transaction has completed.

A second reason for using implicit transactions relates to the amount of effort required to create a distributed application. Why would a programmer hard-code transaction demarcation within code if transaction boundaries can be controlled dynamically by MTS? Using explicit transactions introduces unnecessary code into an application or component, as well as a potential maintenance burden. The implicit or automatic transaction model is more flexible: MTS helps your components respond better to a variety of usage scenarios.

The following examples show how an MTS component can send a message as part of a transaction. Each example uses the Sample Bank application that is distributed with MTS. In that application several components interact to credit or debit an account or to move money between two accounts. Eight implementations of components are provided to demonstrate various MTS features and facilities. We'll work with the `Account` component as implemented in the step 8 folder.

A single method, `Post`, is implemented as part of the `Account` component. `Post` constructs a string describing the result of a credit, debit, or transfer operation. The string is passed back to the Sample Bank client and is displayed in the Result text box, as shown in Figure 11-1. In the examples we will place a copy of the result string into a message and send the message to a transactional queue. MSMQ sends the message only if the transaction commits.

11.2.2.1 Using COM Components

The following declarations are added at the module level of `Account`:

```
Const QGUID = "{03926690-8233-11d1-83B6-006097C4CEFC}"
Const MLabel = "External Transaction Message :: "
Dim exTxnQ As MSMQQueueInfo
Dim openETQ As MSMQQueue
```

The GUID is used to look up a transactional queue by service type. Since this is a transaction processing example, we treat the message label as a statically defined constant to maximize performance. An `MSMQQueueInfo` component reference will be returned, using `locateQueueByType()` as described in Chapter 4. An `MSMQQueue` component references the queue after it has been opened. These MSMQ components are defined at the module level so that an open reference to the transactional queue is retained. This helps to maximize performance.

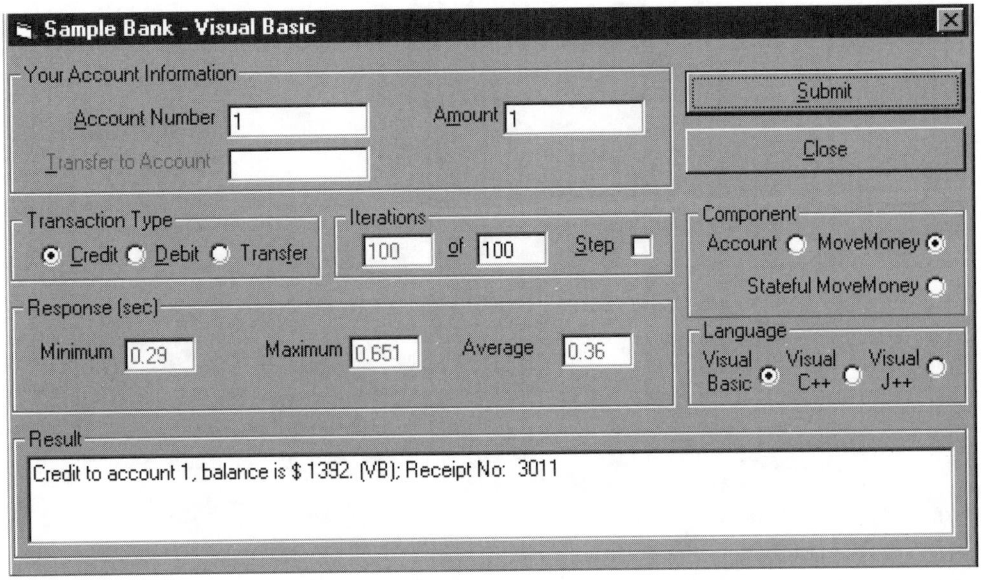

Figure 11-1   The MTS Sample Bank client

Inside the `Post` method a string is declared. The transaction result is returned to the Sample Bank client, using that string. We declare an `MSMQMessage` component that is used to send a message.

```
Public Function Post(ByVal lngAccountNo As Long, _
            ByVal lngAmount As Long) As String
    Dim strResult As String      ' In the original component code
    Dim Msg As New MSMQMessage  ' New declaration
```

In the original `Post` method the component checks security; obtains a connection to the resource manager, using the ActiveX Data Objects (ADO) interface; updates the account's balance; and constructs a string that indicates the result of the operation. The variable `strResult` contains the result. If the account is overdrawn, an error is raised. Otherwise the component releases the database connection and calls `SetComplete`.

After the string result is created and before `SetComplete` is called, we will copy the string `strResult` into the message body and will send the message to the transactional queue. If this is the first time the `Account` component has been activated, it will locate and open the transactional queue. On subsequent calls it will skip these operations. Then we simply copy the string result into the message body, assign a message label, and send the message.

```
' Locating transactional queue
If exTxnQ Is Nothing Then
    Set exTxnQ = locateQueueByType(QGUID)
End If


' Open queue
If openETQ Is Nothing Then
    Set openETQ = exTxnQ.Open(Access:=MQ_SEND_ACCESS, _
        ShareMode:=MQ_DENY_NONE) If openETQ Is Nothing Then ' Check for errors
    ' Handle any errors
    End If
End If


' Send request message
Msg.Body = strResult
Msg.Label = MLabel
Msg.Send openETQ, Transaction:=MQ_MTS_TRANSACTION
```

MQ_MTS_TRANSACTION must be used as the optional transaction parameter in the MSMQMessage.Send method, because we are operating within an MTS transaction.

An administrator can set the transactional control property, based on the requirements of a component. In this example the Account component must be configured to use transactions in order for the message to be sent within an MTS transaction. Otherwise the send operation will fail. Figure 11-2 shows the MTS Explorer window for setting the transactional attribute of a component. We have selected Requires a transaction.

It is possible to check whether the component is running in a transaction and to adjust behavior accordingly. In the following example we call GetObjectContext to get the current component's object context and check to see whether it is in a transaction. If it is we send the message with the MQ_MTS_TRANSACTION constant. Otherwise we use MQ_SINGLE_MESSAGE to send the message.

```
Dim OC As ObjectContext
Set OC = GetObjectContext()
If OC.IsInTransaction Is TRUE Then
    Msg.Send openETQ, Transaction:=MQ_MTS_TRANSACTION
Else
    Msg.Send openETQ, Transaction:=MQ_SINGLE_MESSAGE
End If
```

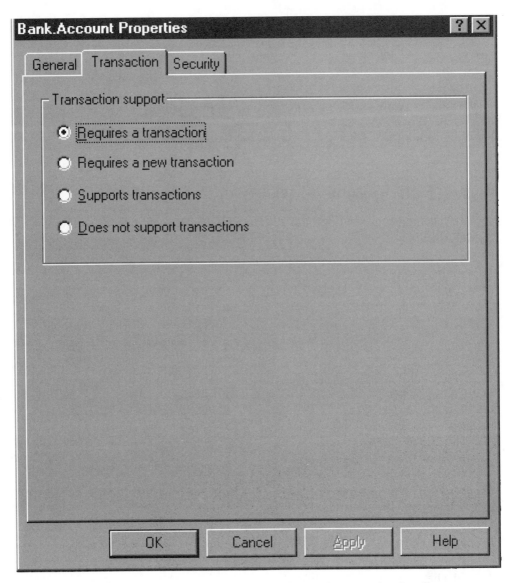

Figure 11-2 The MTS window for setting a component's transactional attributes

You may be wondering why we didn't use MQ_NO_TRANSACTION when sending the message if it is not part of an MTS transaction. The reason is that the message is being sent to a transactional queue.

If we were receiving a message from a transactional queue on the local host, we would use MQ_MTS_TRANSACTION, as follows:

```
Public Function Post(ByVal lngAccountNo As Long, _
   ByVal lngAmount As Long) As String
Dim Msg As New MSMQMessage ' Message that is received

' check security, update account, get for overdraw
' locate and open transactional queue if necessary

Set Msg = openEtxQ.Receive(Transaction:= MQ_MTS_TRANSACTION)
```

11.2.2.2 Using the MSMQ API

Now we'll demonstrate sending a message in an MTS transaction by using the MSMQ API.

```
/* Data definitions */
MQPROPVARIANT propVar[PROPERTIES];   // Array of msg property variants
MSGPROPID     propId[PROPERTIES];    // Array of msg property
                                     // identifiers
HRESULT       stats[PROPERTIES];     // Array of status indicators
MQMSGPROPS    mProps;                // Structure of msg properties &
                                     // values
DWORD         nProps;                // Property counter
QUEUEHANDLE   mQHandle;              // Message queue handle
HRESULT       hResult;               // A status variable

// Set up message properties

mProps.cProp   = nProps;             // Construct the MSGPROPS structure
mProps.aPropID = propId;
mProps.aPropVar = propVar;
mProps.aStatus = 0;       // Status values are ignored
// Derive mQHandle - a handle to a message queue
// Send the message
hResult = MQSendMessage(
   mQHandle,              // Message queue handle
   &mProps,               // Message properties
   MQ_MTS_TRANSACTION);   // Use an MTS transaction
PRINTERROR("Sender :: Could not release transaction", hResult, RESUME);
```

When an MTS component needs to send a message, programming is pretty straight-forward. The client creates the component and then interacts with it. If a message needs to be sent by the component, it creates a message, locates and opens a queue, and sends the message. This model also works fine if the component wants to *synchronously* receive a message. That is, the component is willing to wait—potentially a very long time—for a message (but not a response) to arrive in a queue before proceeding with its work. This interaction is illustrated in Figure 11-3(a). But what happens if an MTS component tries to asynchronously receive a message through one of the notification mechanisms? Since MTS recycles threads when they exit a component method, the thread may never receive an event notification. The asynchronous receive model of MSMQ does not mesh well with the MTS thread-pooling model.

As Chapters 1 and 10 illustrate, there are many situations in which it is useful to receive messages and to update other resources under the control of an MTS transaction. In work flow, for example, it is useful for applications to receive event notifications when a message arrives in a queue.

If you want to combine asynchronous notification with MTS components, an MTS client will need to receive the event notification on behalf of the MTS component, as illustrated in Figure 11-3(b). The client registers to receive an event when

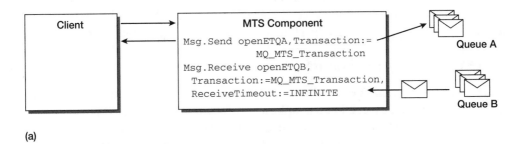

(a)

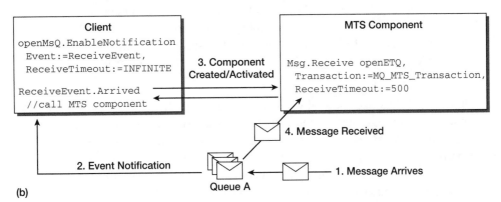

(b)

Figure 11-3 MSMQ and MTS component interactions for (a) sending and (b) receiving a message

a message arrives on a queue. When a message arrives, the client receives an event notification and invokes a method of an MTS component. The MTS component can receive the message and then update resources as part of an MTS transaction. Don't forget that the client needs to reregister for new notifications when it uses an `MSMQEvent` component. A variation of this design might have the MTS client receive the message and pass the message data on to one or more MTS components. The component interfaces would need to be structured to accept data under this design.

11.2.3 XA Transactions

So far we've talked about transaction processing with Microsoft technologies exclusively. For many users, however, working in an all-Microsoft world is not an option. They have existing transaction processing applications. How can they integrate MSMQ and other Microsoft technologies into those environments?

DTC provides the answer. It supports the XA interface defined by X/Open. The XA interface enables TP monitors to coordinate updates managed by one or more XA-compliant resource managers. I call XA a system-level interface, because application developers don't use it; TP monitor and database developers are the only programmers who work with it.

DTC can invoke or respond to XA interface calls.

- DTC invokes XA calls when it needs to coordinate updates to XA-compliant resource managers. For example, a company may want to use MTS with the Oracle database. Oracle cooperates with TP monitors in ensuring ACID properties by responding to XA calls. When an MTS component makes updates to an Oracle database, DTC coordinates the changes, using the XA interface.

- DTC responds to XA calls when MSMQ and SQL Server need to participate in an XA transaction. A company may need to integrate MSMQ applications and SQL Server data with transactional applications written for XA-compliant transaction processing monitors.[1] This is the scenario outlined next.

Figure 11-4 illustrates how MSMQ can be used in an XA transaction. An application makes calls to SQL Server to update data and sends a transactional message with MSMQ. The application brackets these operations in a transaction managed by a third-party TP monitor. The TP monitor controls the transaction by informing DTC when they are in a transaction and when work can be committed or aborted. DTC relays this information to SQL Server and MSMQ.

---

1. These include CICS/6000 and Encina from IBM and BEA's TOPEND and Tuxedo.

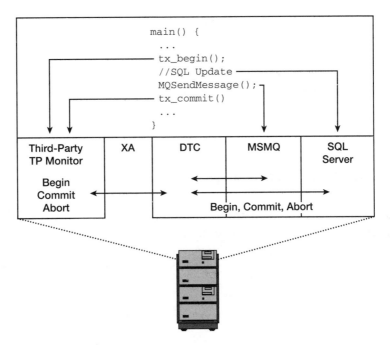

Figure 11-4 An XA transaction

The application will typically create and commit or abort a transaction by using the transaction demarcation API provided by the TP monitor. Most TP monitors support the TX interface defined by X/Open as an option. The syntax in Figure 11-4 conforms to the X/Open TX API.

11.2.3.1 Using COM Components

When sending or receiving an MSMQ message in an XA transaction, you need to use the `MQ_XA_TRANSACTION` constant. Its use for sending a message by using an `MSMQMessage` component is as follows:

```
Msg.Send openITQ, Transaction:= MQ_XA_TRANSACTION
```

11.2.3.2 Using the MSMQ API

The following code shows how to receive a message within an XA transaction by using the MSMQ API:

```
hResult = MQReceiveMessage(
    mQHandle,              // Message queue handle
    INFINITE,              // Wait a long time for a message
```

```
MQ_ACTION_RECEIVE,        // No peeking
&mProps,                  // Message properties
NULL,                     // Overlapped structure
NULL,                     // Asynchronous callback routine
NULL,                     // No cursor
MQ_XA_TRANSACTION);       // An XA transaction
```

11.3 Internal Transactions

An internal transaction is coordinated by MSMQ. When they are used, MSMQ, MTS, and SQL Server operations do not share an "all-or-nothing" quality. Only MSMQ operations are controlled by an internal transaction.

MSMQ provides the following three ways to create an internal transaction:

- MSMQTransactionDispenser, a COM component
- MQBeginTransaction, an MSMQ API call
- Sending a single transactional message with COM components or the MSMQ API

11.3.1 Using COM

MSMQTransactionDispenser, a transaction dispenser similar in purpose to MSMQCoordinatedTransactionDispenser, dispenses internal transactions rather than external transactions. Like MSMQCoordinatedTransactionDispenser, it is possible to hold several transactions at one time. Of course, it's also possible to hold transactions dispensed by each dispenser at the same time.

You call the BeginTransaction method of an MSMQTransactionDispenser component to create a transaction. BeginTransaction returns an MSMQTransaction component. Each instance of an MSMQTransaction component in a program represents a separate transaction. Since all the transactions were dispensed by an MSMQTransactionDispenser component, each is an internal transaction.

The following example demonstrates how to create an internal transaction. A transactional queue is located, an MSMQTransactionDispenser component dispenses a transaction, four messages are prepared and sent, the transaction is committed, and the transactional queue is closed.

```
Private Sub Send()
    Dim Msg1 As New MSMQMessage
    Dim Msg2 As New MSMQMessage
    Dim Msg3 As New MSMQMessage
    Dim Msg4 As New MSMQMessage
    Dim openITQ As MSMQQueue
    Dim txnDisp As New MSMQTransactionDispenser
    Dim intTxn As MSMQTransaction

    ' Locate transactional queue - as demonstrated in Chapter 4.
    ' Open the queue - openITQ represents the open queue

    ' Create internal transaction
    Set intTxn = txnDisp.BeginTransaction

    ' Prepare message 1 (not shown), then send
    Msg1.Send openITQ, Transaction:=intTxn
    ' Prepare message 2 (not shown), then send
    Msg2.Send openITQ, Transaction:=intTxn
    ' Prepare message 3 (not shown), then send
    Msg3.Send openITQ, Transaction:=intTxn
    ' Prepare message 4 (not shown), then send
    Msg4.Send1 openITQ, Transaction:=intTxn

    ' Now commit the transaction - only now are messages actually sent
    intTxn.Commit
    openITQ.Close
End Sub
```

To receive a message using a transaction created by an
`MSMQTransactionDispenser` component, you need to open the queue with
`MQ_RECEIVE_ACCESS` access and to replace an `MSMQMessage.Receive`
method with the following:

```
Set Msg = openITQ.Receive(ReceiveTimeout:=500, Transaction:=intTxn)
```

Of course, it is also possible to send and receive messages within the same internal
transaction.

11.3.2   Using the MSMQ API

MQBeginTransaction behaves like the BeginTransaction method of transaction dispensers, creating an internal transaction object and returning a pointer to it. The data type of the internal transaction is ITransaction.

The following example demonstrates how to create an MSMQ internal transaction and to send a message by using the MSMQ API:

```
void Sender() {
    ITransaction *txnObj;        // MSMQ internal transaction object
    HRESULT hResult;             // Status variable
    HRESULT txResult;            // Transaction status variable
                                 // MSMQ and other declarations


    // Create a transaction
    hResult = MQBeginTransaction(& txnObj); // Returns a transaction
    PRINTERROR("Sender :: Could not create transaction", hResult, ABORT);

    // Create a message

    // Send the message
    hResult = MQSendMessage(
        mQHandle,        // Message queue handle
        &mProps,         // The message
        txnObj);         // Use the internal transaction object
    if (FAILED(hResult)) {
        // Abort the transaction and call an error routine
        txResult = txnObj->Abort(
            0,                     // Not used by DTC
            FALSE,                 // Not used by DTC
            FALSE);                // Perform an asynchronous abort
        PRINTERROR("Sender :: Could not abort transaction!",
            txResult, RESUME);
        PRINTERROR("Sender :: Could not send message!",
            hResult, ABORT);
    }

    // Commit the transaction
    txResult = txnObj->Commit(
            FALSE,       // Not used by DTC
            0,           // No XACTTC enumeration values
            FALSE);      // RM
```

```
    PRINTERROR("Sender :: Could not commit transaction - aborting!",
        txResult, ABORT);

    // Now clean up - Release transaction (inherited from IUnknown)
    hResult = txnObj->Release();
    PRINTERROR("Sender :: Could not release transaction",
        hResult, RESUME);
}
```

11.3.3 Single-Message Internal Transactions

MSMQ also provides a special way to send a single message by using an internal transaction. This is an excellent way to send a message with exactly-once semantics. To minimize programming complexity, a single-message transaction follows an implicit transaction model. You don't have to create, commit, or abort a transaction.

11.3.3.1 Using COM Components

To send a single transactional message, MSMQMessage.Send is called with the MQ_SINGLE_MESSAGE constant. The following example demonstrates its use:

```
Private Sub SendOne()
    Dim Msg As New MSMQMessage
    Dim openITQ As MSMQQueue

    ' Locate a transactional queue - as demonstrated in Chapter 4.
    ' Open the queue - openITQ represents the open queue

    ' Prepare the message (not shown) - then send it
    Msg.Send openITQ, Transaction:=MQ_SINGLE_MESSAGE
    openITQ.Close
End Sub
```

There is no analogous single-message retrieval transaction.

11.3.3.2 Using the MSMQ API

The following code shows how send a single transaction message by using MQSendMessage():

```
hResult = MQSendMessage(
    mQHandle,                  // Message queue handle
    &mProps,                   // Message properties
    MQ_SINGLE_MESSAGE);        // Send a single transactional message
PRINTERROR("Sender :: Could not send message!", hResult, RESUME);
```

11.4 In-Order Delivery

The code in Section 11.3.1 illustrates an important feature of MSMQ: in-order delivery. In that example, message 1 is sent before message 2, message 2 before message 3, and message 3 before message 4. All messages are addressed to the same target queue. Because they are sent within the same transaction, MSMQ guarantees that the messages will arrive and be placed in the target queue in that order: message 1 before message 2, message 2 before message 3, and message 3 before message 4, as shown in Figure 11-5(a).

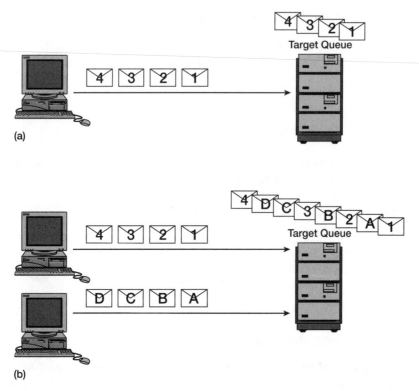

Figure 11-5 In-order delivery (a) with (b) multiple senders

In the sample code in Section 11.3.1 messages are sent within an internal transaction. It is also possible to use external or XA transactions to send the four messages in order. MSMQ guarantees in-order delivery under any type of transaction.

Note, however, that MSMQ does not *guarantee* that the messages are placed next to each other in the target queue. The reason is that a lot of other applications may be sending messages to the target queue at the same time. It is possible that the messages of other applications will be interleaved in the target queue, as shown in Figure 11-5(b).

Under certain conditions MSMQ does guarantee that the messages of two transactions will be serialized. Suppose that one application sends messages to a local or a remote queue. Suppose that the application executes two transactions, T1 and T2. Two messages, M1 and M2, are sent as part of T1. Two messages, M3 and M4, are sent as part of T2. If the application allows T1 to complete before beginning to commit T2, MSMQ guarantees that M1 and M2 will be placed in the queue ahead of M3 and M4. If T2 begins to commit before T1 has finished committing, the messages from each transaction may be interleaved.

11.5   Conclusion

Wow! Chapter 10 described the differences between on-line distributed transaction processing and transactional queued messaging. In this chapter we looked at using MSMQ transactional queued messaging with on-line distributed transaction processing and by itself.

Application designers have a large number of choices for integrating MSMQ applications with legacy transaction processing applications.

- Level 8 Systems provides FalconMQ Client libraries for sending and receiving messages from applications running on UNIX, CICS, and other transaction processing environments.

- Level 8 Systems provides the FalconMQ Bridge for exchanging messages between MSMQ and IBM's MQSeries. Thus an MSMQ application can send messages to and receive messages from MQSeries applications running on CICS, IMS, AS400, Tandem Guardian, various flavors of UNIX, and OS/2.

- SNA Server enables your applications to invoke CICS mainframe application programs, using standard LU 6.2 verbs. And with version 4 of SNA Server, there is support for wrapping the transactions in a COM interface. The COM interfaces can be "exported" to remote clients through MTS.

- Applications executing under the control of third-party TP monitors, such as BEA's Tuxedo or TOPEND, can be integrated with MSMQ, using XA transactions.

11.6 Resources and References

Jennings, R., S. Gray, and R. Lievano, 1997. *Microsoft Transaction Server 2.0.* Indianapolis, IN: SAMS Publishing.

Microsoft Message Queue Explorer Administrator's Online Help.

Microsoft Message Queue Server Online Help.

Microsoft SQL Server Books Online.

Microsoft Transaction Server Online Help.

Sessions, R. 1998. *COM and DCOM: Microsoft's Vision for Distributed Objects.* New York: Wiley.

X/Open. 1991. *X/Open CAE Specification: Distributed Transaction Processing: The XA Specification.* Cambridge, MA: X/Open.

———. 1996. *X/Open Guide: Distributed Transaction Processing: Reference Model, Version 3.* Cambridge, MA: X/Open.

A
Appendix

COM Component and

MSMQ API Reference

This appendix provides a quick reference to COM components and MSMQ API calls. A full reference is provided
with the MSMQ Software Developers Kit On-line Help. This appendix also lists
values that can be assigned to queue and message properties.

A.1   COM Components

Methods for the nine MSMQ COM components are described in Table A-1. Queue
and message properties are outlined in Section A.3.

Table A-1   **Methods for the Nine COM Components**

Methods	Parameters
MSMQMessage	

Send—Sends a message to a designated queue.
Usage:
`Dim MyQ As New MSMQQueue`
`Dim Msg As New MSMQMessage`
`Msg.Send MyQ`
	DestinationQueue—An
	   `MSMQQueue` reference.
	pTransaction—An
	   `MSMQTransaction` object or one of
	   the following constants:

continued

281

Table A-1 *continued*

Methods	Parameters
	• *MQ_NO_TRANSACTION:* Not part of a transaction.
	• *MQ_MTS_TRANSACTION:* Default; part of the current MTS transaction.
	• *MQ_SINGLE_MESSAGE:* Sends a single message as a transaction.
	• *MQ_XA_TRANSACTION:* Part of an XA-compliant transaction.

MSMQQueue

Methods	Parameters

Close—Closes the queue.
Usage:
`Dim MyQ As New MSMQQueue`
`MyQ.Close`	

EnableNotification—Starts event notification for asynchronously reading or peeking messages from the queue represented by the MSMQQueue instance.
Usage:
`Dim openJnlQ As MSMQQueue`
`Dim WithEvents JEvent As MSMQEvent`
`openJnlQ.EnableNotification _`
`   Event:=JEvent, _`
`   ReceiveTimeout:=5000`
	pqevent—An MSMQEvent object.
	msgcursor—Optional; specifies the action of the cursor.
	• *MQMSG_FIRST:* Default; start notification when a message is in the queue.
	• *MQMSG_CURRENT:* Start notification when a message is at the current location of the cursor.
	• *MQMSG_NEXT:* Move the cursor and start notification.
	ReceiveTimeout—Optional; specifies wait time (in milliseconds) for a message to arrive.

Peek—Performs a nondestructive read on the first message in the queue.
Usage:
`Dim MyQ As New MSMQQueue`
`Dim Msg As MSMQMessage`
`Set Msg = MyQ.Peek _`
`   (ReceiveTimeout:=1000)`
	ReceiveTimeout—Optional; specifies wait time (in milliseconds) for a message to arrive.
	WantDestinationQueue—Optional; default is FALSE.

Methods	Parameters
	• *TRUE:* Updates `DestinationQueueInfo` when the message is read. • *FALSE:* Does not update `DestinationQueueInfo` when the message is read. `WantBody`—Optional; default is `TRUE`. • *TRUE:* Reads `Body` as part of the peek. • *FALSE:* Does not read `Body` as part of the peek.

`PeekCurrent`—Performs a nondestructive read on the message at the current cursor position in the queue.
Usage:
`Dim MyQ As New MSMQQueue`
`Dim Msg As MSMQMessage`
`Set Msg = MyQ.PeekCurrent _`
`  (ReceiveTimeout:=1000)`
	`Receive Timeout`—Optional; specifies wait time (in milliseconds) for a message to arrive.
	`WantDestinationQueue`—Optional; default is `FALSE`.
	• *TRUE:* Updates `DestinationQueueInfo` when the message is read.
	• *FALSE:* Does not update `DestinationQueueInfo` when the message is read.
	`WantBody`—Optional; default is `TRUE`.
	• *TRUE:* Reads `Body` as part of the peek.
	• *FALSE:* Does not read `Body` as part of the peek.

`PeekNext`—Performs a nondestructive read on the next message in the queue.
Usage:
`Dim MyQ As New MSMQQueue`
`Dim Msg As MSMQMessage`
`Set Msg = MyQ.PeekNext _`
`  (ReceiveTimeout:=1000)`
	`ReceiveTimeout`—Optional; specifies wait time (in milliseconds) for a message to arrive.
	`WantDestinationQueue`—Optional; default is `FALSE`.
	• *TRUE:* Updates `DestinationQueueInfo` when the message is read.
	• *FALSE:* Does not update `DestinationQueueInfo` when the message is read.

continued

Methods	Parameters
	WantBody—Optional; default is TRUE.
	• *TRUE:* Reads Body as part of the peek.
	• *FALSE:* Does not read Body as part of the peek.

Receive—Performs a destructive read on the first message in the queue.
Usage:
`Dim MyQ As New MSMQQueue`
`Dim Msg As MSMQMessage`
`Set Msg = MyQ.Receive _`
`  (ReceiveTimeout:=1000)`
	pTransaction—An MSMQTransaction object or one of the following constants:
	• *MQ_NO_TRANSACTION:* Not part of a transaction.
	• *MQ_MTS_TRANSACTION:* Default; part of the current MTS transaction.
	• *MQ_XA_TRANSACTION:* Part of an XA-compliant transaction.
	WantDestinationQueue—Optional; default is FALSE.
	• *TRUE:* Updates DestinationQueueInfo when the message is read.
	• *FALSE:* Does not update DestinationQueueInfo when the message is read.
	WantBody—Optional; default is TRUE.
	• *TRUE:* Reads Body as part of the read.
	• *FALSE:* Does not read Body property as part of the read.
	ReceiveTimeout—Optional; specifies wait time (in milliseconds) for a message to arrive.

ReceiveCurrent—Performs a destructive read on the message at the current cursor position in the queue.
Usage:
`Dim MyQ As New MSMQQueue`
`Dim Msg As MSMQMessage`
`Set Msg = MyQ.ReceiveCurrent _`
`  (ReceiveTimeout:=1000)`
	pTransaction—An MSMQTransaction object or one of the following constants:
	• *MQ_NO_TRANSACTION:* Not part of a transaction.
	• *MQ_MTS_TRANSACTION:* Default; part of the current MTS transaction.
	• *MQ_XA_TRANSACTION:* Part of an XA-compliant transaction.

Methods	**Parameters**
	WantDestinationQueue—Optional; default is FALSE.
	• *TRUE:* Updates DestinationQueueInfo when the message is read.
	• *FALSE:* Does not update DestinationQueueInfo when the message is read.
	WantBody—Optional; default is TRUE.
	• *TRUE:* Reads Body as part of the read
	• *FALSE:* Does not read Body as part of the read.
	ReceiveTimeout—Optional; specifies wait time (in milliseconds) for a message to arrive.

Reset—Moves the cursor to the start of the queue.

Usage:

```
Dim Msg As MSMQMessage
MyQ.Reset
```

MSMQQuery

LookupQueue—Returns an MSMQQueueInfos instance (collection of queues), based on search criteria specified in the call.

Usage:

```
Const QGUID = ' a GUID
Dim aQQuery As New MSMQQuery
Dim okQs As MSMQQueueInfos
Set okQs = aQQuery.LookupQueue _
  (ServiceTypeGuid:=QGUID)
```

Search criteria:

• QueueGuid—Optional; a queue identifier.

• ServiceTypeGuid—Optional; type of service provided by applications that receive messages from the queue.

• Label—Optional; queue label.

• CreateTime—Optional; specifies when the queue was created.

• ModifyTime—optional; specifies when the queue properties were last modified.

Relationship parameters modifying one of the preceding search criteria:

• RelServiceType—Optional; modifies ServiceTypeGuid; default is REL_EQ.

continued

Table A-1 *continued*

Methods	Parameters
	• RelLabel—Optional; modifies Label; default is REL_EQ.
	• RelCreateTime—Optional; modifies CreateTime; default is REL_EQ.
	• RelModifyTime—Optional; modifies ModifyTime; default is REL_EQ.
	Values for relationship parameters:
	• REL_EQ—Equal to the search criterion.
	• REL_NEQ—Not equal to the search criterion.
	• REL_LT—Less than the search criterion.
	• REL_GT—Greater than the search criterion.
	• REL_LE—Less than or equal to the search criterion.
	• REL_GE—Greater than or equal to the search criterion.
	• REL_NOP—Ignore the search criterion.

MSMQQueueInfos

Next—Returns the next queue in the collection of
   queues returned by MSMQQuery.

Usage:

```
Const QGUID = _
  "{B9C36050-8142-11d1-83B3-006097C4CEFC}"
Dim aQQuery As New MSMQQuery
Dim okQs As MSMQQueueInfos
Dim anOkQ As MSMSQQueueInfo
Set okQs = aQQuery.LookupQueue _
  (ServiceTypeGuid:=QGUID)
okQs.Reset
Set anOkQ = okQs.Next
```

Methods	**Parameters**

Reset—Moves the cursor to the start of the
   MSMQQueueInfos collection of queues
   returned by MSMQQuery.

Usage:

```
Const QGUID = _
  "{B9C36050-8142-11d1-83B3-006097C4CEFC}"
Dim aQQuery As New MSMQQuery
Dim okQs As MSMQQueueInfos
Set okQs = aQQuery.LookupQueue _
  (ServiceTypeGuid:
  =QGUID)
okQs.Reset
```

MSMQQueueInfo

Create—Creates a queue based on properties
   specified by the MSMQQueueInfo object.

Usage:

```
Dim MyQInfo As New MSMQQueueInfo
MyQInfo.PathName = _
  "pswtech\TPservices"
MyQInfo.Create
```

IsWorldReadable—Optional; default
   is FALSE.

- *TRUE:* Anyone can read messages in
  the queue and its queue journal.
- *FALSE:* Only the owner can read the
  messages.

IsTransactional—Optional; default
   is FALSE.

- *TRUE:* The queue is strictly
  transactional.
- *FALSE:* The queue is strictly nontransactional.

Delete—Deletes an existing queue.

Usage:

```
Dim MyQInfo As New MSMQQueueInfo
MyQInfo.PathName = "pswtech\TPservices"
MyQInfo.Delete
```

continued

Table A-1 *continued*

Methods	Parameters

Open—Opens a queue.
Usage:
`Dim MyQInfo As New MSMQQueueInfo`
`Dim MyQ As MSMQQueue`
`MyQInfo.PathName = _`
`   "pswtech\TPservices"`
`MyQInfo.Create`
`Set MyQ = MyQInfo.Open _`
`   (MQ_SEND_ACCESS, MQ_DENY_NONE)`
	`Access`—Desired access rights; cannot be changed while the queue is open; can be set to one of the following:
	• *MQ_PEEK_ACCESS:* Only nondestructive reads may be performed.
	• *MQ_SEND_ACCESS:* Messages can only be sent to the queue.
	• *MQ_RECEIVE_ACCESS:* Destructive and nondestruction reads may be performed.
	`ShareMode`—Specifies how access to the queue is granted; can be set to one of the following:
	• *MQ_DENY_NONE:* Default. The queue is available to everyone. Must use if `Access` is *MQ_PEEK_ACCESS* or *MQ_SEND_ACCESS*.
	• *MQ_DENY_RECEIVE_SHARE:* Only this process can receive messages from the queue. Applicable only when `Access` is set to *MQ_RECEIVE_ACCESS*. Will fail if the queue is already open for receiving messages.

`Refresh`—Retrieves the latest property values for the `MSMQQueueInfo` object. After a queue is created, the properties of an `MSMQQueueInfo` program object are not updated until `Refresh` is explicitly called, except when the queue is closed and reopened.
Usage:
`Dim MyQInfo As New MSMQQueueInfo`
`MyQInfo.PathName = _`
`   "pswtech\TPservices"`
`MyQInfo.Refresh`	

Methods	Parameters

Update Updates queue property values stored by
    MQIS or on the local computer.

Usage:

```
Dim MyQInfo As New MSMQQueueInfo
MyQInfo.PathName = _
   "pswtech\TPservices"
MyQInfo.Authenticate = _
  MQ_AUTHENTICATE_NONE
MyQInfo.Create
MyQInfo.Authenticate = _
  MQ_AUTHENTICATE
MyQInfo.Update
```

MSMQCoordinatedTransactionDispenser

BeginTransaction—Creates an external trans-
    action represented by an MSMQTransaction
    object that can be used to send or to receive
    a message.

Usage:

```
Dim xTxnDisp As New _
  MSMQCoordinatedTransactionDispenser
Dim txn As MSMQTransaction
Dim MyQInfo As New MSMQQueueInfo
Dim MyQ As MSMQQueue
Dim Msg As New MSMQMessage
Set txn = xTxnDisp.BeginTransaction
MyQInfo.PathName = _
   "pswtech\TPservices"
MyQInfo.Create _
  IsTransactional:=True
Set MyQ = _
  MyQInfo.Open(MQ_SEND_ACCESS, _
    MQ_DENY_NONE)
Msg.Body = "Some important information"
Msg.Send MyQ, txn
txn.Commit
```

continued

Table A-1 *continued*

Methods	Parameters

MSMQTransactionDispenser

BeginTransaction—Creates an internal transaction represented by an MSMQTransaction object that can be used to send or to receive a message.

Usage:

```
Dim iTxnDisp As New _
  MSMQTransactionDispenser
Dim txn As MSMQTransaction
Dim MyQInfo As New MSMQQueueInfo
Dim MyQ As MSMQQueue
Dim Msg As New MSMQMessage
Set txn = iTxnDisp.BeginTransaction
MyQInfo.PathName = _
  "pswtech\TPservices"
MyQInfo.Create _
  IsTransactional:=True
Set MyQ = _
  MyQInfo.Open(MQ_SEND_ACCESS, _
    MQ_DENY_NONE)
Msg.Body = "important information"
Msg.Send MyQ, txn
txn.Commit
```

MSMQTransaction

Abort—Aborts all operations controlled by the MSMQTransaction object.

Usage:

```
Dim iTxnDisp As New _
  MSMQTransactionDispenser
Dim txn As MSMQTransaction
Dim MyQInfo As New MSMQQueueInfo
Dim MyQ As MSMQQueue
Dim Msg As New MSMQMessage
Set txn = iTxnDisp.BeginTransaction
MyQInfo.PathName = _
  "pswtech\TPservices"
```

fRetaining—Optional; reserved by Microsoft DTC.

fAsync—Optional; default is FALSE.
- *TRUE:* An asynchronous abort is performed, and Abort returns immediately.
- *FALSE:* A synchronous abort is performed; control is returned when the Abort completes.

Methods	Parameters
| ```
MyQInfo.Create _
   IsTransactional:=True
Set MyQ = _
   MyQInfo.Open(MQ_SEND_ACCESS, _
      MQ_DENY_NONE)
Msg.Body = "important information"
Msg.Send MyQ, txn
txn.Abort
``` | |

Commit—Commits all operations controlled by the MSMQTransaction object.

Usage:

```
Dim xTxnDisp As New _
   MSMQCoordinatedTransactionDispenser
Dim txn As MSMQTransaction
Dim MyQInfo As New MSMQQueueInfo
Dim MyQ As MSMQQueue
Dim Msg As New MSMQMessage
Set txn = xTxnDisp.BeginTransaction
MyQInfo.PathName = _
   "pswtech\TPservices"
MyQInfo.Create _
   IsTransactional:=True
Set MyQ = _
   MyQInfo.Open(MQ_SEND_ACCESS, _
      MQ_DENY_NONE)
Msg.Body = "important information"
Msg.Send MyQ, txn
txn.Commit
```

fRetaining—Optional; reserved by Microsoft DTC.

grfTC—Optional; default is XACTTC_SYNCPHASEONE; can be one of two constants:

- *XACTTC_ASYNC:* The commit returns as soon as the two-phase commit protocol is initiated.
- *XACTTC_SYNCPHASEONE:* The commit returns after phase 1 of the two-phase commit protocol.

grfRM Optional; reserved by Microsoft DTC.

MSMQEvent

Arrived—User defined; invoked when a message arrives at a queue. A program must register for event notification before this method is called.

Queue—An MSMQQueue object representing an open queue is passed into the event.

Cursor—A cursor constant passed into the event. The value equals MQMSQ_FIRST, MQMSQ_CURRENT, or MQMSQ_NEXT.

continued
```

Table A-1 *continued*

Methods	Parameters
`ArrivedError`—User-defined; invoked when an error is returned while reading messages asynchronously. A program must register for event notification before this method is called.	`Queue`—An `MSMQQueue` object representing an open queue is passed into the event. `ErrorCode`—Error code returned by `MQReceiveMessage`. `Cursor`—A cursor constant passed into the event. The value equals `MQMSQ_FIRST`, `MQMSQ_CURRENT`, or `MQMSQ_NEXT`.

A.2   MSMQ API Functions

MSMQ API functions are described in Table A-2. Message and queue properties are outlined in Section A.3.

Table A-2   MSMQ API Functions

Function	Parameters/Return Codes

Create an internal transaction:
 `HRESULT MQBeginTransaction(`
 `Transaction **ppTransaction`
 `);`
	`ppTransaction`—[out] A pointer to `Transaction` variable that points to the new transaction object.
	
	 Return values:
	 `MQ_OK`—Operation completed successfully.
	 `MQ_ERROR_INSUFFICIENT_RESOURCES`—No resources available to create a new transaction.

Close a cursor for a queue:
 `HRESULT MQCloseCursor(`
 `HANDLE hCursor`
 `);`
	`hCursor`—[in] A cursor handle for the queue to be closed.
	
	 Return values:
	 `MQ_OK`—Operation completed successfully.
	 `MQ_ERROR_INVALID_HANDLE`—The cursor handle specified in `hCursor` is not valid.

Function	Parameters/Return Codes

Close a queue:
 	
`HRESULT MQCloseQueue(`
`  QUEUEHANDLE hQueue`
`);`
	hQueue—[in] A handle to the queue to be closed.
	
	Return values:
	MQ_OK—Operation completed successfully.
	MQ_ERROR_INVALID_HANDLE—The queue handle specified in hQueue is not valid.

Create a queue cursor:
 	
`HRESULT MQCreateCursor(`
`  QUEUEHANDLE hQueue,`
`  PHANDLE phCursor`
`);`
	hQueue—[in] A handle to the queue for which a cursor will be created.
	phCursor—[out] A pointer variable that will receive the cursor handle.
	
	Return values:
	MQ_OK—Operation completed successfully.
	MQ_ERROR_INVALID_HANDLE—The queue handle specified in hQueue is not valid.
	MQ_ERROR_STALE_HANDLE—Obtain a fresh handle to the queue.

Create a queue:
 	
`HRESULT MQCreateQueue(`
`  PSECURITY_DESCRIPTOR`
`   pSecurityDescriptor,`
`  MQQUEUEPROPS`
`   * pQueueProps,`
`  LPWSTR lpwcsFormatName,`
`  LPDWORD`
`   lpdwFormatNameLength`
`);`
	pSecurityDescriptor—[in] A pointer to a SECURITY_DESCRIPTOR structure. A NULL pointer indicates to use default values.
	pQueueProps—[in, out] A pointer to an MQQUEUEPROPS structure of queue properties.
	lpwcsFormatName—[out] A pointer to the buffer that receives the format name for the created queue (or a NULL pointer).
	lpdwFormatNameLength—[in, out] When MQCreateQueue is called, the Unicode character length of the lpwcsFormatName buffer. NULL pointer is not allowed. The length of the format name, including the null-terminating character, is returned.
	
	Return values:
	MQ_OK—Operation completed successfully.
	MQ_ERROR_ACCESS_DENIED—The process does not have the appropriate rights to create the queue.
	MQ_ERROR_ILLEGAL_PROPERTY_VALUE—An illegal property value was specified.

continued

Table A-2 *continued*	
Function	**Parameters/Return Codes**
	MQ_ERROR_ILLEGAL_QUEUE_PATHNAME— PROPID_Q_PATHNAME contains an illegal MSMQ pathname string.
	MQ_ERROR_ILLEGAL_SECURITY_ DESCRIPTOR—The security descriptor has an invalid structure.
	MQ_ERROR_INSUFFICIENT_PROPERTIES— No pathname was specified.
	MQ_ERROR_INVALID_OWNER—The specified queue contains the name of an unrecognized machine.
	MQ_ERROR_NO_DS—Cannot access the MQIS.
	MQ_ERROR_PROPERTY—There were errors with one or more properties.
	MQ_ERROR_PROPERTY_NOTALLOWED—A specified property is not valid when creating the queue.
	MQ_ERROR_QUEUE_EXISTS—A queue with the identical pathname or instance already exists.
	MQ_ERROR_SERVICE_NOT_AVAILABLE— Cannot connect to the queue manager.
	MQ_ERROR_WRITE_NOT_ALLOWED—Cannot add a queue to MQIS while an MSMQ information store server is being installed.
	MQ_INFORMATION_FORMATNAME_BUFFER_ TOO_SMALL—The queue was created successfully. The buffer for receiving the format name is too small.
	MQ_INFORMATION_PROPERTY—The queue was created successfully, but one or more properties resulted in a warning.

Function	Parameters/Return Codes
Delete a queue: HRESULT MQDeleteQueue(LPCWSTR lpwcsFormatName);	lpwcsFormatName—[in] A pointer to a buffer containing the queue's format name. Return values: MQ_OK—Operation completed successfully. MQ_ERROR_ACCESS_DENIED—The process does not have the appropriate rights to delete the queue. MQ_ERROR_ILLEGAL_FORMATNAME—The format name specified in lpwcsFormatName is illegal. MQ_ERROR_NO_DS—Cannot access the MQIS. MQ_ERROR_SERVICE_NOT_AVAILABLE—Cannot connect to the queue manager. MQ_ERROR_UNSUPPORTED_FORMATNAME_OPERATION—Cannot use a direct format name to delete a queue. MQ_ERROR_WRITE_NOT_ALLOWED—Cannot delete a queue; MQIS not in write mode.
Free memory: VOID MQFreeMemory(PVOID pvMemory); This function can be used whenever the application passes VT_NULL in an MQPROPVARIANT structure and MSMQ allocates memory outside the array, that is, where puuid and pwszVal are required.	pvMemory—[in] A pointer to the memory to be freed.
Free the security context allocated by MQGetSecurityContext: VOID MQFreeSecurityContext(HANDLE hSecurityContext);	hSecurityContext—[in] A handle to a security context.

continued

Table A-2 *continued*

Function	Parameters/Return Codes

Retrieve queue manager properties for an MSMQ host:
 	
HRESULT
 MQGetMachineProperties(
  LPCWSTR lpwcsMachineName,
  GUID pguidMachineID,
  MQQMPROPS pQMProps
);
	lpwcsMachineName—[in] The name of the queue manager whose properties should be returned. Set pguidMachineID to NULL if this parameter is used.
	pguidMachineID—[in] The identifier of the queue manager whose properties should be returned. Set lpwcsMachineName to NULL if this parameter is used.
	pQMProps—[in, out] A pointer to a property structure of properties to retrieve.
	
	Return values:
	MQ_OK—Operation completed successfully.
	MQ_ERROR_ACCESS_DENIED—The process does not have the appropriate rights to the computer.
	MQ_ERROR_INVALID_PARAMETER—lpwcsMachineName and pguidMachineID were specified.
	MQ_ERROR_ILLEGAL_MQQMPROPS—No properties were specified or pQMprops was NULL.
	MQ_ERROR_ILLEGAL_PROPERTY_VT—An invalid type was supplied for one or more property values in pQMProps.
	MQ_ERROR_MACHINE_NOT_FOUND—The specified computer was not found in MQIS.
	MQ_ERROR_NO_DS—Cannot access the MQIS.
	MQ_INFORMATION_UNSUPPORTED_PROPERTY—An unsupported property was specified in pQMProps.
	MQ_INFORMATION_DUPLICATE_PROPERTY—A duplicate property identifier was specified in pQMProps. The second entry is ignored.

Function	Parameters/Return Codes

Return queue properties:
HRESULT
 MQGetQueueProperties(
  LPCWSTR lpwcsFormatName,
  MQQUEUEPROPS
    * pQueueProps
);
	lpwcsFormatName—[in] A pointer to the queue's format name. A direct format name cannot be used.
	pQueueProps—[in, out] A pointer to the MQQUEUEPROPS structure that specifies properties to be retrieved.
	
	Return values:
	MQ_OK—Operation completed successfully.
	MQ_ERROR_ACCESS_DENIED—The process does not have the appropriate access rights to the queue's properties.
	MQ_ERROR_ILLEGAL_FORMATNAME—The format name specified in lpwcsFormatName is illegal.
	MQ_ERROR_ILLEGAL_PROPERTY_VT—An invalid type was supplied for one or more property values in pQueueProps.
	MQ_ERROR_NO_DS—Cannot access the MQIS.
	MQ_ERROR_PROPERTY—One or more properties resulted in an error.
	MQ_ERROR_SERVICE_NOT_AVAILABLE—Cannot connect to the queue manager.
	MQ_ERROR_UNSUPPORTED_FORMATNAME_OPERATION—A direct format name cannot be used to get queue properties.
	MQ_INFORMATION_DUPLICATE_PROPERTY—The same property appears more than once in pQueueProps.
	MQ_INFORMATION_PROPERTY—Queue properties were returned successfully, but one or more properties resulted in a warning.
	MQ_INFORMATION_UNSUPPORTED_PROPERTY—Not a valid property identifier. The property is ignored.

continued

Table A-2 *continued*

Function	Parameters/Return Codes

Retrieve the security descriptor for a queue:
 	
HRESULT MQGetQueueSecurity(
  LPCWSTR lpwcsFormatName,
  SECURITY_INFORMATION *
   SecurityInformation,
  PSECURITY_DESCRIPTOR *
   pSecurityDescriptor,
  DWORD nLength,
  LPDWORD lpnLengthNeeded
);
	lpwcsFormatName—[in] A pointer to the queue's format name. A direct format name cannot be used.
	SecurityInformation—[in] A SECURITY_INFORMATION structure that indicates access control information to be returned.
	pSecurityDescriptor—[out] A pointer to the buffer to which the security descriptor should be returned.
	nLength—[in] The size, in bytes, of the security descriptor buffer.
	lpnLengthNeeded—[out] A pointer to a variable that was used to indicate whether any additional buffer length is needed for the security descriptor. If the security descriptor fits in the buffer, this variable indicates the size of the security descriptor.
	
	Return values:
	MQ_OK—Operation completed successfully.
	MQ_ERROR_ACCESS_DENIED—The process does not have the appropriate access rights to the queue's properties.
	MQ_ERROR_FUNCTION_NOT_SUPPORTED—MQGetQueueSecurity is not supported on this platform.
	MQ_ERROR_ILLEGAL_FORMATNAME—An illegal format name is specified by lpwcsFormatName.
	MQ_ERROR_NO_DS—Cannot access the MQIS.
	MQ_ERROR_PRIVILEGE_NOT_HELD—The process does not have the proper privilege to read the queue's system access control list.
	MQ_ERROR_SECURITY_DESCRIPTOR_BUFFER_TOO_SMALL—The buffer pointed to by pSecurityDescriptor is too small.
	MQ_ERROR_UNSUPPORTED_FORMATNAME_OPERATION—lpwcsFormatName is a direct format name, or it specifies a journal, dead letter, or connector queue.

Function	**Parameters/Return Codes**

Retrieve security information needed to authenticate messages:
 	
```VOID MQGetSecurityContext(```
``` LPVOID lpCertBuffer,```
``` DWORD dwCertBufferLength,```
``` HANDLE* hSecurityContext```
```);```
	`lpCertBuffer`—[in] A pointer to a buffer containing a security certificate. External certificates must be encoded in ASN.1 DER. The internal security certificate provided by MSMQ is used if `NULL` is used.
	`dwCertBufferLength`—[in] The length of the security certificate buffer *r.*
	`hSecurityContext`—[out] A handle to a security context buffer.
	
	Return values:
	`MQ_OK`—Operation completed successfully.
	`MQ_ERROR_COULD_NOT_GET_USER_SID`—MSMQ could not get the security identifier.
	`MQ_ERROR_NO_DS`—Cannot access the MQIS.
	`MQ_ERROR_INVALID_PARAMETER`—Either `pCertBuffer` or `dwCertBufferLength` is not valid.
	`MQ_ERROR_INSUFFICIENT_RESOURCES`—Insufficient resources; operation failed.
	`MQ_ERROR_INVALID_CERTIFICATE`—Security certificate is invalid or is not correctly placed in the Microsoft Internet Explorer personal certificate store.
	`MQ_ERROR_CORRUPTED_INTERNAL_CERTIFICATE`—Internal certificate is corrupted.
	`MQ_ERROR_CORRUPTED_SECURITY_DATA`—A CryptoAPI function has failed.

Return a format name for a queue using a queue handle:
 	
```HRESULT```
``` MQHandleToFormatName(```
``` QUEUEHANDLE hQueue,```
``` LPWSTR lpwcsFormatName,```
``` LPDWORD lpdwCount```
```);```
	`hQueue`—[in] A queue handle.
	`lpwcsFormatName`—[out] The buffer to receive the format name.
	`lpdwCount`—[in, out] The Unicode character length of `lpwcsFormatName` on input requires at least 54. `NULL` pointer is not allowed. MSMQ returns the length of the format name string, including the null-terminating character, on output.

continued

Table A-2 *continued*

Function	Parameters/Return Codes
	Return values:
	MQ_OK—Operation completed successfully.
	MQ_ERROR_FORMATNAME_BUFFER_TOO_ SMALL—The `lpwcsFormatName` buffer is too small for the format name.
	MQ_ERROR_INVALID_HANDLE—hQueue is not valid.
	MQ_ERROR_SERVICE_NOT_AVAILABLE— Cannot connect to the queue manager.
	MQ_ERROR_STALE_HANDLE—Obtain a fresh handle to the queue.

Return a format name for a queue, using its instance GUID:
`HRESULT`
`MQInstanceToFormatName(`
`GUID * pGUID,`
`LPWSTR lpwcsFormatName,`
`LPDWORD lpdwCount`
`);`
	`pGUID`—[in] A pointer to the queue identifier.
	`lpwcsFormatName`—[out] The buffer to receive the format name.
	`lpdwCount`—[in, out] The Unicode character length of `lpwcsFormatName` on input requires at least 54. NULL pointer is not allowed. MSMQ returns the length of the format name string, including the null-terminating character, on output.

	Return values:
	MQ_OK—Operation completed successfully.
	MQ_ERROR_SERVICE_NOT_AVAILABLE— Cannot connect to the queue manager.
	MQ_ERROR_FORMATNAME_BUFFER_TOO_ SMALL—The `lpwcsFormatName` buffer is too small for the format name.

Start an MQIS query to locate public queues:
`HRESULT MQLocateBegin(`
`LPCWSTR lpwcsContext,`
`MQRESTRICTION`
`* pRestriction,`
	`lpwcsContext`—[in] Must be NULL.
	`pRestriction`—[in] The search criteria for the query. NULL indicates no restrictions.
	`pColumns`—[in] Queue properties to be returned by the query. Cannot be set to NULL.
	`pSort`—[in] The sort order for the query results. NULL indicates no sort order. PROPID_Q_PATHNAME cannot be a sort key.

Function	Parameters/Return Codes
| ```
MQCOLUMNSET * pColumns,
MQSORTSET * pSort,
PHANDLE phEnum
);
``` | phEnum—[out] A pointer to a query handle to use when calling `MQLocateNext` and `MQLocateEnd`.<br><br>Return values:<br>MQ_OK—Operation completed successfully.<br>MQ_ERROR_ILLEGAL_CONTEXT—`lpwcsContext` is not NULL.<br>MQ_ERROR_ILLEGAL_MQCOLUMNS—`pColumns` is NULL.<br>MQ_ERROR_ILLEGAL_PROPERTY_VALUE—An illegal property value was specified in `pRestriction`.<br>MQ_ERROR_ILLEGAL_PROPID—An illegal property was specified in `pColumns`.<br>MQ_ERROR_ILLEGAL_RELATION—An invalid relationship value was specified in `pRestriction`.<br>MQ_ERROR_ILLEGAL_RESTRICTION_PROPID—An illegal property identifier was specified in `pRestriction`.<br>MQ_ERROR_ILLEGAL_SORT_PROPID—An illegal property was specified in `pSort`.<br>MQ_ERROR_NO_DS—Cannot access the MQIS. |
| End an MQIS query:<br>```
HRESULT MQLocateEnd(
 HANDLE hEnum
);
``` | hEnum—[in] Query handle returned by a call to `MQLocateBegin`.<br><br>Return values:<br>MQ_OK—Operation completed successfully.<br>MQ_ERROR_INVALID_HANDLE—`hEnum` is not valid. |
| Return the next queue located as part of a query:<br>```
HRESULT MQLocateNext(
 HANDLE hEnum,
 DWORD * pcProps,
 PROPVARIANT aPropVar[]
);
``` | hEnum—[in] A query handle returned by `MQLocateBegin`.<br>pcProps—[in, out] On input a pointer to a variable indicating the number of elements (columns) in the `aPropVar[]` array. On return `pcProps` holds the number of properties returned by the |

continued
```

Table A-2 *continued*	

Function	Parameters/Return Codes
	query. A returned value of 0 indicates that no queues were found. aPropVar—[out] The property values retrieved in a PROPVARIANT array. Return values: MQ_OK—Operation completed successfully. MQ_ERROR_INVALID_HANDLE—hEnum is not valid. MQ_ERROR_NO_DS—Cannot access the MQIS. MQ_ERROR_RESULT_BUFFER_TOO_SMALL—A supplied buffer for aPropVar is too small.
Open a public or private queue: HRESULT MQOpenQueue(LPCWSTR lpwcsFormatName, DWORD dwAccess, DWORD dwShareMode, LPQUEUEHANDLE phQueue);	lpwcsFormatName—[in] A pointer to a public, private, or direct queue format name string of the queue to be opened. dwAccess—[in] The desired queue access mode, specified with one of the following constants: • *MQ_PEEK_ACCESS*—Messages can be only looked at. They cannot be removed from the queue. • *MQ_SEND_ACCESS*—Messages can be only sent to the queue. • *MQ_RECEIVE_ACCESS*—Messages can be looked at and removed from the queue. Whether a message is removed from the queue or looked at depends on the dwAction parameter of MQReceiveMessage. dwShareMode—[in] Indicates whether the queue will be shared, specified with one of the following constants: • *MQ_DENY_NONE*—Default. The queue is available to everyone. This setting must be used if dwAccess is set to *MQ_PEEK_ACCESS* or *MQ_SEND_ACCESS*.

Function	**Parameters/Return Codes**
	• *MQ_DENY_RECEIVE_SHARE*—Limits those who can receive messages from the queue to this process. If the queue is already opened for receiving messages by another process, this call fails and returns *MQ_ERROR_SHARING_VIOLATION*. Applicable only when dwAccess is set to *MQ_RECEIVE_ACCESS*.
	phQueue—[out] A handle to the opened queue.
	Return values:
	MQ_OK—Operation completed successfully.
	MQ_ERROR_SERVICE_NOT_AVAILABLE— Cannot connect to the queue manager.
	MQ_ERROR_ILLEGAL_FORMATNAME— lpwcsFormatName contains an illegal format name.
	MQ_ERROR_NO_DS—Cannot access the MQIS.
	MQ_ERROR_INVALID_PARAMETER—One of the IN parameters is not valid.
	MQ_ERROR_SHARING_VIOLATION—The queue has already been opened by another process in a conflicting access or share mode.
	MQ_ERROR_ACCESS_DENIED—The calling process does not have the appropriate access rights to open the queue with the access mode specified by dwAccess.
	MQ_ERROR_UNSUPPORTED_ACCESS_MODE— The access mode is not supported.
	MQ_ERROR_UNSUPPORTED_FORMATNAME_ OPERATION—lpwcsFormatName is not supported by the access rights specified in dwAccess.

continued

Table A-2 *continued*

Function	Parameters/Return Codes
Return a format name for a queue, using its pathname: HRESULT MQPathNameToFormatName(LPCWSTR lpwcsPathName, LPWSTR lpwcsFormatName, LPDWORD lpdwCount);	pwcsPathName—[in] A public or private pathname of the queue. lpwcsFormatName—[out] A pointer to a buffer to receive the format name for the queue. lpdwCount—[in, out] The Unicode character length of lpwcsFormatName on input; at least 54. NULL pointer is not allowed. MSMQ returns the length of the format name string, including the null-terminating character, on output. Return values: MQ_OK—Operation completed successfully. MQ_ERROR_SERVICE_NOT_AVAILABLE—Cannot connect to the queue manager. MQ_ERROR_ILLEGAL_PATHNAME—lpwcsPathName contains an illegal MSMQ pathname string. MQ_ERROR_NO_DS—Cannot access the MQIS. MQ_ERROR_FORMATNAME_BUFFER_TOO_SMALL—lpwcsFormatName is too small to contain the format name.

Perform a destructive or a non-destructive read of a message in a queue:
 	
HRESULT MQReceiveMessage(
 QUEUEHANDLE hSource,
 DWORD dwTimeout,
 DWORD dwAction,
 MQMSGPROPS
  * pMessageProps,
 LPOVERLAPPED lpOverlapped,
 PMQRECEIVECALLBACK
  fnReceiveCallback,
 HANDLE hCursor,
 Transaction * pTransaction
);
	hSource—[in] A queue handle that contains the message.
	dwTimeout—[in] The wait time, in milliseconds, for the message or *INFINITE*.
	dwAction—[in] How to read the message; must be one of the following:
	• *MQ_ACTION_RECEIVE*—Perform a destructive read of the message at the current cursor location.
	• *MQ_ACTION_PEEK_CURRENT*—Perform a nondestructive read of the message at the current cursor location and leave the cursor pointing at the current message. If hCursor is NULL, the queue's cursor points at the first message in the queue.

Function	Parameters/Return Codes
	• *MQ_ACTION_PEEK_NEXT*—Perform a nondestructive read of the next message in the queue. If hCursor is NULL, the queue's cursor points at the first message in the queue.
	pMessageProps—[in, out] A pointer to an MQMSGPROPS structure of message properties on input. The structure contains the message properties when the call returns.
	lpOverlapped—[in, out] A pointer to an OVERLAPPED structure. Use NULL for synchronous receive and for transactions.
	fnReceiveCallback—[in] A pointer to the callback function. Use NULL for synchronous receive and for transactions.
	hCursor—[in] A cursor handle for looking at messages in the queue, or NULL.
	pTransaction—[in] A pointer to a transaction object, a constant, or NULL if a message is not to be retrieved as part of a transaction. Constants include:
	• *MQ_NO_TRANSACTION*—The call is not part of a transaction.
	• *MQ_MTS_TRANSACTION*—The current MTS transaction is used to retrieve the message.
	• *MQ_XA_TRANSACTION*—The call is part of an externally coordinated, XA-compliant transaction.
	Return values:
	MQ_OK—Operation completed successfully.
	MQ_ERROR_ACCESS_DENIED—The dwAction action conflicts with the queue access rights of the process.
	MQ_ERROR_BUFFER_OVERFLOW—The message body buffer is too small. Part of the message body was copied to the buffer, but the message is not removed from the queue.
	MQ_ERROR_SENDERID_BUFFER_TOO_SMALL —The sender identification buffer is too small.

continued

Table A-2 *continued*	
Function	**Parameters/Return Codes**
	MQ_ERROR_SYMM_KEY_BUFFER_TOO_SMALL —The symmetric key buffer is too small.
	MQ_ERROR_SENDER_CERT_BUFFER_TOO_ SMALL—The sender certificate buffer is too small.
	MQ_ERROR_SIGNATURE_BUFFER_TOO_ SMALL—The signature buffer is too small.
	MQ_ERROR_PROV_NAME_BUFFER_TOO_ SMALL—The provider name buffer is too small.
	MQ_ERROR_LABEL_BUFFER_TOO_SMALL— The message label buffer is too small.
	MQ_ERROR_FORMATNAME_BUFFER_TOO_ SMALL—The format name buffer is too small.
	MQ_ERROR_DTC_CONNECT—MSMQ was unable to connect to the MS DTC.
	MQ_ERROR_INSUFFICIENT_PROPERTIES— One or more message properties were specified without an associated length property.
	MQ_ERROR_INVALID_HANDLE—The hSource is not valid.
	MQ_ERROR_IO_TIMEOUT—The dwTimeout timeout period was reached.
	MQ_ERROR_MESSAGE_ALREADY_RECEIVED— The message pointed at by the cursor has been removed.
	MQ_ERROR_OPERATION_CANCELLED—The operation was canceled before it could be completed.
	MQ_ERROR_PROPERTY—One or more message properties in pMessageProps resulted in an error.
	MQ_ERROR_QUEUE_DELETED—The queue was deleted before the message could be read.
	MQ_ERROR_ILLEGAL_CURSOR_ACTION— MQ_ACTION_PEEK_NEXT cannot be executed with the current cursor position.
	MQ_ERROR_SERVICE_NOT_AVAILABLE— Cannot connect to the queue manager.

Function	Parameters/Return Codes
	MQ_ERROR_STALE_HANDLE—The queue handle was obtained in a previous session of the queue manager service. MQ_ERROR_TRANSACTION_USAGE—The state of the transaction queue is not appropriate for reading messages. MQ_INFORMATION_PROPERTY—One or more of the properties in pMessageProps resulted in a warning code.
Send a message: HRESULT MQSendMessage(QUEUEHANDLE hDestinationQueue, MQMSGPROPS * pMessageProps, ITransaction * pTransaction);	hDestinationQueue—[in] A handle representing the queue to which the message is to be sent. pMessageProps—[in] A pointer to an MQMSGPROPS structure of message properties. pTransaction—[in] A pointer to a transaction object, a constant, or NULL if the message is not sent as part of a transaction. Admissible constants include • *MQ_NO_TRANSACTION*—The call is not part of a transaction. • *MQ_MTS_TRANSACTION*—The call is part of the current MTS transaction. • *MQ_SINGLE_MESSAGE*—The message should be sent as a single transactional message. • *MQ_XA_TRANSACTION*—The call is part of an XA-compliant transaction. Return values: MQ_OK—Operation completed successfully. MQ_ERROR_ACCESS_DENIED—The queue was not opened with MQ_SEND_ACCESS rights. MQ_ERROR_BAD_SECURITY_CONTEXT—The security context buffer is invalid. MQ_ERROR_CORRUPTED_INTERNAL_CERTIFICATE—The internal security certificate provided by MSMQ is corrupted. MQ_ERROR_CORRUPTED_PERSONAL_CERT_STORE—The Internet Explorer personal certificate store is corrupted.

continued

Table A-2 *continued*

Function	Parameters/Return Codes
	MQ_ERROR_CORRUPTED_SECURITY_DATA— An error was encountered when calling a CryptoAPI function.
	MQ_ERROR_COULD_NOT_GET_USER_SID— Could not retrieve the user identifier specified by PROPID_M_SENDERID.
	MQ_ERROR_DTC_CONNECT—MSMQ was unable to connect to DTC.
	MQ_ERROR_ILLEGAL_FORMATNAME—The administration or response queue format name is illegal.
	MQ_ERROR_INVALID_CERTIFICATE—The external security certificate is invalid or was not placed in the Internet Explorer personal certificate store.
	MQ_ERROR_INVALID_HANDLE—The hDestinationQueue is not valid.
	MQ_ERROR_MESSAGE_STORAGE_FAILED— An error occurred while storing a recoverable message on the local computer.
	MQ_ERROR_NO_INTERNAL_USER_CERT— The user's internal security certificate provided by MSMQ is not registered.
	MQ_ERROR_PROPERTY—One or more properties resulted in an error.
	MQ_ERROR_SERVICE_NOT_AVAILABLE— Cannot connect to the queue manager.
	MQ_ERROR_STALE_HANDLE—The queue handle was obtained in a previous session of the queue manager service.
	MQ_ERROR_TRANSACTION_USAGE—A transactional message cannot be sent to a non-transactional queue, or the message is not part of a transaction, and the target queue is expecting transactions.
	MQ_INFORMATION_PROPERTY—One or more properties resulted in a warning, but the function completed.

Function	Parameters/Return Codes
Set the properties for a queue: ```\nHRESULT\n MQSetQueueProperties(\n LPCWSTR lpwcsFormatName,\n MQQUEUEPROPS *\n pQueueProps\n);\n```	pwcsFormatName—[in] A pointer to the public or private queue format name. pQueueProps—[in] A pointer to the MQQUEUEPROPS structure specifying the properties to be set. Return values: MQ_OK—Operation completed successfully. MQ_ERROR_ACCESS_DENIED—The process does not have appropriate access rights to set the properties of the queue. MQ_ERROR_ILLEGAL_FORMATNAME—lpwcsFormatName specifies an illegal format name. MQ_ERROR_ILLEGAL_PROPERTY_VALUE—An illegal property value is specified. MQ_ERROR_NO_DS—Cannot access the MQIS. MQ_ERROR_PROPERTY—One or more properties resulted in error. MQ_ERROR_SERVICE_NOT_AVAILABLE—Cannot connect to the queue manager. MQ_ERROR_UNSUPPORTED_FORMATNAME_OPERATION—The lpwcsFormatName specified a direct format name. MQ_ERROR_WRITE_NOT_ALLOWED—MQIS was unavailable to set queue properties. MQ_INFORMATION_PROPERTY—One or more of the properties resulted in a warning, but the function completed.
Set queue access controls: ```\nHRESULT MQSetQueueSecurity(\n LPCWSTR lpwcsFormatName,\n SECURITY_INFORMATION *\n SecurityInformation,\n PSECURITY_DESCRIPTOR *\n pSecurityDescriptor\n);\n```	pwcsFormatName—[in] A pointer to the public or private queue format name. securityInformation—[in] A SECURITY_INFORMATION structure indicating access control information to be set. pSecurityDescriptor—[in] A pointer to a SECURITY_DESCRIPTOR structure.

continued

Table A-2 *continued*

Function	Parameters/Return Codes
	Return values:
	MQ_OK—Operation completed successfully.
	MQ_ERROR_ACCESS_DENIED—The process does not have appropriate access rights to set the queue security information.
	MQ_ERROR_FUNCTION_NOT_SUPPORTED— MQSetQueueSecurity is not supported on this platform.
	MQ_ERROR_ILLEGAL_FORMATNAME— lpwcsFormatName specifies an illegal format name.
	MQ_ERROR_NO_DS—Cannot access the MQIS.
	MQ_ERROR_PRIVILEGE_NOT_HELD—The process owner does not have the proper privilege to set the queue's system access control list.
	MQ_ERROR_SERVICE_NOT_AVAILABLE— Cannot connect to the queue manager.
	MQ_ERROR_UNSUPPORTED_FORMATNAME_ OPERATION—lpwcsFormatName uses a direct format name, or the process is attempting to set the access controls for a journal, dead letter, or connector queue.

A.3   Queue and Message Properties

Table A-3 provides a short reference on each queue property. *Note for MSMQ API users:* Two fields are associated with each MSMQ API property: data type and MQPROPVARIANT. Data type is used to represent a property value; MQPROPVARI-ANT indicates a field within a variant record in which the value is placed. Table A-4 lists five categories of message properties: basic messaging; acknowledgments, journals, and reports; security; additional message-handling properties; and connector applications. Note that VT_NULL can be used as the data type tag for selected properties. When the programmer passes VT_NULL as the data type tag, MSMQ allocates memory to hold the property value.

A connector exchanges messages between MSMQ and foreign messaging environments. However, you may want to integrate MSMQ with proprietary messaging systems. If so, you will need to understand and to use the connector application message properties that enable connector applications to be created. Note that these properties do not have COM equivalents; a connector application must be developed by using the MSMQ API.

Table A-3   Queue Properties

Queue Property	COM Equivalent	Description
PROPID_Q_AUTHENTICATE • Data type: VT_UI1 • MQPROPVARIANT: bVal	MSMQQueueInfo. Authenticate	Indicates whether a queue accepts nonauthenticated messages: • MQ_AUTHENTICATE_ NONE—The default; authenticated and nonauthenticated messages are accepted. • MQ_AUTHENTICATE— Only authenticated messages are accepted.
PROPID_Q_BASEPRIORITY • Data type: VT_I2 • MQPROPVARIANT: iVal	MSMQQueueInfo. BasePriority	The base priority for the queue. A queue's base priority is used when routing messages over the network. Messages addressed to a queue with a higher priority are sent before messages addressed to queues with a lower base priority. Public queues can have a base priority between –32768 and +32767 (the default is 0). The base priority of private queues, as well as public queues accessed using a direct format name, is always 0.

continued

Table A-3 *continued*

Queue Property	COM Equivalent	Description
PROPID_Q_CREATE_TIME • Data type: VT_I4 • MQPROPVARIANT: lVal	MSMQQueueInfo. CreateTime	A read-only property indicating the time and date when the queue was created. The time returned is the number of seconds elapsed since midnight (00:00:00), January 1, 1970 (Coordinated Universal time). Visual Basic automatically converts this time to the local system time and date. In C ctime() converts the time and date for display.
PROPID_Q_INSTANCE • Data type: VT_CLSID • MQPROPVARIANT: *puuid	MSMQQueueInfo. QueueGuid	Identifies a *public* queue instance. It is set by MSMQ when a queue is created. Once a queue is created, the queue identifier can be examined, printed, and used to obtain a format name.
PROPID_Q_JOURNAL • Data type: VT_UI1 • MQPROPVARIANT: bVal	MSMQQueueInfo.Journal	Determines whether messages removed from a queue are also copied to a journal queue. This property can take one of the following values: • MQ_JOURNAL—All messages removed from the queue are stored in its journal queue. • MQ_JOURNAL_NONE—The default; messages are not stored in a journal queue. MSMQ creates a journal queue when a queue is created.

Queue Property	COM Equivalent	Description
PROPID_Q_JOURNAL_ QUOTA • Data type: VT_UI4 • MQPROPVARIANT: ulVal	MSMQQueueInfo. JournalQuota	The maximum size, in kilo-bytes, of a target journal queue. The default is INFINITE. The size of a journal queue can be set during creation and can be reset later.
PROPID_Q_LABEL • Data type: VT_LPWSTR • MQPROPVARIANT: pwszVal	MSMQQueueInfo.Label	A queue label. It does not have to be unique, and applications can use it as a search criterion when locating public queues. The label's maximum string length is 124 Unicode characters. If the type for PROPID_Q_LABEL is set to VT_NULL and is passed to MQGetQueueProperties, MSMQ will allocate the memory needed for the pathname.
PROPID_Q_MODIFY_TIME • Data type: VT_I4 • MQPROPVARIANT: lVal	MSMQQueueInfo. ModifyTime	A read-only property indicating the last time the properties of a queue were modified. The time returned is the number of seconds elapsed since midnight (00:00:00), January 1, 1970 (Coordinated Universal time). Visual Basic automatically converts this time to the local system time and system date. In C ctime() converts the time and date for display.

continued

Table A-3 *continued*

Queue Property	COM Equivalent	Description

PROPID_Q_PATHNAME
• Data type: VT_LPWSTR
• MQPROPVARIANT:
   pwszVal
	MSMQQueueInfo.
	   PathName
		A required property specifying the MSMQ pathname of the queue. The pathname includes the name of the machine on which the queue's messages are stored, whether the queue is public or private, and the name of the queue.
		
		   If the type for PROPID_Q_PATHNAME is set to VT_NULL and is passed to MQGetQueueProperties, MSMQ will allocate the memory needed for the pathname.

PROPID_Q_PRIV_LEVEL • Data type: VT_UI4 • MQPROPVARIANT: ulVal	MSMQQueueInfo. PrivLevel	The privacy level required by the queue. The privacy level determines how the queue handles encrypted messages. This property can take one of the following values: • MQ_PRIV_LEVEL_NONE—Only nonprivate, or clear text, messages are accepted • MQ_PRIV_LEVEL_BODY—Only private, that is, encrypted, messages are accepted. • MQ_PRIV_LEVEL_OPTIONAL—The default; private and nonprivate messages are accepted.

Queue Property	COM Equivalent	Description
PROPID_Q_QUOTA • Data type: VT_UI4 • MQPROPVARIANT: ulVal	MSMQQueueInfo.Quota	The maximum size, in kilobytes, of the queue storage. The default is INFINITE. The size of a queue can be set during creation and can be reset later. An MQ_ERROR_QUEUE_ EXCEEDS_QUOTA error is returned to a sending application if placing a message on the queue will cause the quota to be exceeded.
PROPID_Q_TRANSACTION • Data type: VT_UI1 • MQPROPVARIANT: bVal	MSMQQueueInfo. IsTransactional	Specifies whether the queue is transactional or nontransactional. It cannot be reset once the queue is created. This property can have one of the following values: • MQ_TRANSACTIONAL—All send operations performed on the queue must be done through an MSMQ transaction. Messages can be received without a transaction. • MQ_TRANSACTIONAL_ NONE—The default; no transaction operations can be performed on the queue. In COM the property is set when the MSMQQueueInfo. Create() method is called and examined using MSMQQueueInfo. IsTransactional. Admissible values in both instances are TRUE or FALSE.

continued

Table A-3 *continued*

Queue Property	COM Equivalent	Description
PROPID_Q_TYPE • Data type: VT_CLSID • MQPROPVARIANT: *puuid	MSMQQueueInfo. ServiceTypeGuid	The type of service, represented as a GUID value, that receivers support and senders can request. The default is NULL_GUID. 　　Only one service type can be assigned to a queue. If more than one service type is defined by an application, a queue must be created for each service.

Table A-4 Message Properties

Property	COM Equivalent	Description
		Basic Messaging
PROPID_M_BODY • Data type: VT_VECTOR | VT_UI1 • MQPROPVARIANT: caub	MSMQMessage.Body	The body of the message, consisting of any type of information. The sending and receiving applications are responsible for understanding the type of information in the message. COM automatically interprets types assigned to MSMQMessage.Body. The following types are supported: VT_I2, VT_UI2, VT_I4, VT_UI4, VT_R4, VT_R8, VT_CY, VT_DATE, VT_BOOL, VT_I1, VT_UI1, VT_BSTR, VT_ARRAY, VT_STREAMED_OBJECT (a serialized object of type IPersistStream), and

Queue Property	COM Equivalent	Description
		`VT_STORED_OBJECT` (a serialized object of type `IPersistStorage`).
		Using the MSMQ API, sending and receiving applications can use `PROPID_M_BODY_TYPE` to indicate or determine the type of array elements used in the message. Otherwise applications should assume that the message contains an array of bytes.
		Receiving applications can determine the size of a message by examining `PROPID_M_BODY_SIZE` or `MSMQMessage.BodyLength`.
`PROPID_M_BODY_SIZE` • Data type: `VT_UI4` or `VT_NULL` • MQPROPVARIANT: `ulVal`	`MSMQMessage.BodyLength`	The length, in bytes, of a message body. This property is used only when reading a message.
`PROPID_M_BODY_TYPE` • Data type: `VT_UI4` or `VT_NULL` • MQPROPVARIANT: `ulVal`		The type of message body (string, array of bytes, or object).
`PROPID_M_CLASS` • Data type: `VT_UI1` or `VT_NULL` • MQPROPVARIANT: `uiVal`	`MSMQMessage.Class`	The MSMQ message type. The class property indicates whether a message is a normal MSMQ message, one of several positive or negative acknowledgments, or a report. MSMQ typically sets this property. Connector applications may set the class property when they send a message.

continued

Table A-4 *continued*

Queue Property	COM Equivalent	Description
PROPID_M_ CORRELATIONID • Data type: VT_VECTOR|VT_UI1 • MQPROPVARIANT: caub	MSMQMessage. CorrelationId	An application-defined identifier that enables a sending application to correlate a response message with a request. To facilitate correlation of request and response messages, a responding application will set the correlation ID of a response message to the message ID, PROPID_M_MSGID or MSMQMessage.Id of a request message. MSMQ also does this for acknowledgment messages. The sending application can examine the correlation ID to match the response message to a request.
PROPID_M_DELIVERY • Data type: VT_UI1 or VT_NULL • MQPROPVARIANT: bVal	MSMQMessage.Delivery	Indicates whether message delivery should be recoverable. Applications can specify one of the following values: • MQMSG_DELIVERY_ EXPRESS—The default. The message is stored in memory on systems as it is routed through the network. The message is lost if the computer is rebooted. • MQMSG_DELIVERY_ RECOVERABLE—Delivery is guaranteed. As the message is routed through the network, each system forwards the message or stores it in a backup file.

Queue Property	COM Equivalent	Description
PROPID_M_LABEL • Data type: VT_LPWSTR • MQPROPVARIANT: pwszVal	MSMQMessage.Label	An application-specific message label specified by the message creator. A message label is often used as a user-friendly annotation, but labels can also be used as search criteria when receiving messages. The maximum string length of a label is 250 Unicode characters.
PROPID_M_LABEL_LEN • Data type: VT_UI4 • MQPROPVARIANT: ulVal		The length of the message label in Unicode characters. This property, used only when reading a message, is required if PROPID_M_LABEL is specified when a message is received.
PROPID_M_MSGID • Data type: VT_VECTOR | VT_UI1 • MQPROPVARIANT: caub	MSMQMessage.Id	A read-only 20-byte message identifier generated by MSMQ when a message (of any class) is sent. The sending application reads the message ID if it needs to correlate a request and a response. MSMQ and the receiving application use the message ID value of a request as a correlation ID value in a response.
PROPID_M_PRIORITY • Data type: VT_UI1 or VT_NULL • MQPROPVARIANT: bVal	MSMQMessage.Priority	The message priority, assigned by the message sender, affects message placement in a queue. A priority between 7 and 0 can be assigned; the default is 3. A priority of 0 is automatically assigned to transactional messages.

continued

Table A-4 *continued*

Queue Property	COM Equivalent	Description
		When a message is sent to a public queue, MSMQ adds the target queue's base priority (`PROPID_Q_ BASEPRIORITY` or `MSMQQueueInfo. BasePriority`) to this property to establish a routing priority.
`PROPID_M_RESP_QUEUE` • Data type: `VT_LPWSTR` • MQPROPVARIANT: `pwszVal`	`MSMQMessage. ReponseQueueInfo`	The format name of the queue to which application-generated response messages are to be returned. This property can also be used to send the format name of a private queue to another application. This is done if the sending application wants to make a private queue available to other applications. An `MSMQQueueInfo` component is returned by `MSMQMessage. ReponseQueueInfo`.
`PROPID_M_RESP_QUEUE_ LEN` • Data type: `VT_UI4` • MQPROPVARIANT: `ulVal`		The Unicode character length of the format name for the response queue; required if `PROPID_M_RESP_QUEUE` is specified when a message is received.
`PROPID_M_SRC_MACHINE_ ID` • Data type: `VT_CLSID` • MQPROPVARIANT: `*puuid`	`MSMQMessage. SourceMachineGuid`	A read-only property attached to a message by MSMQ to indicate the computer from which a message originated. Its value is the GUID of the source machine.

Property	COM Equivalent	Description
	Message Acknowledgment, Journal, and Report Properties	
PROPID_M_ACKNOWLEDGE • Data type: VT_UI1 or VT_NULL • MQPROPVARIANT: bVal	MSMQMessage.Ack	Indicates the types of acknowledgment messages MSMQ should return to a sender. Sending applications can specify one of the following values: • MQMSG_ ACKNOWLEDGMENT_ FULL_REACH_QUEUE— Return positive and negative acknowledgments indicating that the message has reached the destination queue. • MQMSG_ ACKNOWLEDGMENT_ FULL_RECEIVE—Return a positive or negative acknowledgment indicating that the message was retrieved before its time-to-be-received timer expired. • MQMSG_ ACKNOWLEDGMENT_ NACK_REACH_QUEUE— Return a negative acknowledgment if the message cannot reach the destination queue. • MQMSG_ ACKNOWLEDGMENT_ NACK_RECEIVE—Return a negative acknowledgment if the message cannot be retrieved from the destination queue before its time-to-be-received timer expires.

continued

Table A-4 *continued*

Queue Property	COM Equivalent	Description
		• MQMSG_ ACKNOWLEDGMENT_ NONE—The default. No acknowledgment messages (positive or negative) are returned.
		When asking for acknowledgments, an administration queue must be specified through PROPID_M_ADMIN_QUEUE or an MSMQQueueInfo component associated with the MSMQMessage. AdminQueueInfo property.
PROPID_M_ADMIN_QUEUE • Data type: VT_LPWSTR • MQPROPVARIANT: pwszVal	MSMQMessage. AdminQueueInfo	The format name of the queue to which an acknowledgment message is sent, when requested through PROPID_M_ACKNOWLEDGE or MSMQMessage.Ack. The property must contain a format name of the administration queue.
PROPID_M_ADMIN_QUEUE_ LEN • Data type: VT_UI4 • MQPROPVARIANT: ulVal		The Unicode character length of the format name for the administration queue; required if PROPID_M_ADMIN_QUEUE is specified when a message is received.

Queue Property	COM Equivalent	Description
PROPID_M_DEST_QUEUE • Data type: VT_LPWSTR • MQPROPVARIANT: pwszVal	MSMQMessage. DestinationQueueInfo	A read-only property attached to a message by MSMQ, indicating the queue to which the message is to be sent. This property would typically be used by an application that inspects messages in a journal or dead letter queue. PROPID_M_DEST_QUEUE contains the format name of the destination queue. MSMQMessage. DestinationQueueInfo returns this information in an MSMQQueueInfo component.
PROPID_M_DEST_QUEUE_ LEN • Data type: VT_UI4 • MQPROPVARIANT: ulVal		The Unicode character length of the format name for the destination queue; required if PROPID_M_DEST_QUEUE is specified when a message is received.
PROPID_M_JOURNAL • Data type: VT_UI1 • MQPROPVARIANT: bVal	MSMQMessage.Journal	Indicates whether a message should be kept in the machine journal, sent to a dead letter queue, or neither. The property can be set to one or more of the following values: • MQMSG_DEADLETTER—If a message is not delivered to a receiving application, it is placed on the dead letter queue on the computer on which the message is located.

continued

Queue Property	COM Equivalent	Description
		• MQMSG_JOURNAL—If a message is transmitted from the originating machine, a copy is placed on the originating machine's journal queue.
		• MQMSG_JOURNAL_NONE— The default; the message is not maintained in the originating machine's journal queue.
		MSMQ automatically sends transactional messages to the transactional dead letter queue (DEADXACT) on the source machine if the message is not delivered.
PROPID_M_TRACE • Data type: VT_UI1 | VT_NULL • MQPROPVARIANT: bVal	MSMQMessage.Trace	Indicates whether the route of the message should be traced. The elements of the report are the source queue manager, message identifier, target queue, time, and next hop. The report message is sent to the report queue specified by the source queue manager. This property can be set to one of the following values: • MQMSG_SEND_ROUTE_ TO_REPORT_QUEUE— MSMQ should generate a report for each hop made by the message. • MQMSG_TRACE_NONE— The default; no tracing for this message.

Queue Property	COM Equivalent	Description
		If an MSMQ administrator did not define a report queue for the message's source queue manager, this property is ignored.
	Security	
PROPID_M_AUTH_LEVEL • Data type: VT_UI4 • MQPROPVARIANT: ulVal	MSMQMessage.AuthLevel	Defines whether a message should be authenticated. This property is used by the sending application and can take one of the following values: • MQMSG_AUTH_LEVEL_NONE—The default. MSMQ does not sign or authenticate the message. • MQMSG_AUTH_LEVEL_ALWAYS—MSMQ signs and authenticates the message. If this property is set to MQMSG_AUTH_LEVEL_ALWAYS, MSMQ digitally signs the message when it is sent and uses the signature to authenticate the message when it is received. An internal certificate is used to sign the message unless PROPID_M_SENDER_CERT is specified; in that case an external certificate is used.
PROPID_M_AUTHENTICATED • Data type: VT_UI1 | VT_NULL • MQPROPVARIANT: bVal	MSMQMessage.IsAuthenticated	Indicates whether MSMQ could authenticate the message. This property is used by the receiving application only when receiving the message and is set

continued

Table A-4 *continued*

Queue Property	COM Equivalent	Description
		to one of the following values:
		• 0—MSMQ did not authenticate the message when it was received.
		• 1—MSMQ authenticated the message when it was received.
		MSMQMessage. IsAuthenticated returns TRUE or FALSE.
PROPID_M_ENCRYPTION_ ALG • Data type: VT_UI4 • MQPROPVARIANT: ulVal	MSMQMessage. EncryptAlgorithm	Used for encrypting a message body, this property can have one of two values: • CALG_RC2—The default. • CALG_RC4 A private (encrypted) message is sent when a privacy level value of MQMSG_PRIV_LEVEL_BODY is specified for the PROPID_M_PRIV_LEVEL or the MSMQMessage.PrivLevel property. Message encryption is based on public key encryption of an underlying RSA provider.
PROPID_M_HASH_ALG • Data type: VT_UI4 • MQPROPVARIANT: ulVal	MSMQMessage. HashAlgorithm	Used to create a digital signature when authenticating messages. The default value is CALG_MD5. The ALG_ID data type in wincrypt.h defines other values.

Queue Property	COM Equivalent	Description
PROPID_M_PRIV_LEVEL • Data type: VT_UI4 | VT_NULL • MQPROPVARIANT: ulVal	MSMQMessage.PrivLevel	Defines whether the message is private (encrypted). The property can take one of the following values: • MQMSG_PRIV_LEVEL_ BODY—The message body is private. • MQMSG_PRIV_LEVEL_ NONE—The default. The message is not private. When privacy is indicated, the source queue manager encrypts the body of the message, and the target queue manager decrypts the message body. The encryption algorithm specified by PROPID_M_ENCRYPTION_ ALG or MSMQMessage. EncryptAlgorithm is used to encrypt the body of the message.
PROPID_M_SECURITY_ CONTEXT • Data type: VT_UI4 • MQPROPVARIANT: ulVal	MSMQMessage. SecurityContext	Contains security information, represented as an opaque handle, that MSMQ uses to authenticate a message. This property includes the user's external security certificate that MSMQ associates with the message. The application should call the MSMQ API call MQGetSecurity Context() to retrieve the security information from the certificate.

continued

Table A-4 *continued*

Queue Property	COM Equivalent	Description
		This property should be set if a sending application will use a certificate for several messages. Otherwise a certificate should be inserted into the PROPID_M_SENDER_CERT or the MSMQMessage. SenderCertificate property.
PROPID_M_SENDER_CERT • Data type: VT_VECTOR|VT_UI1 • MQPROPVARIANT: caub	MSMQMessage. SenderCertificate	Indicates to use an external security certificate to authenticate the message. This property is used if a sending application will use a certificate only once (for one message). Otherwise the application should set MSMQMessage. SecurityContext or PROPID_M_SECURITY_ CONTEXT.
PROPID_M_SENDER_CERT_ LEN • Data type: VT_UI4 • MQPROPVARIANT: ulVal		The Unicode character length of the sender certificate buffer.
PROPID_M_SENDERID • Data type: VT_VECTOR|VT_UI1 • MQPROPVARIANT: caub	MSMQMessage.SenderId	The identity of the message sender. MSMQ attaches the sender's identity unless PROPID_M_SENDERID_ TYPE or MSMQMessage.Sender IdType is set to MQMSG_SENDERID_TYPE_ NONE. Receiving applications might use the sender ID to enforce access controls, auditing, and so on.

Queue Property	COM Equivalent	Description
PROPID_M_SENDERID_LEN • Data type: VT_UI4 • MQPROPVARIANT: ulVal		The length in bytes of the sender ID.

PROPID_M_SENDERID_
  TYPE
• Data type: VT_UI4 |
  VT_NULL
• MQPROPVARIANT: ulVal
	MSMQMessage.
	SenderIdType
		The type of sender identifier found in PROPID_M_SENDERID or MSMQMessage.SenderIdType. MSMQ handles only a SID, or security identifier.
		
		The property can be set to one of the following values:
		
		• MQMSG_SENDERID_TYPE_NONE—the sender ID is not attached to the message.
		
		• MQMSG_SENDERID_TYPE_SID—The default. The property contains the SID of the sending user.

Additional Message-Handling Properties

Queue Property	COM Equivalent	Description
PROPID_M_APPSPECIFIC • Data type: VT_UI4 • MQPROPVARIANT: ulVal	MSMQMessage. AppSpecific	An application-specific index value used for sorting messages. A receiving application can use this property to implement a customized sorting method. This property can also be used in combination with others. The property value can be any unsigned integer. The default value is 0.
PROPID_M_ARRIVEDTIME • Data type: VT_UI4 or VT_NULL • MQPROPVARIANT: ulVal	MSMQMessage. ArrivedTime	This read-only property indicates when the message arrived at the queue. The time returned is the number of seconds elapsed since midnight (00:00:00), January 1, 1970 *continued*

Table A-4 *continued*

Queue Property	COM Equivalent	Description
		(Coordinated Universal time). Visual Basic automatically converts this time to the local system time and system date. In C `ctime()` converts the time and date for display.
PROPID_M_SENTTIME • Data type: `VT_UI4` or `VT_NULL` • MQPROPVARIANT: `ulVal`	`MSMQMessage.SentTime`	This read-only property indicates when the message was sent. The time returned is the number of seconds elapsed since midnight (00:00:00), January 1, 1970 (Coordinated Universal time). Visual Basic automatically converts this time to the local system time and system date. In C `ctime()` converts the time and date for display.
PROPID_M_TIME_TO_BE_ RECEIVED • Data type: `VT_UI4` or `VT_NULL` • MQPROPVARIANT: `ulVal`	`MSMQMessage.` `MaxTimeToReceive`	The total time (in seconds) that the message is allowed to live. This time interval, represented as an integer, includes the time needed by the message to get to its destination queue plus the wait time before it is retrieved by an application. By default this property value is `INFINITE`. MSMQ uses two message timers: time to reach queue and time to be received. The latter

Queue Property	COM Equivalent	Description
		timer takes precedence over the former when it is set to a lesser value. Both timers are started as soon as the application sends the message. When applications send several messages within the transaction, MSMQ automatically uses the time-to-be-received timer of the first message for all other messages.
`PROPID_M_TIME_TO_REACH_QUEUE` • Data type: `VT_UI4` • MQPROPVARIANT: `ulVal`	`MSMQMessage.MaxTimeToReachQueue`	The total time (in seconds) that the message is allowed before it reaches its destination queue. MSMQ always gives the message one chance to reach its destination if the queue is waiting for the message. If the queue is local, the message always reaches the queue. If the time-to-reach-queue timer expires before the message reaches its destination, MSMQ discards the message or sends it to the dead letter queue if `PROPID_M_JOURNAL` or `MSMQMessage.Journal` is set to `MQMSG_DEADLETTER`.
`PROPID_M_VERSION` • Data type: `VT_UI4` • MQPROPVARIANT: `ulVal`		This read-only property indicates the version of MSMQ used to send the message.

continued

Table A-4 *continued*

Queue Property	COM Equivalent	Description
Connector Application Properties		
PROPID_M_CONNECTOR_ TYPE • Data type: VT_CLSID • MQPROPVARIANT: *puuid	No COM equivalent.	A GUID identifying the external application that generated PROPID_M_CLASS, PROPID_M_SENDERID, PROPID_M_SIGNATURE, PROPID_M_PROV_NAME, and PROPID_M_DEST_SYMM_ KEY.
PROPID_M_DEST_SYMM_ KEY • Data type: VT_UI1 | VT_VECTOR • MQPROPVARIANT: caub	No COM equivalent.	Specifies the symmetric key used to encrypt a message when sending it to a foreign queue. The key is encrypted with the public key of the receiving queue manager. A connector application receives the encrypted message and forwards it to the receiving application. The receiving application is required to decrypt the symmetric key and the message body.
PROPID_M_DEST_SYMM_ KEY_LEN • Data type: VT_UI4 • MQPROPVARIANT: ulVal	No COM equivalent.	The length in bytes of the symmetric key used to encrypt the messages. This property is set by MSMQ.

Queue Property	COM Equivalent	Description
PROPID_M_EXTENSION* • Data type: VT_UI1 | VT_VECTOR • MQPROPVARIANT: caub	No COM equivalent.	Enables applications to exchange additional data as part of a message. This property, used primarily when applications send messages to or receive messages from foreign queues, holds application-specific information associated with the message. Applications are responsible for understanding the content of this property.
PROPID_M_EXTENSION_ LEN • Data type: VT_UI4 • MQPROPVARIANT: ulVal	No COM equivalent.	The length in bytes of PROPID_M_EXTENSION. This property is set by MSMQ.
PROPID_M_PROV_NAME • Data type: VT_LPWSTR • MQPROPVARIANT: pwszVal	No COM equivalent.	The name of the cryptographic provider used to send authenticated messages to foreign queues. The name and type (PROPID_M_PROV_TYPE) are required to validate the digital signature of the message.
PROPID_M_PROV_NAME_ LEN • Data type: VT_UI4 • MQPROPVARIANT: ulVal	No COM equivalent.	The Unicode character length of the cryptographic provider name. MSMQ automatically sets PROPID_M_PROV_NAME_ LEN to the length of the provider name when PROPID_M_PROP_NAME is specified.

continued

Table A-4 *continued*

Queue Property	COM Equivalent	Description
PROPID_M_PROV_TYPE • Data type: VT_UI4 • MQPROPVARIANT: ulVal	No COM equivalent.	The type of cryptographic provider used to send authenticated messages to foreign queues. The name and type (PROPID_M_PROV_TYPE) are required to validate the digital signature of the message. Possible values are defined in wincrypt.h. The default is PROV_RSA_FULL.
PROPID_M_SIGNATURE • Data type: VT_UI1 | VT_VECTOR • MQPROPVARIANT: caub	No COM equivalent.	A digital signature forwarded by a connector server to a receiving application to enable it to authenticate the message. MSMQ attaches PROPID_M_SIGNATURE to the message when it is sent. The digital signature is used to determine who sent the message. When used, the signature length, PROPID_M_SIGNATURE_LEN, is also required.
PROPID_M_SIGNATURE_ LEN • Data type: VT_UI4 • MQPROPVARIANT: ulVal	No COM equivalent.	The length of the digital signature used for authenticating a message.

Queue Property	COM Equivalent	Description
PROPID_M_XACT_STATUS_ QUEUE • Data type: VT_LPWSTR • MQPROPVARIANT: pwszVal	No COM equivalent.	The transaction status queue on the source computer. This property is used when sending messages to a foreign queue. A connector application uses the property to send acknowledgments back to the MSMQ sending application. This property's value must contain a format name.
PROPID_M_XACT_STATUS_ QUEUE_LEN • Data type: VT_UI4 • MQPROPVARIANT: ulVal	No COM equivalent.	The Unicode character length of the format name for the transaction status queue.

*Level 8 Systems provides a FalconMQ Extension API that can be used in conjunction with FalconMQ Bridge. Using the Extension API, MSMQ and MQSeries applications can exchange the complete contents of an MQSeries MQMD data structure.

B
Appendix

Configuring Visual C++

and Visual Basic for MSMQ

To configure Microsoft's Visual C++ or Visual Basic for MSMQ, you need to create and to configure a project workspace. This appendix uses Visual C++ 5.0 and Visual Basic 5.0; if you are using previous versions of either product, refer to the help pages for configuring new project workspaces and defining include and library files.

B.1 Creating and Configuring a Project in Visual C++

To use Microsoft's Visual C++ with MSMQ, you need to create a project and then configure it to be able to use MSMQ header and library files. Start by opening Visual C++. On most computers you do this by clicking on the Start button, selecting Programs, and then choosing the Microsoft Visual C++ 5.0 menu of options. Click on Microsoft Visual C++ 5.0 to start the program.

Once Visual C++ is loaded, you need to create a new project. From the File menu from the toolbar, click on New. This brings up the set of tabs pictured in Figure B-1. Select the Projects tab. You have a choice of several project types. You need to take the following steps:

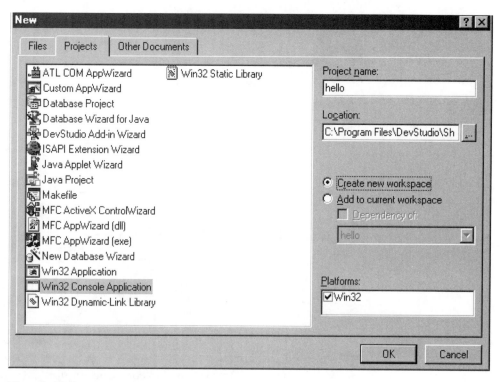

Figure B-1 Creating a project workspace

- Assign a project name in the text box for Project name.
- Define the directory in which the project is to be created in the Location text box.
- Make sure you select the radio button option for Create new workspace.
- Double click the icon for the type you will create.

For simple executable programs that use `printf` statements, select the Win32 Console Application icon. This creates a new project workspace.

B.1.1 Defining Header Files

MSMQ applications will include an MSMQ header file, such as `MQ.H`. Visual C++ needs to be told where those header files can be found. MSMQ header files for Visual C++ are located in the `...\MSMQ\SDK\INCLUDE` folder. (In this example the MSMQ header files are located in `C:\Program Files\MSMQ\SDK\INCLUDE`.)

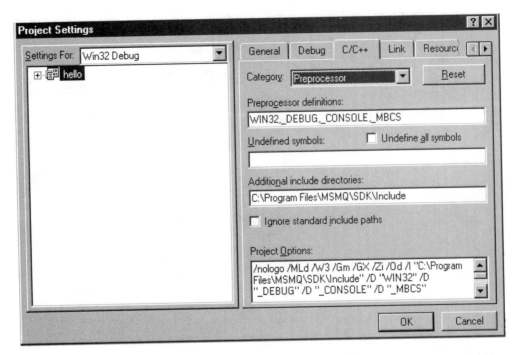

Figure B-2 Configuring Visual C++ for MQ.H

To tell Visual C++ how to locate a header file, select the Project menu from the toolbar and choose Settings. The Project Settings dialog box will be displayed (see Figure B-2). The dialog box contains several tabs. Click on the C/C++ tab. In the Category box select Preprocessor. Define the appropriate include folder in the text box for Additional include directories. (To specify more than one directory, you would use a comma to separate directory names.) Then click OK.

If you return to the Project Settings dialog box, click on the C/C++ tab, and choose the General option in the Category box, you will see the directory defined in the Project Options text box with a /I compiler switch. The /I switch tells Visual C++ to search for include files in the directory following the switch. A /I switch is needed for each directory to be searched.

B.1.2 Defining Library Files

In order to create an executable MSMQ program, Visual C++ needs to be told where to find libraries. MSMQ libraries for Visual C++ are located in the ...\MSMQ\SDK\LIB folder. (In this example the MSMQ library files are located in C:\Program Files\MSMQ\SDK\LIB.)

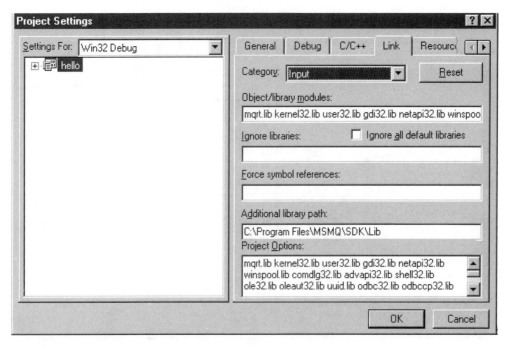

Figure B-3 Configuring Visual C++ for MQRT.LIB

To tell Visual C++ how to locate MSMQ libraries, select the Link tab in the Project Settings dialog box. In the Category box select Input. Define the appropriate library folder in the text box for Additional library path. (To specify more than one directory, you would use a comma to separate directory names.) Then click OK.

In the Object/Library modules text box enter mqrt.lib (see Figure B-3). For console applications you may also want to add entries for the kernel32.lib, user32.lib, gdi32.lib, and netapi32.lib libraries if they are not already there.

B.2 Creating and Configuring a Project in Visual Basic

To use Microsoft's Visual Basic with MSMQ, you need to create a project and then configure it to be able to use the MSMQ library file. Start by opening Visual Basic. On most computers you do this by clicking on the Start button, selecting Programs, and then choosing the Microsoft Visual Basic 5.0 menu of options. Click on Microsoft Visual Basic 5.0 to start the program.

B.2.1 Creating a New Project Workspace

When Visual Basic is loaded, it presents the New Project window shown in Figure B-4. You have a choice of several project types. For a simple Windows application, choose Standard EXE and click the Open button. This sets up a new project to create an executable program and places you into the Visual Basic Integrated Development Environment (IDE). To give the project a name and save it, select the File menu from

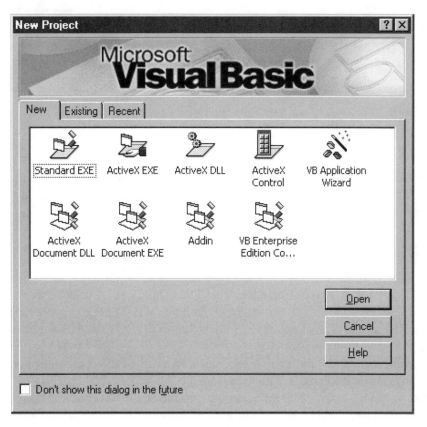

Figure B-4   Visual Basic's New Project window

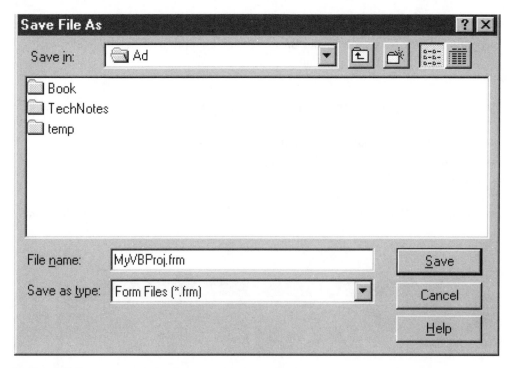

Figure B-5 The Visual Basic Save Project As window

the toolbar and choose Save Project. This will bring up the Save Project As window (see Figure B-5). Choose the folder in which the project files will be saved, and assign a project name.

B.2.2 Defining the Library File

In order to compile or to create an executable MSMQ program, Visual Basic needs to be told where to find MSMQ libraries. By default the MSMQ library for Visual Basic is located in the \WINNT\system32 folder. (In this example the MSMQ library is located in C:\WINNT\system32.)

To define the MSMQ library to Visual Basic, select the Project menu from the toolbar and choose References. This brings up the References window (Figure B-6). Scroll down the list of available references, check the box for Microsoft Message Queue Object Library, and click the OK button. You can now begin to use COM objects defined for MSMQ.

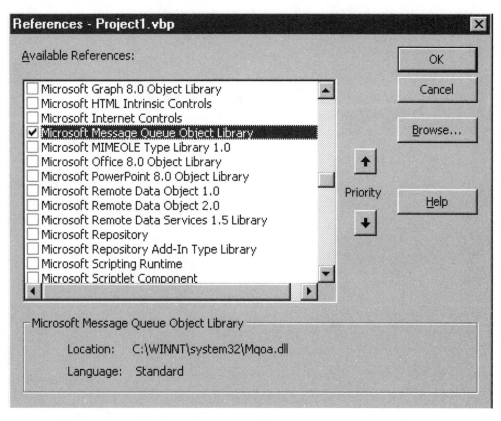

Figure B-6 Defining the MSMQ library to Visual Basic

C
Appendix

MSMQ Performance

This appendix, intended for IS managers and developers, discusses the performance costs associated with express, recoverable, and transactional messages. It also identifies ways to tune your systems to optimize MSMQ performance.

Messaging is typically used by distributed applications that require high-performance communications. Some of the reasons were outlined in Chapter 10. Message queuing applications typically incur much less communications and transaction processing overhead relative to on-line direct communications between applications across a network.

MSMQ should satisfy the performance requirements of some of the most stringent performance standards. For example, I have been able to send 20,000 messages per second to a local queue on a Pentium 200. That's remarkably fast!

Let's begin by looking at some performance numbers. Then we'll discuss ways of improving the performance of your MSMQ applications.

C.1   Messaging Performance

In the performance numbers reported in Table C-1, an MSMQ application repeatedly sends 10-byte messages. Each test is executed with an empty target queue. For non-transactional messaging each thread in a test case sends 1,000 10-byte messages; thus 3,000 messages are sent if three threads are used. In transactional tests each thread sends 100 10-byte messages. Each test is repeated five times. Table C-1 reports the best result out of the five tests. In general, there was not a substantial variation between throughput of the best run and the worst run.

Table C-1 Local and Remote Message Performance

Messages Sent per Second	Local (Number of Threads:)				Remote (Number of Threads:)			
	1	3	5	Change	1	3	5	Change
Express	19,971	17,622	17,831	—	11,095	14,978	16,106	—
Recov.	489	1,074	1,486	12–40x	298	441	540	29–37x
Single	156	207	280	3–5x	127	179	292	~2x
DTC	5	52	72	4–31x	5	57	63	5–25x

All tests were executed on a computer built by Handley Computers. The computer is a Pentium Pro 200MHz with 64MB RAM, a single IDE 5.1GB disk, and a Novell NE2000–compatible Ethernet card. In remote tests messages are sent through a TRENDnet TE-910 hub to a Dell Dimension XPS, which is a Pentium 200MHz with 64MB RAM, one IDE 2GB disk, and one IDE 1GB disk, plus a 3COM Fast EtherLink card. These are desktop machines rather than server-class machines, and makes MSMQ performance all the more impressive.

Three comments about the configuration are in order.

- Each system is configured with MSMQ and DTC files on the same disk. When an external transaction is used to send a message, MSMQ writes the message to disk and MSMQ and DTC write and flush log records as each transaction progresses. This is far from an optimal configuration. If the message files and transaction logs were configured on separate disks, we could expect to see better performance results.

- My disk drives and controllers are not exceptionally fast. High-performance servers will deliver better throughput. It is not unusual to see a tenfold (10x) performance improvement with hardware-stripped disks and hard-caching controllers.

- There was no background network traffic during these tests. These benchmark tests would suffer higher network overhead in many typical production network environments.

The quantity, quality, and configuration of every system component impact performance. For example, a system will perform better with several high-speed disk drives configured in a way that minimizes contention for an individual drive. The axiom of quantity, quality, and configuration applies to memory and to other system resources, as well as how you deploy your software applications across a set of systems and how you configure the software components they use.

I exercised care in running benchmarks, but these tests were far from scientific. In a truly rigorous benchmark one would run hundreds of iterations to test a messaging scenario. My purpose in executing these tests was to derive some general rules to save you time. The tests demonstrate that MSMQ delivers quite good performance under all messaging scenarios, but the tests do not indicate the performance limits of MSMQ!

First, let's look at the performance numbers when messages are sent to local queues. As you can see in Table C-1, sending express messages is extremely fast. This is understandable, because a message is immediately stored in memory. No performance is gained by using multiple threads. The cost of switching thread contexts degrades messaging performance.

MSMQ also delivers great performance when recoverable messages are sent, even though they are stored to disk via memory-mapped files. Between 12 and 20 times fewer recoverable message were sent per second relative to express messages. Performance improvements can be realized by using multiple threads, even though thread context switches are incurred. While one thread is blocked as a message is stored to disk, other threads can still perform send operations. In effect, NT is able to optimally schedule MSMQ and I/O operations with more and more threads.

Performance is still quite good when messages are sent within internal transactions. Sending messages within an internal transaction reduces throughput per second by three to five times in comparison with recoverable messages. In order to guarantee transactional semantics, MSMQ behaves as a communications provider and a database. Transactional state changes must be controlled by using locks, and state changes must be logged to disk. Applications can realize substantial gains in throughput by using multiple threads.

External or general-purpose transactions incur 4 to 31 times the overhead of internal transactions. The overhead has a lot to do with background logging of transaction status. When using external transactions, both DTC and MSMQ log transactional status. As noted earlier, external transactions are not specifically optimized for MSMQ. You can also realize substantial gains in throughput when multiple threads or multiple applications run in parallel.

Looking at the performance when messages are sent across a network, you see that the network adds some overhead to express and recoverable messaging. When messages are sent to remote queues within internal or external transactions, the impact of network overhead is less substantial. The reason is that so much file I/O is also occurring. The relative throughput of express recoverable and transactional messaging is similar to the local case.

C.2 Conclusions and Recommendations

Several rules of thumb can be derived from the performance numbers.

- Using overlapping I/O improves overall MSMQ throughput. The design of high-performance MSMQ applications should take advantage of Windows' multithreading and multiprocess capabilities. Tune the number of threads or processes based on the kind of message sent or received.

- If you are procuring hardware for applications that will send and receive express messages, try to buy enough memory so that memory pages are rarely swapped to disk by NT. Estimating total system memory requirements will be difficult, since the requirements of individual applications can vary substantially. However, it is not too difficult to estimate the memory requirements.

  A message header is added to every message sent—an additional 136 bytes per message, on average. Other message properties also need to be included. An NT security identifier (SID) of 28 bytes is sent with every message (unless the sending application explicitly specifies that the SID should not be sent). A 68-byte SID is sent when there are many trusted domains (up to 15). Response and administrative queue format names require at least 44 Unicode characters, 54 for private queues. A correlation identifier is 40 bytes. You should include a minimum of 264 bytes to every message that will reside in memory at any instant. With acknowledgments, responses, correlation, a label, and other properties, 0.5K to 0.75K per message is not unreasonable.

- If you are procuring hardware for applications that will send and receive recoverable or transactional messages, you should try to minimize disk seeks and I/O contention. Consider purchasing high-performance disks and controllers with large caches.

  Performance of recoverable and transactional messaging can also be improved by placing MSMQ message, MSMQ message logger, MSMQ transaction logger, DTC log, and application data or SQL Server files on separate physical disks. The MS Message Queue program in the NT control panel allows you to specify Message File, Message Logger, and Transaction Logger folders for MSMQ. Consider placing those folders on separate disks.

- Choose your message delivery options carefully. In making a selection, you will trade off performance and reliability.

Express messages deliver excellent performance, but messages are lost whenever the system they reside on is shut down or fails. In addition, the messages are not guaranteed to arrive at the target queue, and duplicates are possible.

Recoverable messages deliver great performance and are recoverable in the event of a system shutdown or failure. Like express messages, they are not guaranteed to arrive at the target queue, and duplicates are possible.

Internal transactions offer very good performance. Also, duplicates are eliminated, and delivery is guaranteed.

External transactions incur much higher overhead. But they are absolutely required when other resource managers participate in a transaction.

- Use transactions only when they are necessary, for example, if you need to guarantee message delivery and cannot afford to have duplicate messages. Express and recoverable messages are already highly reliable, and recoverable messages can survive shutdowns and failures. Several disk writes are needed to guarantee exactly-once semantics. Thus, transactions place substantial I/O demands on systems. Use internal transactions when only MSMQ operations are part of the transaction. Use external transactions when sending or receiving a message needs to be coordinated with other activities.

- Assign message priorities so that important messages are processed before other messages. A message with a higher priority is placed in a queue ahead of messages with a lower priority.

- Assign queue priorities so that important messages are given a higher transmission priority relative to other messages. The priority assigned to messages as they are routed across the network is determined by the relative priority of the destination queue. Queue priorities can be tuned to lower the routing latency of important messages.

- Use session concentration to route messages across high-speed or uncongested network segments. MSMQ gives administrators considerable flexibility in determining how messages pass across their networks.

All forms of MSMQ messaging offer great programming simplicity, so that should not be part of your selection criteria.

Security can also impact performance. However, applications do not necessarily incur overhead when using MSMQ security features. When sending authenticated messages, the digital signature is calculated in the user context, by the MSMQ runtime, and therefore does have a slight impact on performance. However, sending private messages does not directly impact the performance of the send operation, as the encryption is done by the MSMQ queue manager. On the receiving end any signature validation or decryption is performed by the receiving queue manager when the message arrives, so from the application's point of view, the receive operation is also not directly impacted by security features.

Applications do incur direct overhead when using an external certificate for authentication. On the receiver side the application is free to impose any criteria it wants when determining whether to trust the sending application. The application incurs overhead, but the amount of overhead depends on how it processes the external certificate.

Index

MFC Programming

Alan R. Feuer

This book provides an in-depth introduction to writing 32-bit Windows applications using C++ and the Microsoft Foundation Class (MFC) library. The text builds from the ground up: first describing the Windows architecture and showing how MFC works with that architecture; then covering the document/view framework that simplifies the creation of industrial-strength programs; and finally illustrating advanced concepts like the usage of dynamic link libraries (DLL), creating Internet clients, and building form-based applications. *MFC Programming* answers the hard questions—diving below the surface presented in the Reference Manual—by building comprehensive, detailed chapters on all types of controls, all of the common dialogs (along with the various methods of customization), serialization, printing and previewing, and customization of the Page Setup dialog. The accompanying CD-ROM contains source code for all the programs in the book.

0-201-63358-2 • Hardcover • 480 pages • ©1997

The MFC Answer Book

Solutions for Effective Visual C++ Applications
Eugène Kain

Microsoft Foundation Class (MFC) Library is becoming increasingly more popular among Windows programmers—more than one million developers use MFC. Although there are many tutorials covering MFC programming, there are few texts that teach you to build sophisticated and professional user interfaces that go beyond Wizard-supplied functionality. *The MFC Answer Book* is specifically designed to help programmers solve their MFC programming problems, in the most efficient way possible, both in immediate answer form and through detailed explanations. The techniques covered in this book will save the MFC programmer several hours (or even days) of frustration looking for the right answer to a pressing question. The accompanying CD-ROM contains more than one hundred sample programs demonstrating the various solutions discussed in the book, enabling the pro-grammer to immediately reuse those proven techniques in their own projects.

0-201-18537-7 • Paperback • 704 pages • 1998

Extending the MFC Library

*Add Useful Reusable Features to the
Microsoft Foundation Class Library*
David A. Schmitt

MFC allows you to code for new or customized capabilities by extending the application framework and creating your own reusable classes. *Extending the MFC Library* brings C and C++ programmers quickly up to speed on MFC's implementation of traditional C++ features, then presents numerous extension projects, discussing how they are created and used, and how to further customize them for use in your own projects. The extension projects are included ready-to-run on disk.

0-201-48946-5 • Paperback • 384 pages • ©1996

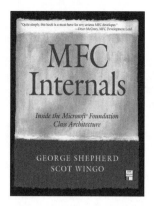

MFC Internals

Inside the Microsoft® Foundation Class Architecture
George Shepherd and Scot Wingo

According to Dean McCrory, Microsoft's MFC Development Lead, "Quite simply, this book is a must-have for any serious MFC developer." This guide to the inner workings of the Microsoft Foundation Classes gives you in-depth information on undocumented MFC classes, utility functions and data members, useful coding techniques, and analyses of the way MFC classes work together. The book covers both graphical user interface classes and extensions to the basic Windows support. You will learn about such specific topics as MFC's document/view architecture, undocumented aspects of MFC serialization and classes, how OLE controls are implemented, and more.

0-201-40721-3 • Paperback • 736 pages • ©1996

Essential COM

Don Box

Essential COM helps developers go beyond simplistic applications of COM and become truly effective COM programmers. You will find comprehensive coverage of the core concepts of Distributed COM (interfaces, classes, apartments, and applications), including detailed descriptions of COM theory, the C++ language mapping, COM IDL (Interface Definition Language), the remoting architecture, IUnknown, monikers, threads, marshalers, security, and more. Written by the premier authority on the COM architecture, this book offers a thorough explanation of COM's basic vocabulary, provides a complete Distributed COM application to illustrate programming techniques, and includes the author's test library of COM utility code. By showing you the why of COM, not just the how, Don Box enables you to apply the model creatively and effectively to everyday programming problems.

0-201-63446-5 • Paperback • 464 pages • ©1998

Effective COM Programming

50 Ways to Improve Your COM and MTS-based Applications
Don Box, Keith Brown, Tim Ewald, and Chris Sells

Written by *Essential COM* author Don Box in conjunction with three other trainers at DevelopMentor, *Effective COM Programming* offers fifty concrete guidelines for COM based on the communal wisdom that has formed over the past five years of COM-based development. This book is targeted at developers who are living and breathing COM, humbled by its complexity and challenged by the breadth of distributed object computing. Although the book is written for developers who work in C++, many of the topics (e.g., interface design, security) are approachable by developers who work in Visual Basic, Java, or Object Pascal. *Effective COM Programming* takes a practical approach to COM, offering guidelines developers can use immediately to become more effective, efficient COM programmers.

0-201-37968-6 • Paperback • 208 pages • Available winter 1998

Multithreading Applications in Win32
The Complete Guide to Threads
Jim Beveridge and Robert Wiener

Windows® 95 and Windows NT™ allow software developers to use the powerful programming technique of multithreading: dividing a single application into multiple "threads" that execute separately and get their own CPU time. This can result in significant performance gains, but also in programming headaches. Multithreading is difficult to do well, and previous coverage of the subject in Windows has been incomplete. In this book programmers will get hands-on experience about when and how to use multithreading, together with expert advice and working examples in C++ and MFC. The CD-ROM contains the code and sample applications from the book, including code that works with Internet Winsock.

0-201-44234-5 • Paperback • 400 pages • ©1997

Win32® Network Programming
Windows® 95 and Windows NT™ Network Programming Using MFC
Ralph Davis

As a developer of applications that must communicate across Windows® 95 and Windows NT™, you need to know what network capabilities have been implemented across both platforms. *Win32® Network Programming* is a guide to building networked applications for both Windows 95 and Windows NT 4.0, focusing on overlapped I/O, Windows Sockets 2.0, the Registration Service API, RPC, and Named Pipes. The book's disk contains the example code cast as a C++/MFC class library that extends MFC to support overlapped I/O, I/O completion ports, the Windows Sockets Service Registration API, and related functionality.

0-201-48930-9 • Paperback • 832 pages • ©1996

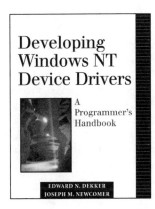

Developing Windows NT Device Drivers
A Programmer's Handbook
Edward N. Dekker and Joseph M. Newcomer

Device drivers are a necessary evil, connecting the operating system with its peripherals. There is not always a need for a custom device driver, but it is difficult to determine when one is necessary until driver fundamentals are clear. This book emphasizes the core techniques of programming device drivers. Without this core knowledge, all of the "advanced" driver techniques (layered drivers, WDM, File System Filters, File System Drivers) are inaccessible. This book covers the components of a Kernel mode device driver for Windows NT. There is also background on the Bus Interfaces the Driver Programmer will use; the ISA and the PCI. The authors tackle both existing drivers (the ISA bus and the PCI bus, the primary buses in today's computers).

0-201-69590-1 • Hardcover • 1104 pages • Available winter 1998

Win32 System Programming

Johnson M. Hart

With this book you can capitalize on your knowledge of high-end operating systems such as Unix, MVS, or VMS to learn Windows system programming quickly. *Win32 System Programming* focuses on the core operating system services of Win32, the common API for the Windows 95 and Windows NT operating systems. The book offers extensive coverage of I/O, security, memory management, processes, threads, and synchronization. You will also find discussions of other advanced topics including file locking, DLLs, asynchronous I/O, fibers, and the registry. In addition, the book includes numerous practical examples and comparisons of Win32 and UNIX functions. The accompanying CD-ROM contains all of the code examples found in the text, a suite of programs for testing system performance, and a collection of UNIX-like utilities.

0-201-63465-1 • Hardcover • 384 pages • ©1997

Windows™ Sockets Network Programming

Bob Quinn and Dave Shute

Windows Sockets (WinSock), a standard network API for use with Windows®, UNIX®, and TCP/IP networking environments, is an extraordinary resource for network programmers. This book shows you how to reap WinSock's full benefits to create network-ready applications. In addition to comprehensive coverage of WinSock 1.1 and 2.0 function calls, you will find information on porting existing BSD Sockets source code to Windows, debugging techniques and tools, common traps and pitfalls to avoid, and the many different operating system platforms that currently incorporate WinSock.

0-201-63372-8 • Hardcover • 656 pages • ©1996

Win32 Programming

Brent E. Rector and Joseph M. Newcomer

This book covers all the material necessary to understand and write 32-bit Windows® applications for both Windows® 95 and Windows NT™ 3.5.1. The book details Win32 application programming concepts, approaches, and techniques for the common Application Programming Interface of Windows 95 and Windows NT. It covers basic methods of Windows message handling, advances in mouse and keyboard input handling, and graphical output using the Graphics Device Interface. The CD-ROM is a gold mine of useful programs, with a C template to create your own Windows applications and dozens of other programs.

0-201-63492-9 • Hardcover • 1568 pages • ©1997

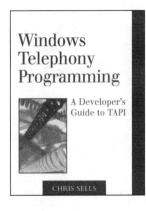

Windows Telephony Programming
A Developer's Guide to TAPI
Chris Sells

TAPI has been called the "assembly language of telephony." TAPI has standardized the interface to telephony hardware under Windows and legitimized the computer telephony industry. In the process, however, TAPI has turned into one of the largest Application Programming Interfaces (APIs) available for Windows. This makes it general and flexible, requiring clear, concise instruction; otherwise it is difficult to learn. The goal of this book is to reduce the high learning curve associated with Windows telephony. The book provides Windows C++ developers with a clear, concise TAPI tutorial, and offers several examples of popular telephony applications and a C++ class library to make Windows telephony more approachable.

0-201-63450-3 • Paperback • 320 pages • Available fall 1998

Windows NT™ Security Guide
Stephen A. Sutton

Weak links in a security system leave the door open to data tampering, virus attacks, and numerous other unpleasant scenarios. This book shows system administrators how to protect their networks from intruders. It contains information on critical security issues by providing practical examples and tutorials on configuring and managing a leak-proof network. *The Windows NT™ Security Guide* provides hands-on advice (in the form of real life examples and tutorials) for setting up and managing a secure network. Perhaps most importantly, it provides guidelines for assessing the effectiveness of a network's defense system.

0-201-41969-6 • Paperback • 384 pages • ©1997

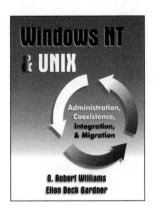

Windows NT & UNIX
Administration, Coexistence, Integration, & Migration
G. Robert Williams and Ellen Beck Gardner

This book will serve as a guidebook in your endeavor to manage a smoothly running system incorporating both UNIX and Windows NT. It clarifies the key issues you are likely to encounter in dealing with the two operating systems, focusing on the three specific areas of interaction: coexistence, integration, and migration. Planning and implementing the introduction of Windows NT into a UNIX environment is discussed in depth, from selecting a topological model and assessing hardware requirements through rollout and training. The book also addresses such topics as accessing data across platforms; user interface emulators; running Windows applications under UNIX and vice versa; ported POSIX commands and utilities; and SNMP. In addition, it presents available tools for porting UNIX applications to Win32, discusses retrofitting UNIX CPUs, and examines CORBA and DCOM interoperability issues.

0-201-18536-9 • Paperback • 768 pages • ©1998

How to scale Microsoft solutions to the enterprise

PSW